CW01190088

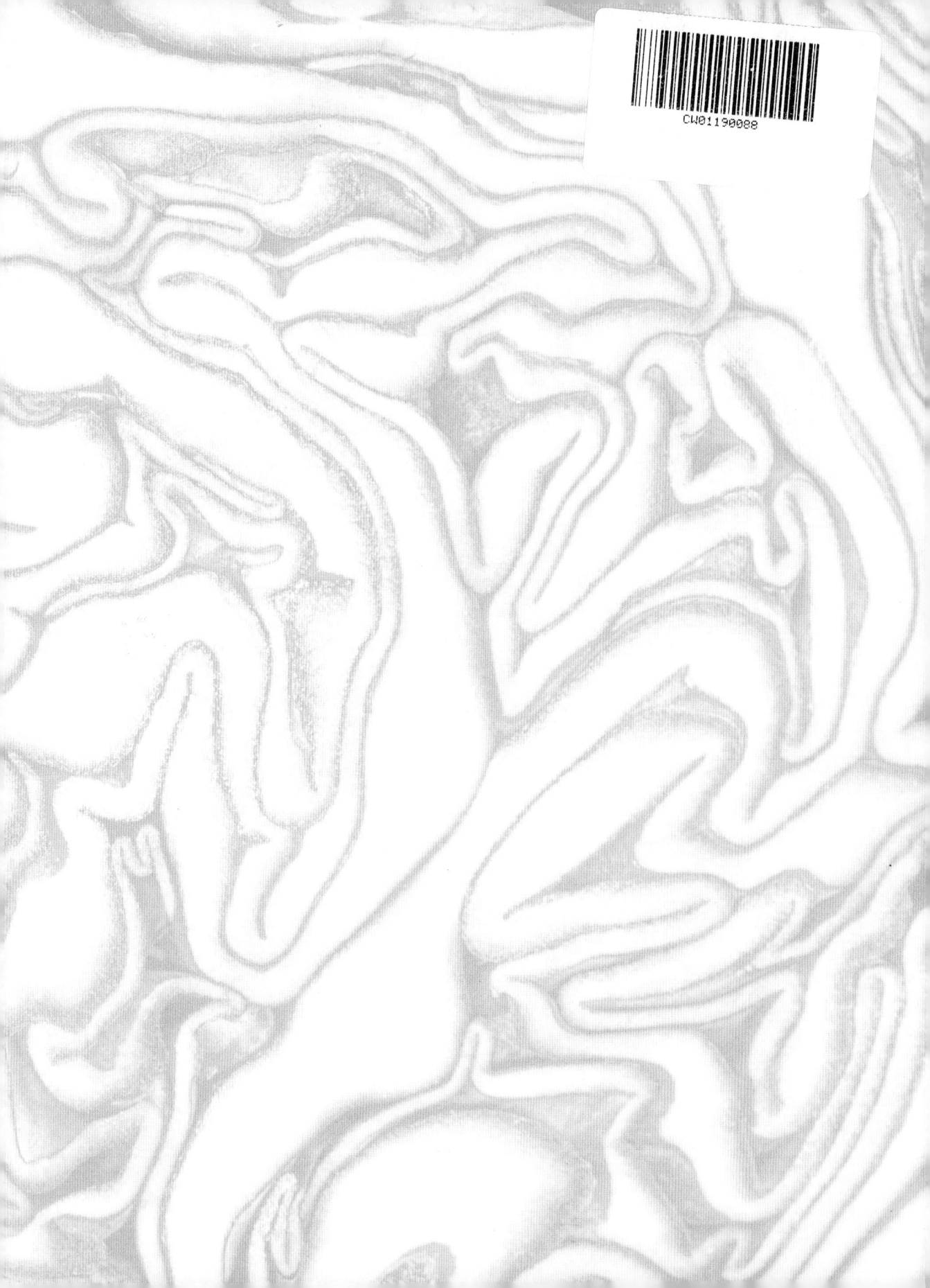

> "TO WANDER
> IS NOT TO BE LOST;
> IT IS SIMPLY
> MAPPING THE WAY."

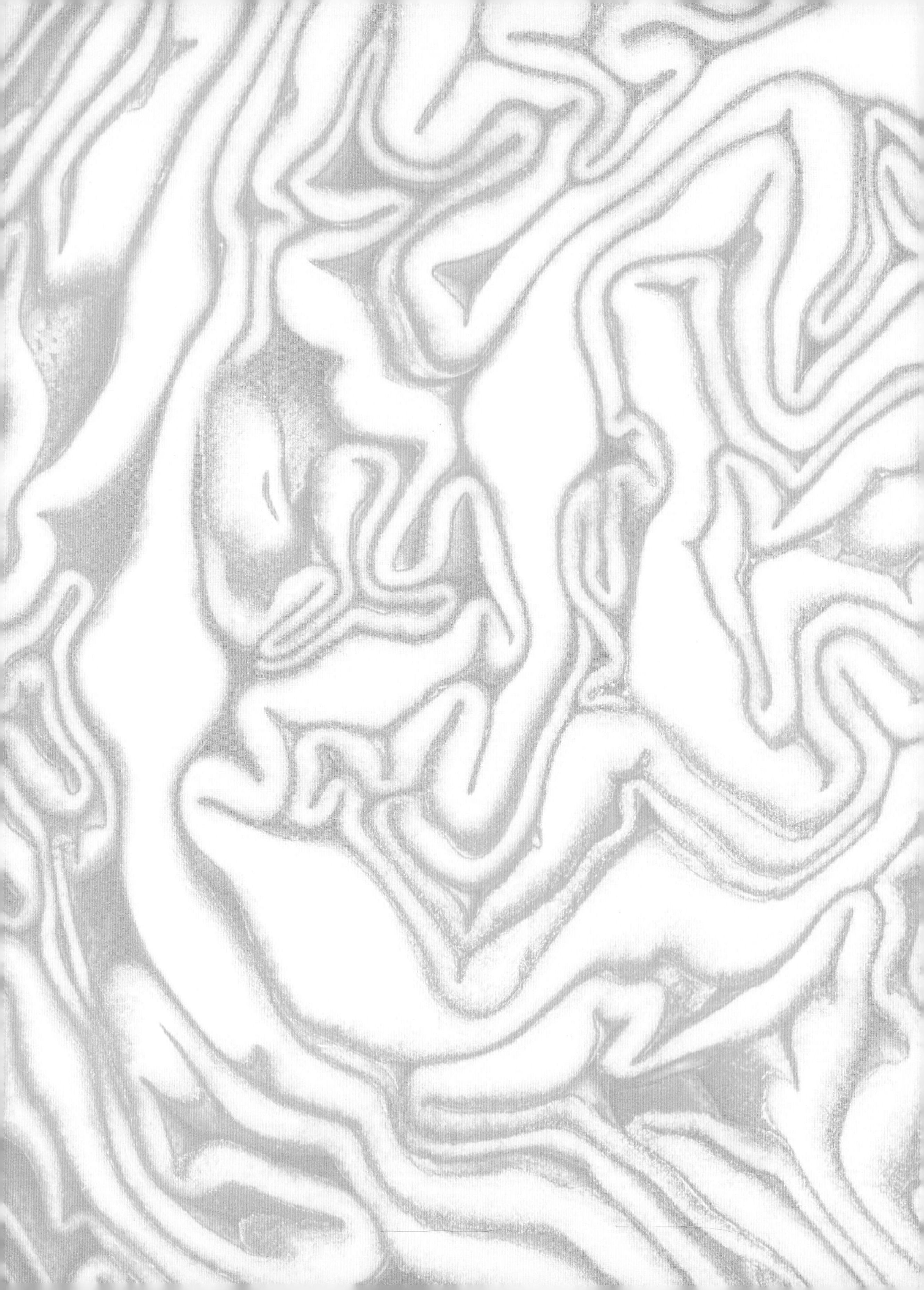

THE MINDFUL KITCHEN MAP

The New System for Ethical Veganism and Neurodiverse Wellbeing

mensch • chef

TOMASO MANNU

NOURISH

EAT WELL, LIVE WELL

The map of a mindful kitchen: break your kitchen down into these key areas and discover new ways to organize and maximize on time, energy and flavor

Cabinets store our shelf-stable essentials, supporting quick, creative decisions— just like the prefrontal cortex helps us plan, problem-solve, and think ahead.

The Cabinets
The Hidden Chambers
The Prefrontal Cortex
Creativity & Decision-Making

Just like the hippocampus stores knowledge, the pantry holds the essential building blocks of our kitchen— ingredients we return to time and time again.

The Pantry
The Library of Ingredients
The Hippocampus
Memory & Storage

The Bin
The Resource Recovery Centre
The Brain's Filtering System
Efficiency & Waste Processing

This is where the kitchen (and the mind) sorts, filters, and repurposes what's useful— turning waste into something valuable.

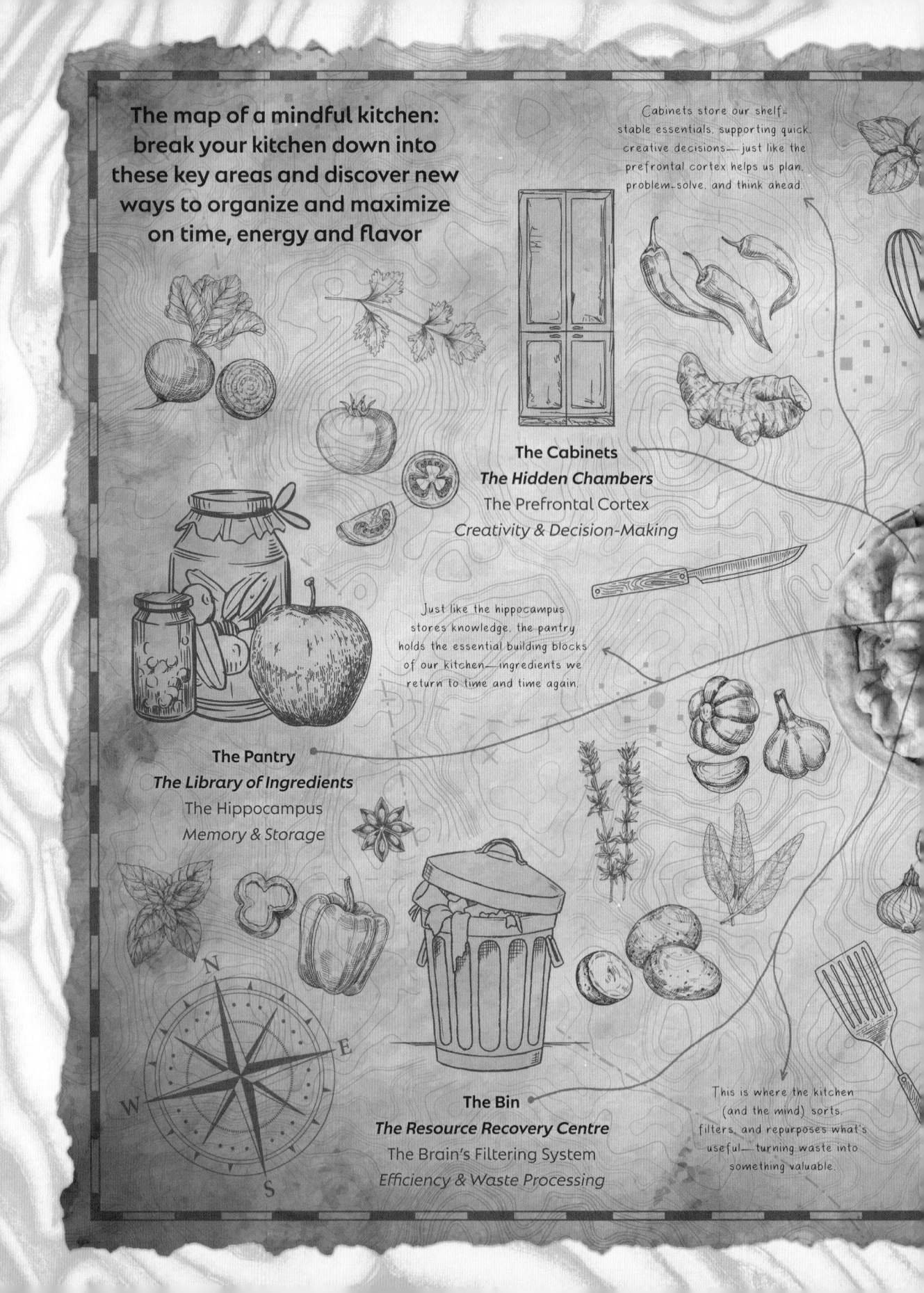

The fridge keeps our most-used ingredients fresh and accessible, much like the basal ganglia reinforces daily habits and routines—shaping the way we eat and live.

The Refrigerator
The Cold Storage Vault
The Basal Ganglia
Repetition & Habits

Freezing meals preserves flavors and nutrients over time, just as the temporal lobe stores memories and processes sensory input for the long haul.

The Freezer
The Time Capsule
The Temporal Lobe
Processing & Long-Term Storage

This chapter brings everything together, much like the parietal lobe helps us process sensory details and connect with the world around us.

Not the End
The Recipe for a Holistic Kitchen
The Parietal Lobe
Integration & Sensory Awareness

Growing food connects us deeply to what we eat—just as the limbic system ties our emotions to our experiences and surroundings.

The Home
Home-Grown Haven
The Limbic System
Emotions & Connection to Nature

INTRODUCTION: A Personal Map

This is not just another cookbook. It doesn't claim to have all the answers, nor is it a prescriptive manual for instant change.

It is something else entirely – a guide, a tool and a map. Think of this book as a compass designed to help you navigate the often overwhelming complexities of your kitchen and, by extension, your life.

I'm not here to transform your diet or impose rigid rules. Instead, I aim to inspire a new way of interacting with the heart of your home – the kitchen.

Before we embark on this journey, I want to make everything easier by clarifying from the start what *The Mindful Kitchen Map* truly is not:

- It's not just another collection of recipes.
- It's not merely a handbook with advice on steps for sustainability.
- It's not the usual story of one of the countless vegan chefs or gurus who have dominated the food world over the last ten years.

Instead, this book is an invitation – a guide to rethinking your relationship with food, your kitchen and, ultimately, yourself.

This is a map designed to help you navigate the unique challenges of neurodivergence, anxiety or simply the demands of a busy life, while creating a lifestyle that prioritizes wellbeing, creativity and mindfulness.

WHY COOKBOOKS FAIL US

If you're like me, you've struggled to find resources that truly resonate; traditional cookbooks often fail us.

You buy them in the hope of transformation – better meals, better skills, or a better relationship with food. But what happens?

You cook two or three recipes, maybe four if you're feeling ambitious and the rest collect dust. Why?

Because most cookbooks aren't designed to be used. They're designed to be admired. Glossy photos and innovative recipes sit untouched, a testament to their inaccessibility.

They expect a uniformity that doesn't exist – built on fixed timelines and unspoken assumptions for a world that assumes everyone, every kitchen, every cook and every lifestyle operates the same way.

But we don't. Especially for those of us navigating neurodivergence. Cookbooks rarely account for the real challenges – be it the chaos of ADHD, the ebb and flow of anxiety or the simple unpredictability of life.

Too often, they fail to acknowledge how deeply our emotional, physical and mental wellbeing are tied to the space where we prepare our meals. Cookbooks focus too much on rigid rules and not enough on the experience of cooking – the part where creativity, intuition and enjoyment come into play.

A MAP, NOT A MANUAL

I wanted this book to be different. Not just in the recipes but in how you experience it.

Not another shelf-help book.

This is a tool designed to meet you where you are, empower you to engage with your kitchen and to make cooking feel intuitive, inspiring and achievable.

Cooking should never be an exercise in stress or perfectionism.

And this is not a race against time, so you won't find prescriptive preparation durations here. Cooking is a rhythm you set yourself – a process that feels as good as it tastes.

This is an invitation to slow down and create. To explore your kitchen not as an obligation but as a sanctuary – a place where mindful practices meet practical tools.

BUILDING THE MAP: Visual and Structural Philosophy

To make this process achievable, I've built this book around three core principles:

1 PHOTOGRAPHY: Visuals that speak without words

Every image is crafted to communicate the essence of the recipe at a glance. The visuals are your first guide, offering an intuitive understanding of the steps and ingredients before you even dive into the written instructions.

For many of us, the brain scans before it processes. We take in the big picture first, trying to make sense of it before diving into the details.

The photography in this book serves as a tool for clarity, rather than a collection of pretty pictures.

The visuals are designed to guide you through the recipe without needing to read every word.

You'll see the final dish alongside the steps that get you there.

The images tell the story of the process, showing you the transformation of ingredients, so you can imagine yourself in the kitchen.

It's about immersion, not aesthetic perfection.

When you look at a photo, you should feel like you're already cooking: whisking the cream, blitzing the pesto, sautéing the vegetables or shaping the dough.

You'll get the core of the recipe just by scanning the page, understanding how doable it is before you've even read the first instruction.

This approach is about confidence and connection. By showing the process or the key achievement, the visuals invite you to engage with the recipe, trust yourself and take that first step.

2 STRUCTURE: A recipe that works for you

Recipes are designed with clarity and simplicity. My experience has taught me the importance of consistency, so every recipe here is structured to be foolproof and adaptable.

Cooking is deeply personal. It's influenced by how you feel, how much time you have and the energy you bring to the process.

Yet traditional recipes often impose a structure that feels suffocating – precise measurements, exact times and rigid instructions that leave no room for adaptation.

That approach doesn't work for everyone – especially not for me.

In this book, recipes are frameworks, not strict formulas. They're designed to be foolproof but flexible and clear but forgiving.

If you have every ingredient and want to follow the recipe to the letter, it will work. However if you need to swap something out, simplify a step or improvise based on what's in your pantry or the equipment you have available, it will still work.

Most importantly, there are no time constraints.

Cooking isn't a sprint. It's about presence, flow and creativity.

Some days, you'll take your time savouring each step as a form of mindfulness. On other days, you'll move quickly, getting food on the table without sacrificing quality.

This book is built for both.

Cooking should feel like an invitation, not an obligation.

That's the ethos behind every recipe in these pages.

3 ACCESSIBILITY: A Layout That Respects Your Brain

Special attention has been given to fonts, spacing and layout, ensuring the book is easy to follow, even for neurodivergent readers.

The structure of this book has been designed with neurodivergent readers in mind because I've walked that path.

Traditional cookbooks often feel cluttered and overwhelming, with dense paragraphs and unbroken instructions and layouts that demand constant re-reading. Here we do things differently.

Every recipe is broken into small, digestible steps and spaced for clarity and flow. The fonts are chosen to reduce cognitive strain, and the overall layout is built to guide your eyes naturally, from one part of the page to the next.

For me, cooking has always been about reducing overwhelm, not adding to it. This layout is a reflection of that philosophy.

It's designed to work with your brain, not against it.

BREAKING THE COOKBOOK NORM

I said it before, but I can't stand the fact that most cookbooks end up being used for just a handful of recipes.

Studies show that readers typically cook fewer than five per cent of the recipes in a given book, leaving the rest untouched.

That's not just wasteful – it's a missed opportunity.

This book is designed to break that norm.

There's no aspirational cooking here. This is a practical book with intuitive recipes that you'll come back to again and again.

Help me in doing that, breaking the circle and ensuring this is not another unused, forgotten cookbook.

This is your map.

A guide. A tool.

It's here to help you engage, explore and create in your kitchen with confidence and curiosity.

Whatever you are making, this book will meet you where you are.

It's not about perfection – it's about presence.

Cooking is something you become a part of.

So let this book be your companion as you navigate your culinary journey, one recipe at a time.

Welcome to *The Mindful Kitchen Map*. Let's begin this journey together.

WHY THE MAP MATTERS

The idea of a "map" emerged from my own journey. For years, I didn't know I had ADHD. I lived undiagnosed, constantly compensating with makeshift tools and coping mechanisms.

Amidst the chaos, I found that the kitchen could be my anchor. It wasn't just a place to prepare meals – it became my sanctuary.

Through trial and error, I crafted systems and routines – not rigid rules, but flexible frameworks – that turned cooking into a creative and stabilizing force in my life.

The Mindful Kitchen Map captures those tools, born from years of learning and shaped by neurodivergence, creativity and mindfulness.

Unlike one-size-fits-all solutions, this map is adaptable.

It's designed to be revisited, revised and reimagined as your needs evolve.

What makes it unique is its holistic approach. In addition to recipes, you'll develop strategies for creating a serene, functional kitchen that nourishes your body, mind and soul.

This is about empowerment – a path that aligns with who you are and where you want to go.

THE POWER OF CHOICE

In a world that is obsessed with speed and efficiency, this book asks you to pause.

To use cooking as a form of expression and connection.

Every recipe and routine is an opportunity to reclaim agency and embrace sustainability – for the environment, of course, but mainly for yourself.

Without unnecessary pressure, you'll discover a style of cooking and living that aligns with who you are.

Whether you are just like me, someone seeking sustainability or simply a person striving to create harmony in their kitchen, this map is for you. It's about progress – learning, evolving and finding joy in the journey.

Welcome to *The Mindful Kitchen Map*.

Let's chart your course to a sustainable, mindful and healthier life.

A BIT OF ME: Living Without Knowing

I grew up in Sardinia but moved to London when I just turned 19, and you know London …

Back then, I didn't understand why life felt the way it did. My mind was a constant whirlwind of thoughts and no matter how hard I tried, the pieces never seemed to fit.

I wasn't lazy or unmotivated – the opposite, in fact. But simple tasks – finishing projects, meeting deadlines, staying consistent – felt like climbing a mountain without a map.

Yet, somehow, when I found something I loved, something that caught my attention, I'd hyperfocus and lose myself in it. I could accomplish in hours what might take others days.

That's the contradiction of undiagnosed ADHD. It's like having a high-performance engine with brakes that don't work.

You're powerful, but you're also unpredictable.

THE EYE OF THE STORM

For me, the kitchen became the calm in my chaos. At first, I didn't realize why. I just knew that when I stepped into it, whether at home or work, things clicked.

The clatter of pans, the rhythm of chopping, the aroma of garlic hitting hot oil – it all made sense. Cooking itself was grounding. It gave me something tangible to hold onto.

Over time, this sanctuary expanded into more than just preparation.

Managing the service during a busy dinner shift, plating dishes to perfection and organizing the pass tickets became an extension of the calm I found in cooking.

Leading the brigade during peak hours was chaos transformed into choreography – every action deliberate, every step purposeful.

Watching dishes leave the pass and seeing the instant feedback in the expressions of diners connected me to the impact of my craft in real time.

The kitchen wasn't just my calm; it became my control, my art, and my way of engaging with the world.

Everything started by turning the raw into something finished. I could start and complete a process without distractions pulling me in a hundred directions.

The rules were clear: prepare, cook, taste, adjust.

There was no noise, no chaos – just me, the ingredients, and the tools I'd built to make it all work.

What started as a way of making meals became more than a necessity – it was my way of navigating life.

> Online I am also known as the Mensch Chef. The word "mensch" is Yiddish, and it means someone who acts with integrity, honor, fairness and transparency. These are the qualities I seek to embody as the Mensch Chef, as an advocate for sustainable living, creativity and wellbeing.
>
> My content is all about showcasing how sustainability and a plant based lifestyle can be practical, enjoyable and deeply fulfilling. Cooking is more than just preparing meals, it's an approach that intertwines the art of cooking with the science of wellbeing. It's also about integrating sustainable practices that do not just reduce waste or promise to save the environment, but are transformational and enhance our wellbeing and the communities around us.
>
> This book is just one part of the Mensch Chef community and movement, where people can discover and share not only recipes but learn the art of living well and responsibly, impacting the world one dish at a time!

THE DIAGNOSIS QUESTION: To Know or Not to Know

For years, I didn't have a name for the chaos that shaped my life.

I didn't know there was a reason for my impulsivity, scattered focus or the energy that came in overwhelming waves. All I knew was that I wasn't like everyone else.

When I finally learned about ADHD, everything clicked. It wasn't just me. There was a framework, a term, an explanation. And yet, knowing didn't solve everything – it raised new questions:

Do I need a diagnosis? What would it mean to have one? How would it change how I saw myself – or how others saw me?

The professionals I consulted gave me answers but not solutions. They validated what I already suspected: I wasn't broken and my struggles weren't failures of effort or willpower.

They explained that ADHD shaped how I experienced the world, for better or for worse.

A diagnosis could provide clarity, open the door to treatment and offer external validation for what I already knew.

But knowing that didn't make the decision easier.

Would a diagnosis really change how I lived my life? Would it change anything at all?

Medication was a key part of the discussion. For many, it provides the stability they need to create meaningful change.

But I knew it wasn't my path.

As someone who had dedicated years to studying natural medicine and becoming a healing diet coach, I believed deeply in the power of holistic approaches.

My ethos has always been to address the root cause of challenges and to align every solution with balance and sustainability.

Medication, while valuable for others, didn't resonate with the way I wanted to approach my life.

UNDERSTANDING THE GUT AND ADHD

What did resonate was something far less explored: the connection between what we eat and how we think.

While traditional approaches to ADHD often focus on behavioural therapy or medication, I found that diet was rarely part of the conversation.

Through my studies, I discovered the profound impact the gut has on the brain.

This connection isn't a passing trend, but it's extensively backed by science.

The gut is often called the "second brain" because it directly communicates with the central nervous system. What we eat doesn't just fuel our bodies; it influences our mental clarity, mood and ability to focus.

For those with ADHD, this connection is even more critical.

Inflammatory foods – those packed with refined sugars, processed ingredients and artificial additives – can worsen symptoms like impulsivity, brain fog and emotional dysregulation.

They create internal chaos that mirrors the external challenges of ADHD.

On the other hand, nutrient-rich, anti-inflammatory diets can bring balance.

Wholefoods, healthy fats and plant-based nutrients support the brain's ability to function clearly and efficiently.

The shift isn't just physical – it's mental and emotional, too.

When I began focusing on my diet, everything started to change.

Eliminating inflammatory foods brought me a sense of calm I hadn't felt in years. Preparing meals from scratch gave me control – not just over my food, but also over my mind.

The process itself became therapeutic.

That's when it clicked: I no longer cook for sustenance but as a way to reset, reconnect with myself and create a foundation for growth.

A CHOICE OF ALIGNMENT

Choosing not to pursue a formal diagnosis wasn't about rejecting the system – not entirely anyway. It was about recognizing that I already had the tools to move forward.

The knowledge I gained, combined with the routines I had built over the years, gave me the clarity I needed to make a decision that aligned with my values.

This choice doesn't diminish the value of diagnosis. For many, it's the key to understanding themselves and accessing the resources they need. But for me, the diagnosis wasn't the goal.

The goal was agency – the ability to choose my path and craft a life that worked for me on my terms.

SHIFTING THE ADHD CONVERSATION

The role of diet in managing ADHD is an area that deserves far more attention.

While behavioural therapy and medication are valuable tools, they're only part of the picture.

The gut-brain connection, the influence of inflammation and the power of wholefoods should be central to any discussion on mental health, especially for those navigating neurodivergence.

We need to shift the conversation. **ADHD isn't just about focus or behaviour – it's about the whole system**: the mind, the body and the choices we make every day.

For me, choosing to focus on diet, mindfulness and holistic practices was a declaration.

It was a way of saying, "I'm not broken. I'm just different. And I can build a life that works for me."

As we move forward, before diving into the cookbook itself, I want to explore this connection further – the relationship between the gut, diet and ADHD, and how understanding this relationship can unlock new possibilities for growth and wellbeing.

BRAIN, GUT AND HEART COHERENCE

The connection between the brain, gut and heart isn't just a poetic metaphor – it's a scientific and energetic reality that shapes how we experience life.

Our thoughts, emotions and physical health are intricately linked, forming a feedback loop that determines our wellbeing. Yet, modern medicine often views these systems in isolation, focusing on symptoms rather than their connections.

Ayurveda and natural medicine, however, have long understood what science is beginning to validate: the gut isn't just a digestive organ. It's central to our mental health, immune function and even our emotional balance.

The energy of the food we consume, the rituals we engage in, and the mindfulness we cultivate can profoundly influence our neurodivergent or non-neurodivergent minds.

THE GUT: A Second Brain

The gut is our "second brain", and for good reason. With its vast network of neurons and direct connection to the central nervous system via the vagus nerve, the gut communicates with the brain constantly.

This communication isn't one-way – signals from the gut influence our mood, focus and emotional resilience just as much as the brain affects our digestion.

Food isn't just fuel from the macros perspective – it's energy that directly shapes how we think, feel and act.

Ayurveda beautifully categorizes foods into three energetic qualities: **sattvic** (pure and calming), **rajasic** (stimulating) and **tamasic** (dulling). Knowing your constitution type isn't just some "woo woo" concept from Ayurveda blogs – it's a game-changer. I highly recommend finding out yours. And if you ever need help, reach out in my community – I've got you!

For a neurodivergent mind, incorporating more sattvic foods can be transformative.

Fresh fruits, vegetables, nuts, seeds and whole-grains not only nourish the body but also bring clarity and calm, creating a foundation for focus and emotional regulation.

Modern research reinforces this ancient wisdom.

Diets high in refined sugars, trans fats and artificial additives increase inflammation, leading to cognitive fog, mood swings and difficulty concentrating.

Is this what's happening to the young generations? Does the recent explosion of diagnosis in children have something to do with the modern diets they have been raised on?

For those of us navigating ADHD or other forms of neurodivergence, avoiding inflammatory foods means not fuelling stress hormones, emotional instability and cognitive chaos.

When I began to eliminate this type of food and replace it with nutrient-dense alternatives, everything changed.

Replacing refined sugars with natural options stabilized my energy, calmed my mind and created a sense of balance I hadn't felt in years.

Cooking was transformative. It allowed me to take control of what entered my body and, in turn, what shaped my thoughts and emotions.

That's why I always refer to cooking as a sanctuary – a sanctuary for growth, that grounded me in the present while empowering me to craft a foundation of clarity and resilience.

While this book introduces key principles, diving deeply into the intricate dance of food combinations and their effects requires another book entirely.

For now, let this serve as a reminder: **the way we nourish ourselves is the way we empower our lives.**

THE HEART:
A Compass for Emotional and Physical Balance

While the gut and brain communicate directly, in my opinion the heart is the third key player in this relationship. Often overlooked, the heart generates the body's largest electromagnetic field, sending signals that influence the gut, brain and entire nervous system.

When our heart rhythms are fast – due to stress, anger or fear – the signals amplify instability.

It's no surprise that this can exacerbate ADHD symptoms like impulsivity and emotional dysregulation. But when the heart's rhythm is coherent, aligning with states of gratitude, calm and focus, it acts as a stabilizing force.

This coherence supports the gut and brain, fostering clarity, balance and a sense of ease.

What does it have to do with food? Well, cooking became the way for me to create heart coherence.

Before meditations, before walking sessions, sound baths and breathworks it's what worked for me – a process that requires focus and care, anchoring me in the present moment, bringing peace and clarity.

Remember, the heart, mind and gut are not separate. They function as one interconnected system. And when they are in harmony, we can experience a profound sense of balance and resilience.

PRACTICAL ROUTINES FOR COHERENCE

I want to share with you a few practices that are very doable and sustainable and that you can easily integrate into your routine.

I am not reinventing the wheel. The following practices have been around forever. They worked for me and didn't require a complete overhaul.

MORNING PRACTICES FOR GUT AND MIND

Begin the day with warm lemon water to awaken digestion and prepare the gut-brain axis for optimal function. This small ritual sets the tone for balance throughout the day.

Then follow with a nutrient-dense breakfast to stabilize energy levels and promote focus.

Incorporate juicing into your morning routine, focusing on fresh, vibrant juices packed with greens, herbs and citrus to energize and detoxify.

Wheatgrass shots, rich in chlorophyll and phytonutrients, are a potent addition that nourishes your cells and support gut health.

For basic grounding and hydration, drink purified water – choose the best quality you can find, as water is the foundation of life and balance.

FERMENTED FOODS FOR BALANCE

Probiotics are essential for a healthy gut microbiome, impacting cognitive function and emotional regulation.

Incorporate living (the plant type) and fermented foods like homemade vegan yogurt, kimchi or miso soup into your daily meals. Favour sprouts and learn not to overcook food.

For a deeper dive into gut health and advanced techniques, explore the Gut Health section in this book (page 186) and check out my advanced fermented cheese recipes on my website www.menschchef.co.uk.

These recipes will get your kitchen to the next level.

HEART-FOCUSED COOKING RITUALS

Without sounding too cheesy, I really believe cooking is an act of care and connection.

While I do not like modern chefs and foodies fetishizing and mystifying food, a little romance goes a long way.

Before you start preparing a meal, take a moment to breathe deeply and set an intention.

Whether it's gratitude for the food or focus for the task ahead, this simple act creates coherence and calms the nervous system.

Do not cook in an intense rush. Take care with every little step, noticing the transformation as the ingredients come together. Watch the colours deepen, the aromas bloom and the textures shift.

This attentiveness will not only bring better cooking but also imprint your care and energy into the food itself.

Think about your grandmother's cooking. It tasted better not just because of skill, but because she cared about you and that energy was infused into the meals she prepared.

This is the essence of heart-focused cooking: a practice of presence, intention and love.

MINDFUL EATING

Eating is not just about fuelling your body; it's an opportunity to deepen your connection with the food you've prepared.

Slow down. Chew each bite fully. Notice the flavours, textures and aromas.

This practice aids digestion and creates a sense of gratitude for the nourishment you're receiving.

Mindful eating transforms a simple meal into an act of self-care and alignment, bridging the connection between the gut, heart and mind.

Macrobiotics and Ayurveda are fascinating subjects to explore more deeply if you wish.

THE TRIANGULAR CONNECTION IN ACTION

Each of these simple practices reinforces one another, creating a cycle of balance and resilience.

Each component creating a harmonious system that thrives when nurtured with care.

Cooking becomes the starting point for this alignment – a tangible, daily practice that shifts the way we think, feel and act.

We move from functional to intentional.

The alignment starts in the kitchen. By turning meal preparation into a mindful ritual, the act of cooking evolves from a necessity into an opportunity for connection – with yourself, with those around you and with the earth that provides your nourishment.

The lessons extend far beyond the kitchen walls. The patience developed while cooking mirrors how we can approach challenges with calm and focus.

The creativity sparked by a recipe fuels innovative thinking in other areas of life. The discipline of following a process translates into a more intentional way of living.

It is a way to cultivate coherence, and to nourish the systems that support your mental and emotional health.

Systems that bring harmony to your life, one step at a time.

THE SYSTEM THAT BUILT ME

I didn't know it at the time, but the systems I created in the kitchen taught me how to navigate everything else in life.

Cooking became a mirror for my existence, a reflection of creativity, discipline and growth.

In the kitchen, the tools – in the food, my medium.

The following principles are lessons I've learned from the stove. And the last words before I leave you with the recipes, I promise.

To those with care, talent and a pure heart, whose minds sometimes feel like their greatest obstacle, I offer these as a simple guide.

Let the kitchen be your sanctuary and food your medium.

Within its walls, you might just uncover your strength, discover your voice and realize your capacity to make a positive impact on the world.

1. START SMALL, DREAM BIG
In the kitchen, perfection doesn't happen overnight.

I didn't set out to master a recipe in one go. Instead, I started with one ingredient and one step.

I didn't need to bake the perfect loaf of bread on day one – I just needed to figure out what yeast does, how it breathes life into dough and what the process feels like when it works.

This philosophy carried into every part of my life. When I opened restaurants, developed concepts, or created resources, I didn't plan for packed venues, millions of followers or thousands of students. I focused on the first task: a single lesson, the first person I could help or one small change I could implement.

Small, clear steps layered with intention create momentum.

Over time, those steps build toward something far greater than you could have imagined at the start.

Dream big, but begin small – that's the trick.

2. RITUALS CREATE FOCUS

Chefs live by a concept called mise en place or "everything in its place". Before service begins, every ingredient is prepped, every tool is ready and every station is clean.

It's not just about efficiency; it's about creating the mental space to focus fully on the work ahead. Chaos during prep leads to chaos during service.

This practice transformed my daily life. I began to notice that a cluttered workspace meant a cluttered mind. A scattered morning led to a scattered day.

So I created rituals: small, intentional acts to anchor myself before stepping into the chaos of life.

Each morning, I take time to meditate, breathe deeply and centre my thoughts. I clear my desk before diving into work, jot down three priorities for the day or simply enjoy a quiet moment with a cup of tea.

These rituals are more than habits – they're acts of self-care. They create clarity and focus, even when life feels overwhelming.

3. EMBRACE THE FAILURES

Every chef will tell you the same thing: every great dish is built on a mountain of failed ones.

Recipes flop. Sauces split. Pastries refuse to rise. But failure is never the end – it's just a step in the process. You adjust, taste, and try again.

Life follows the same messy, looping path.

I've launched projects that didn't take off, closed restaurants that didn't thrive, and watched ideas I believed in fall apart. I've stumbled more times than I can count. Yet, every failure taught me something essential. Each misstep revealed what worked, what didn't and how to improve.

Progress isn't a straight line. It's trial and error, adjustment and persistence.

Failure isn't a mark against you – it's a step forward.

4. ENGAGE FULLY

Cooking demands presence. The sound of onions sizzling in a pan, the feel of dough beneath your fingers, the aroma of a freshly sliced tomato – it's an immersive experience that pulls you into the moment.

You can't rush it or half-heartedly go through the motions. You have to be fully there.

That sense of engagement became a skill I carried into everything else. Whether brainstorming for a project, diving into a new subject, or sharing time with loved ones, I learned to immerse myself completely.

Life isn't about multitasking, as they led us to believe; totally the opposite, it is about showing up fully for whatever is in front of you. Whether it's shaping a loaf of bread, solving a problem or having a meaningful conversation, being present transforms the experience.

5. CREATE FOR YOURSELF FIRST

When I first started cooking, I followed recipes to the letter, afraid to deviate from the instructions. However as I gained confidence, I started trusting my instincts. I adapted flavours, simplified techniques and made dishes my own.

That same mindset shaped how I approach my work now.

I don't try to recreate what's already out there. I focus on building what feels authentic to me, whether it's a recipe, a course or this book. Creating for yourself doesn't mean ignoring others; it means starting from a place of truth, where your work reflects your heart and vision.

When I chose the name Mensch.Chef, it was a declaration.

To be a mensch is to act with integrity, to uplift others and to create with purpose.

That's what I strive for every day.

Use the following pages to slow down, pay attention, and appreciate the process as much as the result – not only to make food but to create something meaningful with your own hands.

When you make your own flour, milk or cheese, you're reclaiming control.

You're saying, "I can do this. I don't need shortcuts or compromises."

That mindset won't just stay in the kitchen – it will spill into everything.

It's about empowerment. It's about mindfulness. It's about realizing that the things you thought were impossible are often just a matter of patience and practice.

And what better place to practice? Transforming your kitchen into a supportive and intuitive space where nourishment begins and creativity thrives.

Think of the map as your guide, one that organizes the kitchen into distinct zones – each with its own purpose, lessons and tools – designed to reduce overwhelm and foster mindfulness.

Book Dedication:

To myself – the one who questioned if this would matter, who made promises to a blank page and kept them, when doubt, setbacks and noise screamed louder than faith – you got it done, and for that, I am proud.

CONTENTS:
Integrating the Kitchen Zones

28 CHAPTER 1:

THE PANTRY
– The Library of Ingredients

The pantry becomes your foundation, a place to stock essential building blocks for nourishing meals. This chapter teaches you how to curate your ingredients with care, from organizing staples to crafting homemade flours and spices.

62 CHAPTER 2:

THE CABINETS
– The Hidden Chambers

Cabinets hold tools and treasures. This chapter shows you how to create efficient systems, and use shelf-stable ingredients for quick, satisfying recipes.

114 CHAPTER 3:

THE BIN
– The Resource Recovery Centre

Waste doesn't belong in a mindful kitchen. This chapter embraces zero-waste cooking, offering strategies to upcycle scraps into broths, sauces and snacks, honouring a sustainable philosophy.

142 CHAPTER 4:

THE REFRIGERATOR
– The Cold Storage Vault

Refrigerators are more than storage – they're systems for maintaining freshness and longevity. You'll learn to preserve dairy-free essentials, craft probiotic-rich foods and explore recipes like meat alternatives and vibrant juices.

214 CHAPTER 5:

THE FREEZER
– The Time Capsule

Freezers capture time, preserving nutrients and flavours. This chapter focuses on freezer-friendly meal prep, seasonal preservation techniques and instant food.

236 CHAPTER 6:

THE HOME
– Homegrown Haven

Gardening, even on a balcony, connects you to your food in profound ways. This chapter introduces home-growing basics and features simple recipes that showcase fresh, homegrown ingredients.

252 CHAPTER 7:

NOT THE END
– The Recipe for a Holistic Kitchen

The final chapter ties it all together, blending elements of food sovereignty, ethical eating, and holistic wellbeing. It's a space for reflection and action, giving you strategies to create a harmonious kitchen and lifestyle.

1 THE PANTRY:
The Library of Ingredients

Your pantry is the starting line of your health. Clear it, organize it and let it work for you – not against you.

The pantry isn't just where you store food – it's the engine room of your kitchen, the core of your journey and the place where clarity begins.

It's not a dumping ground for forgotten ingredients or expired packets; it's a living system. With a bit of time and intention, it can become your secret weapon for nutrition, creativity and organization.

This chapter is all about turning your pantry into what it should be: a curated, functional library of ingredients.

Let's learn how to ditch the junk, stock the essentials, and set up a system that works for your brain, your life and your goals.

FIRST STEP: GET RID OF THE CRAP

A cluttered pantry equals a cluttered mind.

Start with a clean slate. Take every single item out of your pantry and ask yourself:

- Is this nourishing me or is it filler?
- Is it aligned with the way I want to eat?
- Has it expired or have I forgotten about it entirely?

Processed, sugary or additive-heavy products have no place here.

They clutter your space and drain your energy.

Toss the stale crackers, the processed soups and the chemical-laden "quick fixes".

Donate unopened items if they're still usable, compost what you can and free up mental and physical space for what truly matters.

BUT WHAT'S AN OPEN PANTRY?

An open pantry is exactly what it sounds like – a system where everything is visible, accessible and organized. It's a shift from hiding your food behind doors to showcasing it on open shelves or transparent storage containers.

Why does this matter? Because visibility changes behaviour. When you see your ingredients, you're more likely to use them. You reduce waste, improve meal planning and create a sense of order that's especially powerful for those with ADHD or anxiety.

A summary of how it helped me and how it can be useful to you too:

1: Clarity and Control
With everything in sight, you know what you have and need. This reduces the risk of overbuying and ensures older items are used first.

2: Fewer Decisions, More Focus
The open layout eliminates the mental clutter of "Where did I put that?" and streamlines decision-making while cooking.

3: Encourages Healthy Choices
When fresh, whole ingredients like grains, legumes and spices are front and centre, you naturally gravitate toward them.

4: Minimizes Overwhelm
For neurodivergent minds, digging through cluttered shelves can trigger frustration. An open pantry eliminates that stress by making organization intuitive.

5: Energy Efficiency
Less time hunting for items means more time creating, cooking and enjoying.

SECOND STEP: The Power of Organization

Once you've purged the clutter, it's time to build the foundation of your pantry system.

Think of it as designing a library for your kitchen – functional, clear and inspiring.

HOW TO ORGANIZE YOUR PANTRY:

- **Categorize by Type**

Group grains, legumes, spices, nuts and seeds into designated zones. This builds efficiency and flow.

- **Use Clear Containers**

Transfer dry goods into transparent, airtight containers. This preserves freshness and lets you see at a glance how much you have.

- **Label Everything**

Whether they're hand-written or printed, labels create structure. They eliminate guesswork and keep your system running. Add dates and you won't go wrong.

- **Rotate Stock**

Adopt the "first in, first out" method. Place new items behind older ones to keep your pantry fresh and reduce waste.

- **Create a Replenishment List**

Keep a running list of items that need restocking. This prevents "panic shopping" and keeps your pantry in balance.

YOUR PANTRY STAPLES

Stocking your pantry with the right ingredients is more than practical – it's transformative. Here's an idea of what you'll want in your arsenal:

- **Grains & Legumes**
GRAINS: rice, quinoa, oats, millet ...
LEGUMES: chickpeas/garbanzo beans, lentils, beans ...

- **Flours**
BASE FLOURS: chickpea flour, almond flour, whole wheat, rice ...
SPECIALTY FLOURS: teff, sorghum, pea, potato ...

- **Nuts, Seeds & Oils**
Almonds, chia seeds, flaxseeds, sunflower seeds, olive oil, coconut oil

- **Spices**
Turmeric, cumin, smoked paprika, nutritional yeast, dried herbs ...

- **Vinegars & Sweeteners**
Apple cider vinegar, maple syrup, agave nectar ...

This isn't a one-size-fits-all list; it's a starting point.

Adjust it based on your tastes, dietary needs and favourite recipes, but it gives you an idea of what you are looking for.

For an exhaustive guide you can check an old YouTube video of mine titled "Vegan Pantry Secrets" or download my app for a Smart Grocery List.

Needless to say, for neurodivergent individuals, chaos in the kitchen can spill into chaos in the mind, and an organized pantry provides a sense of order that translates into reduced overwhelm.

You want to always look for PSE: Predictability, Simplicity, Empowerment.

The pantry is the starting point for a better relationship with cooking, your health and your home.

When you take control of this space, you take control of your choices. You create an environment that supports the way you want to eat and live.

By investing time in creating an intentional pantry, you're setting the stage for everything else. Meals become easier, waste decreases and you feel more connected to the process.

Clear the clutter. Simplify the system. Transform the way you cook – and the way you live.

LEGUMES & GRAINS FLOURS

"Small, intentional actions lead to transformative outcomes."

Imagine taking control of one of the most fundamental aspects of your vegan kitchen: your flours.

By milling your own legumes and grains, you unlock a world of freshness, flavor, and nutrient density that store-bought products can't compete with.

A step toward healthier eating and mastery over what you put into your body.

Milling your own flour might sound like a niche practice, but it's a game-changer.

With just a manual or small electric mill – or even a sturdy blender – you can create fresh, nutrient-rich flours that become the backbone of your recipes. From chickpeas/garbanzo beans and lentils to brown rice, the possibilities are endless.

Yes, store-bought flours are convenient, but they come with a cost.

Over time, pre-milled flours lose their nutrients and can even contain additives or preservatives. When you mill your own, you're working with the full spectrum of vitamins, minerals and natural flavors inherent in the original legumes and grains.

The beauty of home-milled flour lies in its freshness and purity.

The result? Dishes that taste better and nourish your body more effectively, adding texture and character, elevating your meals from functional to unforgettable.

Milling your own flours is a health upgrade as much as it's an investment in sustainability and savings.

Buying legumes and grains in bulk allows you to cut down on packaging waste while reducing your grocery bill. Over time, the initial cost of a mill or blender pays for itself in versatility and cost-effectiveness.

Think about it: one bag of chickpeas or lentils can transform into countless batches of fresh flour, soups or stews. You're saving money and gaining flexibility.

And in today's world, where food waste and environmental impact are on everyone's radar, this small change can make a big difference.

Not to mention that for anyone with dietary restrictions or food sensitivities, home milling is a revelation.

You control every step of the process, ensuring your flours are free from cross-contamination and perfectly suited to your needs.

Whether you're gluten-free, managing allergies or just looking to avoid additives, milling at home gives you peace of mind.

This is all about the process. There's something deeply satisfying about transforming a simple grain or legume into a foundational ingredient.

It's a way to appreciate its origins and to participate in the alchemy of cooking from scratch – a practice not reserved for culinary experts but for anyone who values intentional living.

Start small. Try milling chickpeas for a flavorful flour or experiment with a blend of lentils and rice for a gluten-free alternative.

The more you explore, the more confident you'll become and soon, milling will feel as natural as chopping vegetables.

Let's now sift through the essence of each of these flours and how to create them.

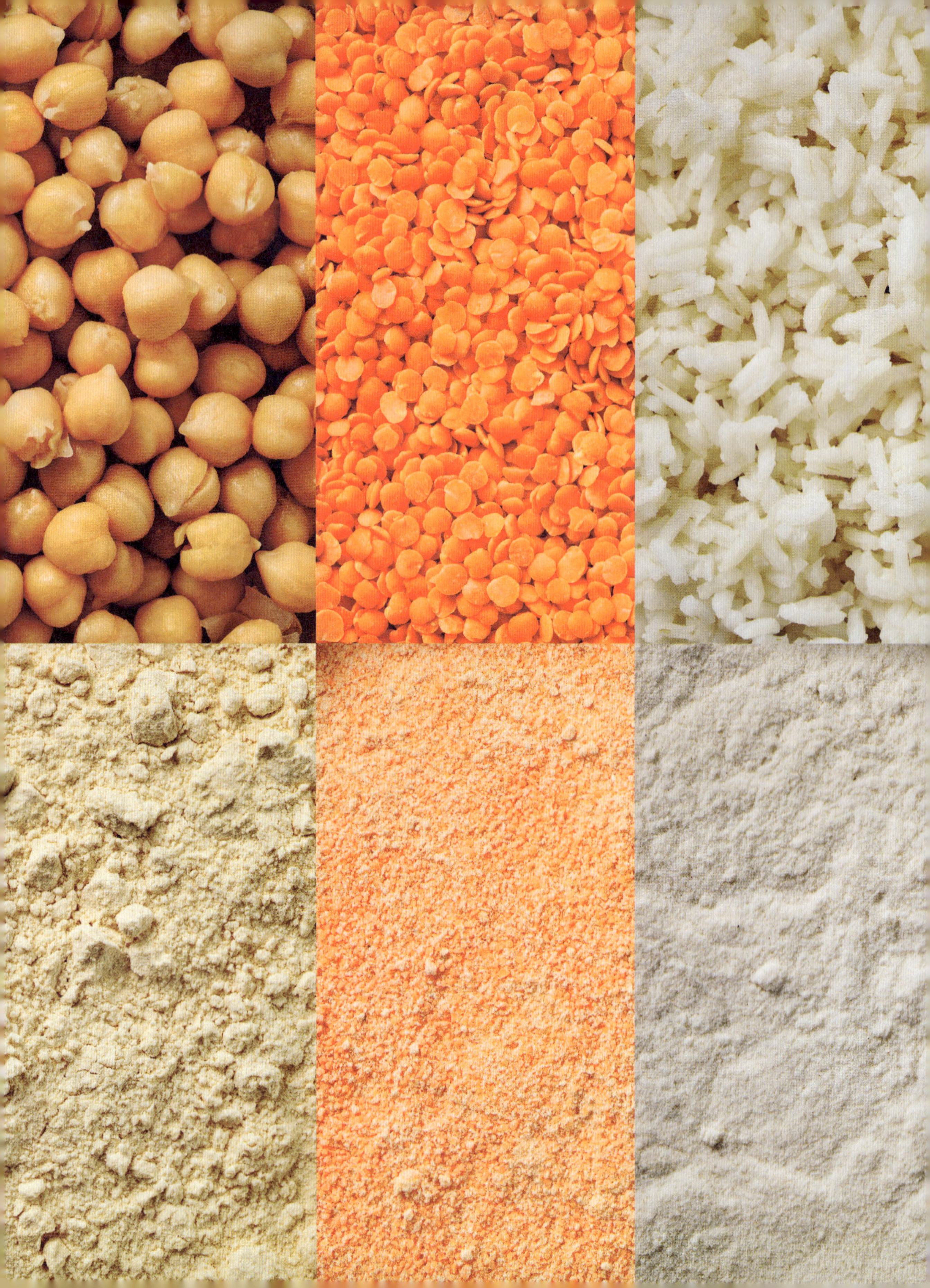

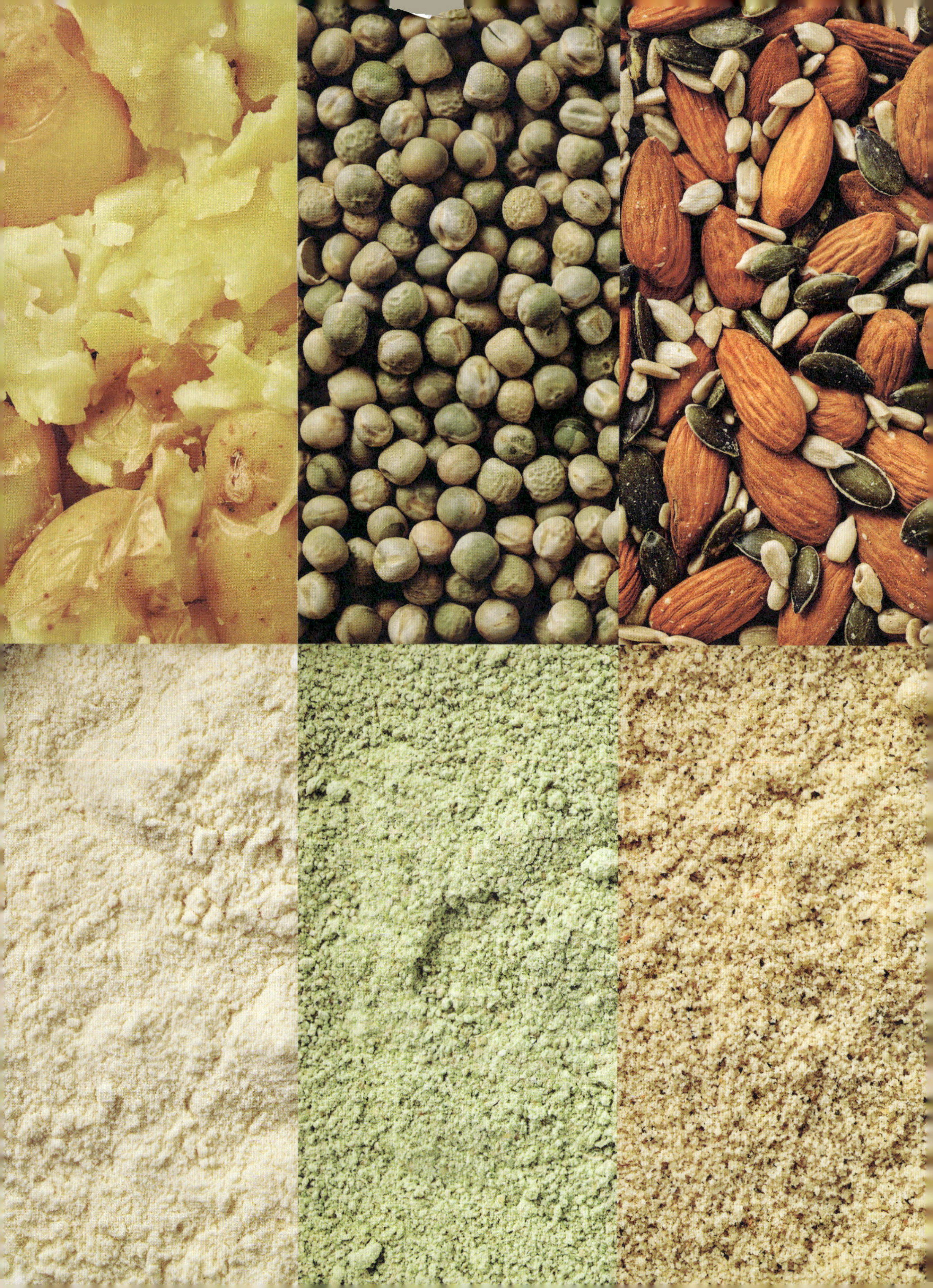

CHICKPEA/ GARBANZO BEAN FLOUR

Chickpea flour, also known as gram flour or besan, is a versatile and nutritious gluten-free flour, a cornerstone of many cuisines. Its nutty flavor, high protein content and adaptability make it a must-have ingredient in any vegan kitchen.

INGREDIENTS

- 400g (14oz/2 cups) dried chickpeas/garbanzo beans

PRO TIP:

- If you're new to milling, start with a small batch to understand the texture you prefer. Over time, you'll develop a rhythm that fits your recipes.

MINDFUL BENEFITS:

- Chickpea flour is rich in protein and fiber, supporting sustained energy and digestion. Its low glycemic index helps stabilize blood sugar levels, promoting better focus and mental clarity.

- High in folate and magnesium, chickpeas contribute to brain health by supporting neurotransmitter function and reducing stress.

Preparation:
Step 1: Spread the dried chickpeas/garbanzo beans on a baking sheet and inspect them for any stones or debris.

Step 2: Ensure the chickpeas are completely dry before grinding to prevent moisture from affecting the flour.

Grinding:
Step 3: Place the chickpeas in a high-powered blender or food processor. Grind in batches if necessary.

Step 4: Blend on high speed until you achieve a fine powder. Pause and stir the mixture occasionally to ensure all chickpeas are ground evenly.

Sifting:
Step 5: Pass the ground chickpea powder through a sieve or fine-mesh strainer to remove any larger particles.

Step 6: Re-grind any large pieces that remain in the sieve. Sifting ensures a smooth and consistent flour texture, which is essential for baking.

Storage:
Step 7: Store the chickpea flour in an airtight container in a cool, dry place.

Step 8: Label the container with the date to keep track of its freshness. It will keep for up to 6 months.

Ideas:
- Use chickpea flour for *socca* (a Mediterranean flatbread), *fainè* (a savory chickpea pancake from Sardinia) or as a batter for pakoras and other fritters.
- It's a fantastic binding agent in gluten-free baking.

RED LENTIL FLOUR

Red lentil flour is the unsung gluten-free hero of every pantry.

With its delicate, earthy flavour and protein-rich profile, it's a versatile ingredient.

Use red lentil flour in gluten-free baking, as a thickener for soups and sauces or to make protein-rich pancakes.

INGREDIENTS

- 400g (14oz/2 cups) red lentils

MINDFUL BENEFITS:

- Red lentils are high in protein and fiber, providing sustained energy and promoting digestive health.

- Rich in iron, they support oxygen transport in the body, which can reduce fatigue and improve focus.

- Folate and magnesium in lentils contribute to brain health by supporting neurotransmitter function and reducing stress.

Preparation:

Step 1: Inspect the red lentils for any stones or debris and rinse thoroughly under cold water.

Step 2: Spread the lentils out on a clean kitchen towel and let them dry completely.

Roasting (Optional):

Step 3: For a nuttier flavour, lightly roast the lentils before grinding.

Step 4: Spread the lentils on a baking sheet and roast at 175°C/350°F/Gas 4 for about 10 minutes, stirring occasionally. Let them cool completely before grinding.

Grinding:

Step 5: Place the dried (or roasted and cooled) lentils in a high-powered blender or food processor. Grind in batches if necessary.

Step 6: Blend on high speed until you achieve a fine powder. Pause and stir the mixture occasionally to ensure even grinding.

Sifting:

Step 7: Pass the ground lentil powder through a sieve or fine-mesh strainer to remove any larger particles.

Step 8: Re-grind any large pieces that remain in the sieve. Sifting ensures a smooth and consistent flour texture.

Storage:

Step 9: Store the red lentil flour in an airtight container in a cool, dry place.

Step 10: Label the container with the date to track freshness. It will keep for up to 6 months.

BROWN RICE FLOUR

Brown rice flour is a nutritious, gluten-free alternative to wheat flour. With its mild, nutty flavour, it's a versatile ingredient that can be used in baking, cooking and as a thickener for soups and sauces or as a base for homemade pasta. Its mild flavour complements both sweet and savoury recipes. An indispensable option for those seeking gluten-free solutions.

INGREDIENTS

- 400g (14oz/2 cups) brown rice

MINDFUL BENEFITS:

- Brown rice flour is high in fiber, which supports digestive health and promotes gut microbiome balance – key for reducing inflammation that can affect mental clarity and mood.

- It is rich in magnesium, essential for brain health, stress reduction and regulating energy levels. Manganese supports healthy cognitive function and helps protect against oxidative stress in the brain.

Preparation:
Step 1: Rinse the brown rice thoroughly under cold water to remove any dust or impurities.

Step 2: Spread the rice out on a clean kitchen towel and let it dry completely.

Roasting (Optional):
Step 3: For a nuttier flavour, lightly roast the rice before grinding.

Step 4: Spread the rice on a baking sheet and roast at 175°C/350°F/Gas 4 for about 10 minutes, stirring occasionally. Let it cool completely before grinding.

Grinding:
Step 5: Place the dried (or roasted and cooled) rice in a high-powered blender or food processor. Grind in batches if necessary.

Step 6: Blend on high speed until you achieve a fine powder. Pause and stir the mixture occasionally to ensure even grinding.

Sifting:
Step 7: Pass the ground rice powder through a sieve or fine-mesh strainer to remove any larger particles.

Step 8: Re-grind any large pieces that remain in the sieve. Sifting ensures a smooth and consistent flour texture.

Storage:
Step 9: Store the brown rice flour in an airtight container in a cool, dry place.

Step 10: Label the container with the date to track freshness. It will keep for up to 6 months.

POTATO FLOUR

Potato flour, made from starchy potatoes, is a gluten-free flour with excellent moisture-retaining properties. It adds elasticity, moisture, and softness to baked goods and acts as a natural thickener for soups and sauces.

INGREDIENTS

- 1kg/35oz potatoes (Russet, Idaho or Maris Piper), unpeeled, washed

MINDFUL BENEFITS:

- Easy to digest, supporting gut health.

Boiling & Preparation:

Step 1: Place the washed, unpeeled potatoes in a large pot and cover with water.

Step 2: Bring to a boil, then simmer for 15-20 minutes until fully cooked and tender.

Step 3: Drain the potatoes and allow them to cool slightly before handling.

Dehydrating:

Step 4: Cut the boiled potatoes into thin slices or mash them into a uniform layer.

Step 5: Spread the potatoes thinly on a dehydrator tray or a lined baking sheet.

Step 6: Dehydrate at 60°C/140°F for 8-12 hours or until completely dry and brittle.

Grinding & Sifting:

Step 7: Allow the dried potatoes to cool for 5 minutes before grinding.

Step 8: Grind in a high-powered blender or food processor until a fine powder forms.

Step 9: Sift the ground potato flour through a fine-mesh sieve to remove any larger particles.

Step 10: Re-grind any coarse pieces that remain in the sieve and pass them through again.

Storage:

Step 11: Transfer the potato flour to a labeled, airtight container.
- Store in a cool, dark place for up to 6 months.
- For extended storage (up to 1 year), use a vacuum pack or add a food-grade desiccant packet to prevent moisture-related clumping.

PEA FLOUR

Pea flour is a high-protein, gluten-free option with a nutty flavour, perfect for boosting the nutritional profile of baked goods, soups and sauces.

INGREDIENTS

- Fully dehydrated peas

MINDFUL BENEFITS:

- **High in protein and fiber, pea flour promotes stable blood sugar levels and sustained energy, which can enhance focus and mental clarity.**

Preparation:
Step 1: Start with whole, dry peas. If you have fresh peas, dry them completely first.

Roasting:
Step 2: Roast the dry peas in the oven for about 10 minutes at 170°C/340°F/Gas 3 to enhance their nutty flavour.

Grinding:
Step 3: Once the roasted peas have cooled completely, grind them to a fine powder in a high-speed blender or food processor.

Sifting:
Step 4: Pass the ground peas through a sieve or fine-mesh strainer to remove any large bits and achieve a fine flour.

Step 5: Re-grind any large pieces that remain in the sieve. Sifting ensures a smooth and consistent flour texture.

Storage:
Step 6: Store the pea flour in a labeled, airtight container away from direct sunlight.

- For longer shelf-life, refrigerate it to prevent rancidity, as its high protein content makes it prone to spoilage.

ALMOND AND SEED FLOUR

Almond and seed flour is a protein-packed, gluten-free option with a subtle, nutty flavour. It's versatile for both sweet and savoury dishes, offering nutrient density while maintaining a light texture.

INGREDIENTS

- Blanched almonds
- Raw and shelled seeds (e.g., sunflower or pumpkin seeds, unsalted and without added oil)

MINDFUL BENEFITS:

- **Provides healthy fats, magnesium and vitamin E, supporting brain health and reducing inflammation linked to stress and anxiety.**

Preparation:
Step 1: Mix equal parts almonds and seeds of your choice (such as sunflower or pumpkin seeds) in a food processor.

Grinding:
Step 2: Pulse until you reach a fine meal consistency, being careful not to over-process and turn it into butter.

Sifting:
Step 3: For a finer texture, sift the meal after processing.

Storage:
Step 4: Transfer the almond and seed flour to a labeled, airtight container.

- Refrigerate or freeze to maintain freshness for several months, as the natural oils can go rancid if stored improperly.

RICE THICKENER

Rice thickener, made from pulverized rice, is a versatile, gluten-free solution for adding body and texture to dishes.

Its neutral flavor and light colour make it ideal for soups, sauces, gravies and even desserts without altering the taste or appearance of your recipes.

To use it, create a slurry by mixing equal parts of rice flour and cold water before adding it to hot liquids. This prevents clumping and ensures a smooth consistency.

With this thickener, you step beyond the usual options like cornstarch or arrowroot, opening doors to new innovations. Mastering the techniques and understanding their unique characteristics will allow you to craft recipes that cater to diverse dietary needs.

INGREDIENTS

- Arborio rice or any other rice variety with a neutral flavour and light colour

UNIQUE BENEFITS:

- Rice flour is a transformative ingredient with unique properties. It produces a clear, glossy finish, enhancing the visual appeal of dishes without altering flavour profiles. Use it thoughtfully to achieve the desired textures while maintaining balance in your recipes.

Preparation:

Step 1: Choose your rice – Arborio or white rice is ideal for its neutral flavour and colour.

Step 2: Rinse the rice under cold water to remove any impurities and surface starch.

Step 3: Spread the rice out on a clean kitchen towel or a layer of paper towels. Allow it to air dry completely or gently pat it dry. The rice must be completely dry to grind properly.

Sifting:

Step 4: Once dry, use a high-powered blender or a coffee/spice grinder to pulverize the rice into a fine powder. Grind in batches if necessary to ensure an even texture.

Step 5: Use a sieve or fine-mesh strainer to sift the ground rice into a fine flour, discarding any larger pieces that don't pass through. Re-grind these pieces or save them for another use.

Storage:

Step 6: Store the rice flour in an airtight container in a cool, dry place until ready to use as a thickener.

MILLED LEGUMES AND GRAINS – OAT, BARLEY, BEANS, SPELT

"The secret to transformation lies in mastering the basics."

Why bother milling grains? A home mill doesn't just create flour – it gives you freedom. The freedom to create unique flaked grains, adding another dimension to your culinary repertoire. This technique involves gently crushing grains to create flakes rather than grinding them into a fine powder.

The result is a product that retains more of the grain's original texture and nutritional profile. It's a small step, but one that transforms the way you think about grains and their possibilities.

The appeal of flaked grains is in their distinct character. Oat flakes are a classic, commonly used in porridge/oatmeal, but there's a world beyond them. Barley flakes add a nutty depth to breakfast bowls. Rye flakes bring a subtle earthiness to rustic loaves. Even rice flakes can be a delicate foundation for creative dishes.

Flaking grains at home isn't complicated. With the right mill or attachment, you can crush grains to create fresh, whole flakes in minutes.

The key is a gentle crush that flattens the grain without completely breaking it down. This method preserves the natural, fibrous structure of the grain, ensuring that you get the maximum nutritional benefit from each flake.

Home-flaked grains have a freshness that can't be matched by store-bought versions. You can flake just the amount you need, ensuring that each bowl of porridge or each batch of granola is made with the freshest, most flavourful grains possible.

The freshness makes all the difference. Pre-flaked grains from the store often sit on shelves for months, losing both flavour and nutrients. Home-flaked grains allow you to use only what you need, ensuring that every meal you prepare starts with the best possible ingredients.

The advantage is control. You determine the quality, quantity and freshness. Each bowl of granola or loaf of bread retains the full flavour and nutrition of the grain, untouched by time or additives.

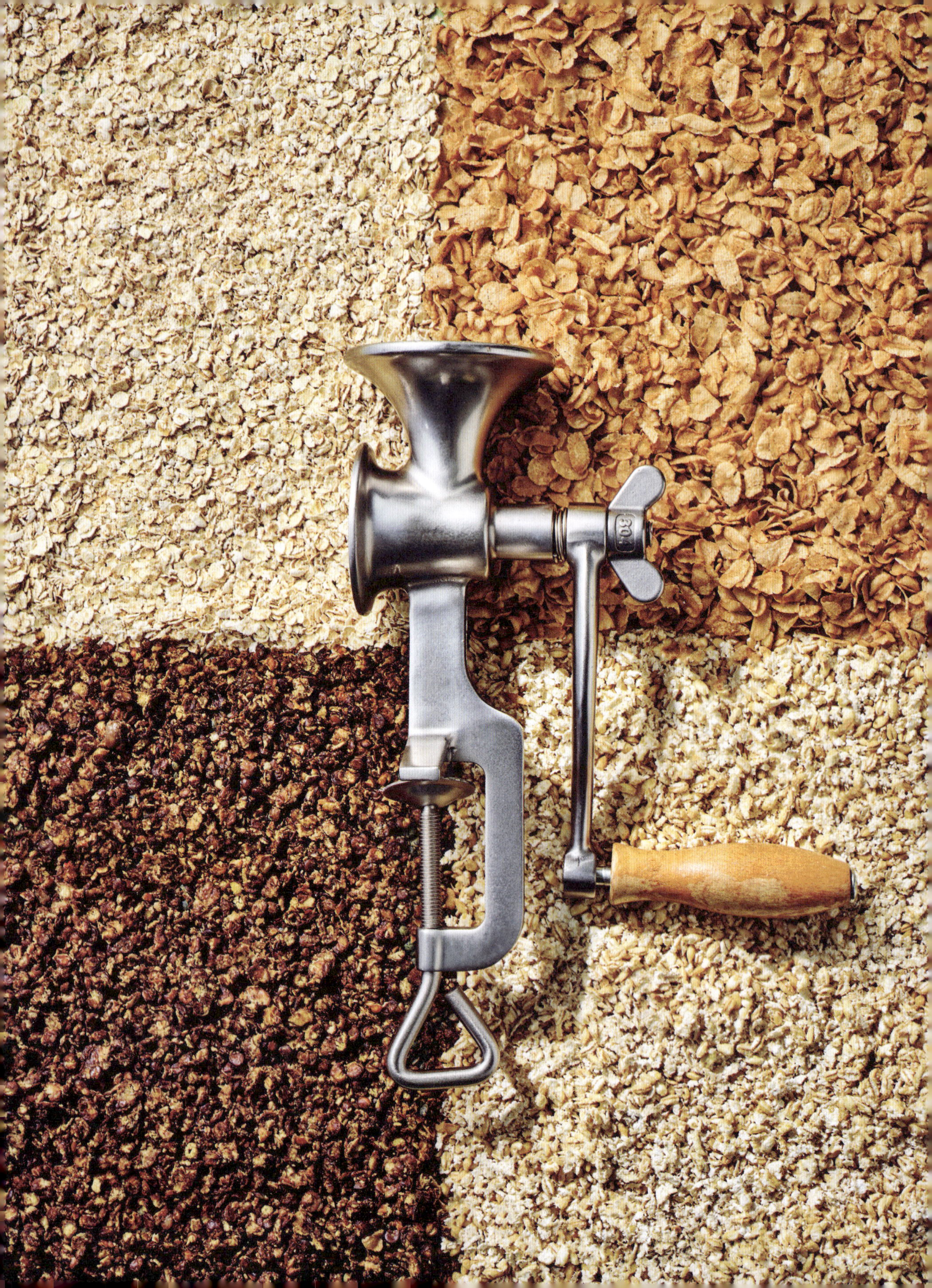

THE FLAKING SYMPHONY:
- Gently crush grains in your mill, preserving their texture and nutrients.
- Create oat flakes for porridge, barley for bread or spelt for muesli.
- Mill beans or lentils to create depth in your "instant meals".

ACTIVATION TIP

To delve deeper into this wholesome world, let's consider the process of activation, a prelude to flaking that can significantly elevate the quality of your grains and beans.

Activation involves soaking oats, barley, beans and spelt to initiate germination, which reduces the levels of phytic acid. This process unlocks nutrients, making them more bioavailable and enhancing digestibility. Adding a splash of apple cider vinegar or lemon juice (about 1 tbsp per 1L of water) to the soaking water further aids in breaking down anti-nutrients, improving mineral absorption.

To activate any grain or bean, soak them in water for 8–12 hours. To dry naturally, either place on kitchen paper between dishcloths, or ideally place in a dehydrator, or in the oven with the fan on set at no more than 30°C/85°F.

After activation, these grains and beans can be flaked, giving you a fresh and nutritious base for a variety of recipes. For more about activation, see page 72.

Jazz up your breakfast with homemade flaked grains and tap into ancient health with a modern twist!

FRESH IDEAS WITH FLAKED GRAINS:
- **Breakfast Revolution:** Start your mornings with oat or barley flakes for hearty porridge/oatmeal or granola.
- **Rustic Breads**: Incorporate spelt or rye flakes into your dough for added texture and depth.
- **Quick Meals**: Use flaked beans or lentils in soups and stews.

DRIED VEGGIES AND FRUITS

"Simplicity is the ultimate sophistication."
Leonardo da Vinci

In the vibrant tapestry of vegan ingredients, dried vegetables and fruits hold a place of honour. They're not flashy, but they are essential.

When done right, they save time, money and your sanity while elevating your cooking game. Think about it – these pantry staples pack the intensity of fresh produce into a long-lasting, shelf-stable form. Plus, you control the process, the flavour and the nutrients.

Beyond convenience, they embody the beauty of sustainability and the timeless wisdom of preserving nature's bounty.

A SHORT HISTORY OF DEHYDRATION

Dehydration is not new – it's ancestral wisdom that has stood the test of time. Thousands of years ago, our ancestors dried fruits, vegetables and even meats using nothing but the sun, the wind and the patience of nature.

These simple methods were essential for survival, enabling us to store food for harsh winters or long journeys.

In arid climates, sun-drying was the preferred method, while in cooler, wetter regions, smoke-drying techniques developed. Fast forward to today and the process has evolved with technology.

Modern dehydrators and ovens now make it possible to replicate this timeless technique with precision, allowing you to bring ancient preservation methods into the heart of your kitchen.

EQUIPMENT FOR DEHYDRATION: WHAT DO YOU NEED?

Dehydration is as much an art as it is a science, and the tools you choose can dramatically impact your results. Whether you're an experienced chef or just dipping your toes into the world of foods, here's how to decide which method is best for you:

1. DEHYDRATORS: The Gold Standard

If you're serious about incorporating dried foods into your kitchen arsenal, a dehydrator is worth the investment. Purpose-built dehydrators offer unparalleled control over temperature and airflow, making it easy to achieve perfect, consistent results every time.

BENEFITS:

PRECISION: The consistent temperature control ensures that nutrients are preserved while flavours are intensified.

EFFICIENCY: Dehydrators are energy-efficient and can handle large batches at once.

RELIABILITY: Unlike ovens or air drying, dehydrators are specifically designed for even moisture removal, so there's no guesswork involved.

2. OVENS: A Versatile Option

For those just starting or working with small batches, your oven can double as a dehydrator. While it may not offer the same precision as a dedicated machine, it's a convenient and accessible option.

BENEFITS:

ACCESSIBILITY: You already own it – no extra equipment required.

EASE OF USE: Ideal for occasional dehydration or experimenting with smaller portions.

DRAWBACKS:

ENERGY COSTS: Ovens consume more energy compared to dehydrators.

MONITORING: Achieving even results often requires manual intervention, like rotating trays or checking temperatures frequently.

3. AIR-DRYING OR SUN-DRYING: The Timeless Classic

For purists or those who prefer a hands-off, minimalist approach, air-drying or sun-drying is a nod to our ancestors' methods. However, it's not without its challenges.

BENEFITS:

SUSTAINABILITY: No electricity required – it's as eco-friendly as it gets.

SIMPLICITY: Perfect for drying herbs or thinly sliced fruits in dry, sunny climates.

DRAWBACKS:

TIME: Air drying can take significantly longer than modern methods.

RISK: Without controlled conditions, there's a higher chance of spoilage or contamination in humid or dusty environments.

IS A DEHYDRATOR ESSENTIAL?

Here's the truth: no, you don't need a dehydrator to get started. But if you're planning to make dehydration a regular part of your lifestyle, it's a game-changer. Think of it as a tool that brings precision, speed and efficiency to the art of preservation. For beginners, an oven or even air-drying is a fantastic way to test the waters before committing to more specialized equipment.

SO WHY CHOOSE DEHYDRATION?

I see dehydration more than a preservation method – it's a lifestyle choice with many flavours and creativity implications. It allows you to enjoy the best of seasonal produce year-round, reduce food waste and take control of what goes into your body.

Unlike many store-bought dried products, home-dried foods are free from unnecessary sugars, preservatives or chemicals, making them a cleaner, healthier option for you and your family. The versatility of dried produce is unmatched.

Picture this: a handful of dried mushrooms turning a simple soup into a robust, umami-packed masterpiece. Or dried tomatoes, rehydrated and blended into a sauce, bursting with the flavour of summer. Dried fruits are nature's candy, perfect for sweetening your morning oats or energizing your mid-day snack.

But here's the best part: when you embrace dehydration, you're not just preserving food – you're preserving time, energy and the planet's resources. Seasonal abundance and a deeper connection to the cycles of nature.

THE FINAL INGREDIENT: YOU

Like everything else, we are not looking for perfection; it's all about experimentation.

Start small and see what works for you. Whether you use a dehydrator, oven or a sunny windowsill, the process is as much about creativity as it is about practicality.

Your kitchen is your lab, and each dried ingredient is a step toward mastery, sustainability and mindful living.

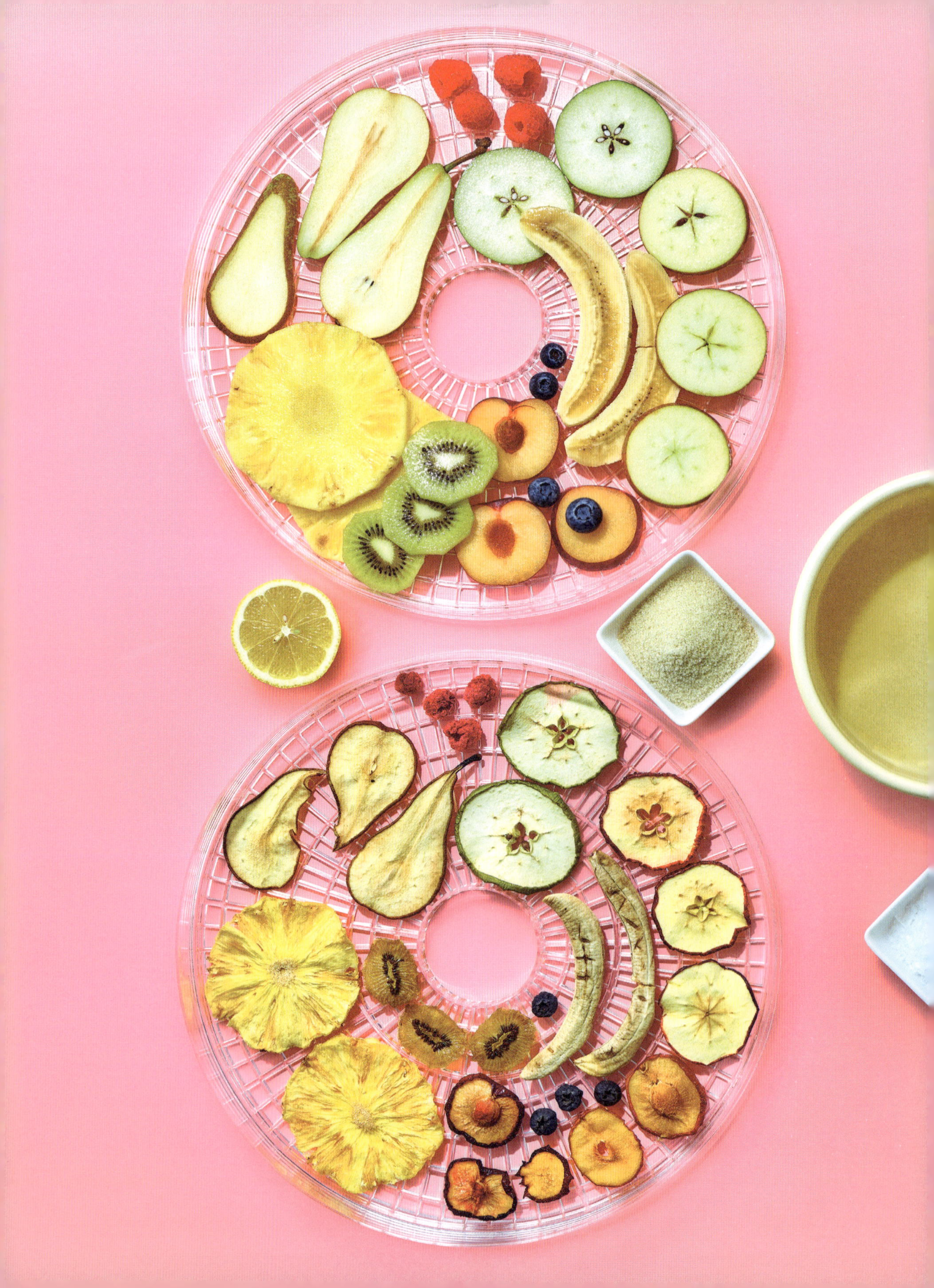

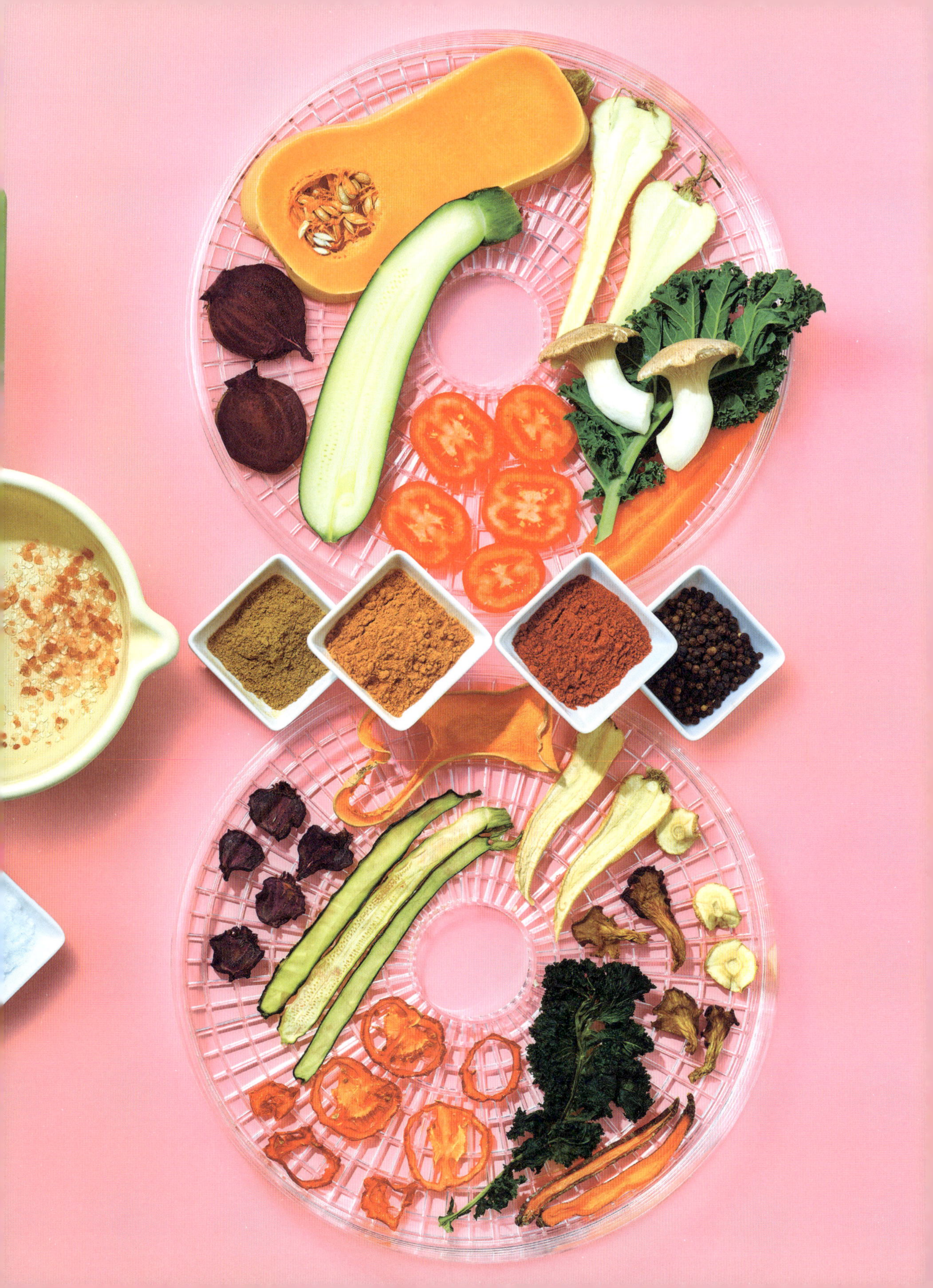

DRIED FRUIT AND VEGETABLES

Drying fruits and vegetables is a natural way to preserve their flavors, nutrients and textures. This method intensifies their taste, making them perfect for snacking, baking or adding to meals. Below are two approaches:

DRIED FRUITS

INGREDIENTS

- 1kg (35oz) seasonal fruit (e.g., strawberries, cherries, apricots, peaches, apples, pears, kiwis, bananas, plums, raspberries, blueberries)

FOR SUGAR-ENHANCED METHOD

- 400ml (14fl oz/1 ⅔ cups) water
- 100g (3½oz/½ cup) raw cane sugar
- 100ml (3½fl oz/scant ½ cup) lemon juice

OPTION 1: Sugar-Enhanced Method
(Best for color retention, flavor enhancement, and softer texture in dried fruit.)

Prepare the Syrup:
Step 1: Bring the water to a boil in a saucepan, then add the sugar and stir until completely dissolved.

Step 2: Turn off the heat and stir in the lemon juice.

Prepare the Fruit:
Step 3: Wash, pit, and slice the fruit into even-sized pieces.

Soak the Fruit:
Step 4: Immerse the fruit in the warm syrup for 10-15 minutes.

Step 5: Drain the fruit well and arrange it in a single layer on a dehydrator rack or lined baking sheet.

Drying:
Step 6: Dehydrate at 60°C/140°F for 6-8 hours (varies by fruit and thickness) until crisp and moisture-free.

Storage:
Step 7: Store the dried fruit in labeled, airtight glass jars for up to 6 months or vacuum-sealed for up to a year.

- **THE SUGAR-ENHANCED METHOD:**
Uses a light syrup to brighten colors, enhance natural sweetness and improve texture.

- **THE RAW METHOD:**
Preserves the fruit or vegetables in their most natural state, perfect for those avoiding added sugar or salt.

OPTION 2: Raw Sliced Method
(Best for a sugar-free, natural drying process.)

Prepare the Fruit:
Step 1: Wash, pit, and slice the fruit into even-sized pieces (around 3-5mm/¼in thick).

Step 2: Arrange the slices in a single layer on a dehydrator rack or a lined baking sheet.

Drying:
Step 3: Dehydrate at 50-55°C/122-131°F for 8-12 hours (depending on fruit type).

Step 4: Check for doneness: The fruit should be slightly pliable but not sticky or moist.

Storage:
Step 5: Store dried fruit in airtight glass jars for up to 6 months. For longer storage (up to 1 year), vacuum-seal or add a food-grade desiccant packet.

MINDFUL BENEFITS:

- Large batches ensure you have a healthy, ready-to-eat snack, reducing decision fatigue and impulsive food choices during busy days.

- Dried fruits are rich in fiber, antioxidants and vitamins like A and C, which support immune health and energy levels.

- The steady source of energy improves focus and reduces fatigue.

DRIED VEGETABLES

INGREDIENTS

- 1kg (35oz) fresh vegetables (e.g., carrots, bell peppers, zucchini, tomatoes, onions, mushrooms, beets, kale, spinach)

FOR BLANCHING METHOD

- 500ml (17fl oz/2 cups) water
- 4 tbsp salt
- Ice water (for refreshing)

OPTION 1: Blanching & Refreshing
(Recommended for Color & Texture Preservation.)

Prepare the Water:
Step 1: Bring a large pot of water to a boil and dissolve the salt.

Prepare an Ice Bath:
Step 2: Fill a large bowl with ice water and set aside.

Prepare the Vegetables:
Step 3: Cut the vegetables into uniform slices, cubes, or preferred shapes (around 3-5mm/¼in thick for even drying).

Blanch the Vegetables:
Step 4: Put the vegetables into the boiling water for the following amount of time:

Leafy greens (spinach, kale): 30 seconds
Root vegetables (carrots, beets): 2-3 minutes
Peppers, zucchini, onions, tomatoes: 1-2 minutes

Refresh the Vegetables:
Step 5: Refresh immediately in ice water for the same amount of time as blanching.

Step 6: Drain well and spread in a single layer on a dehydrator rack.

Drying:
Step 7: Dehydrate at 50-60°C/122-140°F for 6-12 hours (depending on vegetable type and thickness).

OPTION 2: Raw Sliced Method
(For Maximum Nutrient Retention, No Blanching)

Prepare the Vegetables:
Step 1: Wash and slice vegetables into uniform pieces.

Step 2: Arrange in a single layer on a dehydrator rack.

Drying:
Step 3: Dehydrate at 50°C/112°F for 8-14 hours (longer for denser vegetables).

Step 4: Check for doneness: Vegetables should be completely dry and brittle.

Storage
Step 5: Store in airtight glass jars for up to 6 months. For longer storage (up to 1 year), vacuum-seal or add a food-grade desiccant packet.

VARIANTS FOR DRIED FRUITS AND VEGETABLES:

Both dried fruits and vegetables can be ground into a fine powder for versatile uses:

- **Fruit Powder:** Use as a topping for yogurt, oatmeal, or fillings for chocolates.

- **Vegetable Powder:** Add to broths, soups, or roasted dishes for an umami punch.

MINDFUL BENEFITS:

- Dried vegetables retain a significant portion of their vitamins and minerals, such as beta carotene, vitamin C and potassium, which support brain health and immune function.

- Their long shelf life ensures you always have nutritious options available, reducing the reliance on processed foods.

- Organizing your workspace and preparing ingredients before starting the drying process helps reduce overwhelm and makes the task more enjoyable.

SPICES AND CONDIMENTS

"A single spice can tell a story; a blend creates a journey."

In the sanctuary of my kitchen, spices and condiments hold a sacred place. They are the alchemists of flavour, turning the mundane into the extraordinary with a single pinch or sprinkle.

Each jar and bottle is a gateway to a world of flavour, culture and wisdom.

These aromatic treasures carry the echoes of ancient traditions and healing properties that have been passed down through generations.

With their ability to elevate even the simplest ingredients, spices and condiments become the bridge between nourishment and artistry, between tradition and modern innovation.

My fascination with them goes beyond their utility. I'm drawn to the history they embody, the restorative power of their nature and the global stories they represent. To me, a well-stocked spice shelf is a canvas for creativity, a toolbox for health and a testament to the timeless connection between food and humanity.

Here, we'll explore not just the recipes but the philosophy behind them. From the nutty crunch of Gomasio to the bold warmth of Garam Masala and the vibrant tang of Za'atar, we'll dive into the essence of flavour creation. These blends ground us in the moment, inviting mindfulness, connection and a deep appreciation for the process of cooking itself.

An invitation to pause, to create and to connect with something greater.

• Recipes on the next page

GOMASIO

Gomasio, meaning "salt and sesame" in Japanese, is the expression of a philosophy. Born from a culture that values balance and minimalism, this humble condiment is a perfect example of simplicity elevating the everyday. Used as a traditional seasoning in Japanese macrobiotic diets, gomasio embodies the principles of mindful eating, providing flavour and nourishment without overloading the palate or the body. A warm, nutty aroma of toasted sesame seeds, blended with the mineral-rich complexity of sea salt. It's a sensory experience, connecting you to nature and the wisdom of tradition. For me, gomasio is a ritual. Preparing it requires focus: the gentle toasting of the seeds, the rhythmic grinding, the care in balancing salt and sesame. It's a moment to slow down, to appreciate the ingredients and to align with the art of mindful cooking. With many health benefits it is indispensable in my kitchen.

INGREDIENTS

- 144g (5oz/1 cup) sesame seeds (white or black)
- 1 tbsp sea salt

USAGE:

- Sprinkle gomasio over salads, soups, steamed vegetables, rice, or toast for a nutty, salty boost.
- Use it as a healthier alternative to table salt to reduce sodium intake without sacrificing flavour.

MINDFUL BENEFITS:

- Sesame seeds are rich in magnesium, calcium and healthy fats, which support cognitive function, stress reduction and better sleep.

- Sea salt contains essential minerals, adding balance and nourishment.

Preparation:

Step 1: Heat a dry skillet over medium heat. Add the sesame seeds.

Step 2: Toast the sesame seeds, stirring frequently, until they are golden brown and start to pop. This takes about 5–7 minutes. Be attentive to prevent burning.

Grind the Salt:

Step 3: While the sesame seeds toast, grind the sea salt into a fine powder using a mortar and pestle or a spice grinder.

Combine and Grind:

Step 4: Let the toasted sesame seeds cool slightly. Combine them with the ground sea salt.

Step 5: Grind the mixture lightly with a mortar and pestle or spice grinder. Break the seeds slightly without turning them into a paste.

Storage:

Step 6: Store the gomasio in a labeled airtight container in a cool, dry place. It will keep for up to a month.

ZA'ATAR MIX

Za'atar is a Middle Eastern blend of herbs, sesame seeds, sumac and salt that has roots that stretch back thousands of years. Its name derives from the Arabic word for thyme, a key ingredient that lends its distinctive herbal aroma. From ancient times, za'atar was believed to hold medicinal properties and was a staple in the diets of scholars and warriors alike, revered for enhancing mental clarity and strength.

Archaeological evidence points to the use of za'atar-like blends in ancient Egypt and the Levant, where it was mixed with olive oil and eaten with bread – a practice still cherished today. Across generations, za'atar has transcended its origins, becoming a symbol of hospitality and connection. It is sprinkled on flatbreads, stirred into olive oil, or used to season dishes, each variation reflecting local traditions. Za'atar is a reminder of the global language of food.

INGREDIENTS

- 2 tbsp dried thyme
- 2 tbsp dried oregano
- 2 tbsp ground sumac
- 2 tbsp toasted sesame seeds
- 1 tbsp dried marjoram (optional)
- 1 tsp sea salt

MINDFUL BENEFITS:

- **Thyme and oregano are rich in antioxidants that combat free radicals and support immune health.**

- Sumac provides anti-inflammatory properties and vitamin C, making it a great energy booster.

Prepare the Herbs:
Step 1: Ensure all herbs (thyme, oregano and marjoram, if using) are dried and free of moisture.

Toast the Sesame Seeds:
Step 2: Heat a dry skillet over medium heat. Add the sesame seeds and toast them, stirring frequently, until they are golden brown and fragrant, about 3–5 minutes.

Combine the Ingredients:
Step 3: In a bowl, combine the dried thyme, oregano, ground sumac, toasted sesame seeds and sea salt.

Step 4: Mix thoroughly to ensure an even distribution of all ingredients.

Storage:
Step 5: Store the za'atar mix in a labeled airtight container in a cool, dry place. It will keep for up to 6 months.

COOKING TIP:

- Freshly dried herbs will provide the most vibrant flavour.
- Be careful not to burn the seeds; they should have a warm, nutty aroma when ready.

THE PANTRY

GARAM MASALA

Garam masala, the aromatic heart of North Indian cuisine, is a warm and intoxicating symphony.

A celebration of warmth and depth, it's the secret that transforms Indian dishes from good to unforgettable.

Each ingredient – cinnamon, cardamom, cloves and cumin – brings its own story, rooted in ancient traditions and medicinal wisdom. Together, they create a blend that's as flavourful as it is therapeutic with the ability to stimulate digestion and boost metabolism and emotional balance.

Another ritual you don't want to miss in your kitchen.

Add garam masala to curries, soups and marinades for warmth and depth. Sprinkle it on roasted vegetables or use it in desserts like spiced cookies. Just be sure to add it toward the end of cooking to preserve its vibrant flavour.

INGREDIENTS

- 2 tbsp cumin seeds
- 2 tbsp coriander seeds
- 1 tbsp black peppercorns
- 1 tbsp cardamom pods
- 1 tbsp cloves
- 2 cinnamon sticks (5cm/2in each)
- 1 tbsp fennel seeds (optional)
- 2 bay leaves
- 1 tsp ground nutmeg

Toast the Spices:

Step 1: Heat a dry skillet over medium heat. Add the cumin seeds, coriander seeds, black peppercorns, cardamom pods, cloves, cinnamon sticks, fennel seeds (if using) and bay leaves.

Step 2: Toast the spices, stirring frequently, until they are fragrant and slightly darkened, about 3–5 minutes. Avoid burning to prevent bitterness.

Cool the Grind:

Step 3: Transfer the toasted spices to a plate and let them cool completely.

Step 4: Grind the cooled spices into a fine powder using a spice grinder or high-powered blender.

Add Nutmeg:

Step 5: Stir in the ground nutmeg.

Storage:

Step 6: Store the garam masala in a labeled airtight container in a cool, dry place. It will keep for up to 6 months.

MINDFUL BENEFITS:

- **Cumin and Coriander:** Aid digestion and reduce bloating.

- **Cardamom and Cloves:** Have anti-inflammatory and antibacterial properties.

- **Black Pepper and Cinnamon:** Stimulate metabolism and enhance nutrient absorption.

- **Nutmeg:** Offers a calming effect, promoting better sleep and stress relief.

2 THE CABINETS:
The Hidden Chambers

"Organization is not just about storing items; it's about creating access to a life of ease and abundance."

Welcome to The Cabinets, the beating heart of your vegan kitchen, where the ethos of self-reliance merges seamlessly with the convenience of modern practices and mindful living.

This chapter is about creative efficiency; it embodies a realm where every item, from homemade canned foods to essential kitchen staples, is thoughtfully selected.

Behind these cabinet doors, in a cool, dark sanctuary, each ingredient is preserved, free from additives in a practical and cost-effective way, underscoring our commitment to a sustainable, health-conscious lifestyle.

The Cabinets redefine the concept of nutritious cooking and efficient organization.

This section is designed to help you transform long-shelf-life products into pivotal components of your daily meals, offering a diverse array of options for every need.

You can begin your day with some wholesome homemade muesli or granola, a vibrant selection of activated nut butters or, as the day progresses, snack on a satisfying crunch of seed or carob bars.

This chapter unveils a collection of preserved essentials such as a rich passata and whole pelati, along with a variety of instant flavour enhancers like homemade gravy, dashi, bouillon and instant chocolate powder.

The story of The Cabinets continues with its array of preserves and pickles, each jar capturing the essence of seasonal freshness and zest. It celebrates the art of creating homemade essentials as an opportunity to nourish your body and mind while embracing the joy of eating.

Discover in these chambers an innovative assortment of ready-to-go foods, crafted for quick and effortless meal preparation, demonstrating that in the contemporary kitchen, quick meals can be synonymous with quality, and that the true essence of innovation can also be a celebration of mindful living.

MUESLI

Originating in Switzerland, muesli was created by Dr. Maximilian Bircher-Brenner as a healthful, fiber-rich meal for his hospital patients. Over time, this versatile staple has gained widespread acclaim across Europe and the United States. While store-bought muesli often comes with additives like skimmed milk powder, wheat protein or palm oil, making your own is not only healthier but also more cost-effective. This recipe takes muesli back to its roots, emphasizing simple, wholesome ingredients that nourish both body and mind.

By incorporating techniques like activating nuts, you'll unlock even greater nutritional potential, transforming this dish into a powerhouse of health.

Why Activate Nuts?
Nature equips grains and nuts with phytic acid and enzyme inhibitors to preserve their longevity, but these natural compounds can hinder nutrient absorption and digestion. By soaking and activating, you neutralize these inhibitors, making nutrients more bioavailable. In simpler terms: activated nuts are easier to digest and packed with more accessible goodness for your body.

INGREDIENTS

- 3 tbsp mixed nuts of your choice (almonds, walnuts, cashews)
- 1 tsp vinegar or lemon juice
- 300g (10½oz) flaked grains (e.g., oats, barley, spelt) (see page 43)
- 300g (10½oz) mixed dried fruits (e.g., raisins, apricots, dates), chopped if large (see page 46)

COOKING TIP:

- Prepare in small batches to maintain freshness and nutrient retention.

- Dry cereal has a longer shelf life than milled, so proper storage is key.

Activate Your Nuts:

Step 1: Soak your chosen nuts in water for 12–24 hours. Add 1 tsp of vinegar or lemon juice to enhance the activation process.

Step 2: Drain and rinse the nuts, then dehydrate them at a low temperature in your oven (at 60°C/140°F) or a dehydrator until completely dry and crispy. This could take 12–24 hours depending on the method used.

Prepare the Muesli:

Step 3: Mix your choice of flaked grains with the dried fruits in a large bowl.

Step 4: Roughly chop the activated nuts and toss them into the mix for added crunch and nutrition.

Storage:

Step 5: Store your muesli in labeled airtight jars or vacuum-sealed bags to retain freshness. Keep in a cool, dry place out of direct sunlight. Consume activated nuts and homemade muesli within a reasonable time to enjoy their peak nutritional benefits.

CREATIVE TIP:

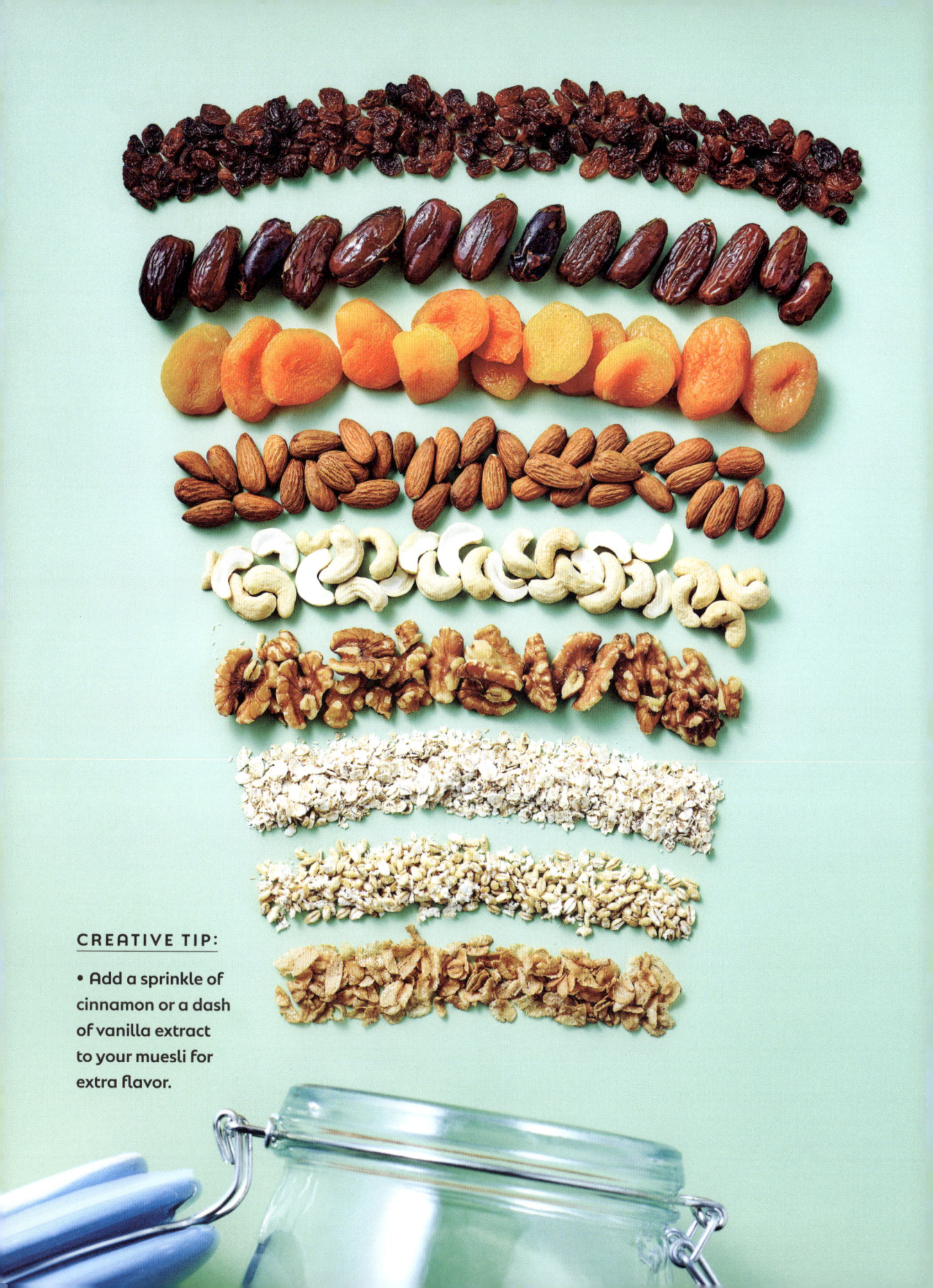

- Add a sprinkle of cinnamon or a dash of vanilla extract to your muesli for extra flavor.

SUPER GRANOLA

Granola, a classic born in the United States during the health food movement of the late 19th century, has evolved into a versatile staple for breakfast and snacks worldwide.

With its toasted mixture of oats, nuts and a hint of sweetness, granola has a comforting familiarity. However the true magic lies in its adaptability – making it at home means you control the sweetness, ensure freshness and, of course, avoid unnecessary preservatives.

By incorporating superfoods such as chia seeds, flaxseeds and goji berries, your granola transforms from a simple snack to a nutrient-dense powerhouse – real fuel for your body and mind. It offers a delicious way to start the day or keep you energized. Enjoy with yogurt, milk or as a topping for smoothie bowls. It's also a great snack on its own or sprinkled over desserts for extra crunch.

INGREDIENTS

- 300g (10½oz/3 cups) rolled oats
- 150g (5oz/1 cup) nuts (almonds, walnuts, pecans), roughly chopped
- 80g (2½oz/½ cup) seeds (pumpkin, sunflower, chia, flaxseeds)
- 85g (3oz/½ cup) dried fruit (raisins, cranberries, apricots, goji berries), chopped
- 180g (6oz/½ cup) honey or maple syrup
- 56g (2oz/¼ cup) coconut oil, melted
- 1 tsp vanilla extract
- ½ tsp ground cinnamon
- ¼ tsp salt
- 25g (¾oz/¼ cup) unsweetened shredded coconut (optional)
- 2 tbsp cacao nibs (optional for a chocolatey twist)

Preheat the Oven:
Step 1: Preheat your oven to 175°C/350°F/Gas 4. Line a large baking sheet with baking parchment.

Mix the Dry Ingredients:
Step 2: In a large bowl, combine the rolled oats, chopped nuts, seeds and shredded coconut (if using).

Combine the Wet Ingredients:
Step 3: In a separate bowl, mix the honey or maple syrup, melted coconut oil, vanilla extract, ground cinnamon and salt.

Mix Everything Together:
Step 4: Pour the wet ingredients over the dry ingredients. Stir well to ensure everything is evenly coated.

Bake the Granola:
Step 5: Spread the mixture evenly on the prepared baking sheet. Bake for 25–30 minutes, stirring halfway through, until the granola is golden brown and fragrant.

Add Dried Fruit and Superfoods:
Step 6: Remove the granola from the oven and let it cool completely. Once cooled, stir in the dried fruit and superfoods like goji berries and cacao nibs (if using).

Bake the Granola:
Step 7: Store the granola in a labeled airtight container at room temperature for up to 2 weeks.

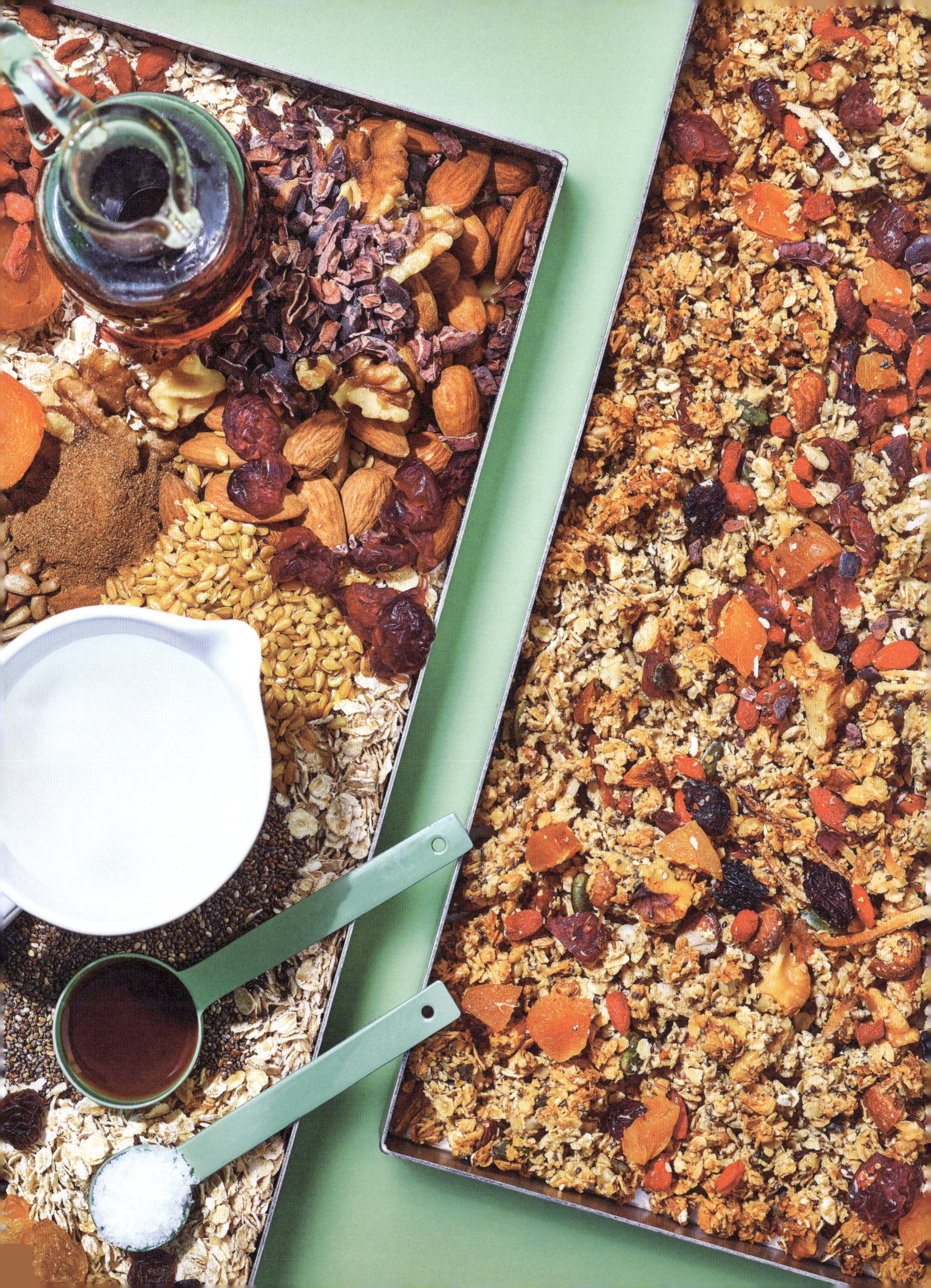

CAROB "CHOCOLATE"

Carob, often overshadowed by its more popular cousin cacao, deserves its own spotlight. Derived from the pod of a Mediterranean tree (*Ceratonia siliqua* tree), carob has a rich history stretching back to ancient Egypt, where it was cherished for its natural sweetness and versatility.

In modern kitchens, carob offers a caffeine-free alternative to chocolate, making it an excellent choice for those sensitive to stimulants or seeking a nourishing treat that supports calm. Rich in calcium and fiber and free from unnecessary additives, this recipe is designed for simplicity and focus.

INGREDIENTS

- 200g (7oz/scant 1 cup) coconut oil
- 90g (3oz/¾ cup) carob powder
- 100g (3½oz/ ⅔ cup) toasted hazelnuts
- 50g (2oz) coconut pulp or coconut flour (Check out my coconut milk recipe on page 148 for this ingredient!)

MINDFUL BENEFITS:

- Carob's natural sweetness eliminates the need for refined sugar, making these bars a healthier alternative to chocolate.

- Rich in calcium and fiber, carob supports bone health and digestion while avoiding caffeine that can cause restlessness.

- These carob bars pair wonderfully with a cup of tea or coffee.

Melt the Coconut Oil:
Step 1: In a small saucepan, gently melt the coconut oil over a low heat until fully liquid.

Combine with Carob Powder:
Step 2: Remove from the heat and stir in the carob powder until smooth and fully incorporated.
Tip: Use a whisk to ensure there are no lumps.

Add the Coconut Pulp/Flour:
Step 3: Stir in the coconut pulp or coconut flour, mixing thoroughly. This will add texture and a mild sweetness to the bars.

Prepare the Hazelnuts:
Step 4: Roughly chop the toasted hazelnuts. You can leave some halves for added crunch.

Combine All Ingredients:
Step 5: Fold the chopped hazelnuts into the carob mixture, ensuring they are evenly distributed.

Mould the Bars:
Step 6: Pour the mixture into a lined or silicone mould (any size or shape works). Use a spatula to spread it evenly
Tip: Tap the mould gently on the counter to remove bubbles.

Chill to Set:
Step 7: Place the mould in the refrigerator for at least 1–2 hours or until the bars are fully set and firm.

Cut and Store:
Step 8: Once set, remove from the mould and cut into bars of your preferred size. Store in a labelled airtight container in the refrigerator. They will keep for to 2 weeks.

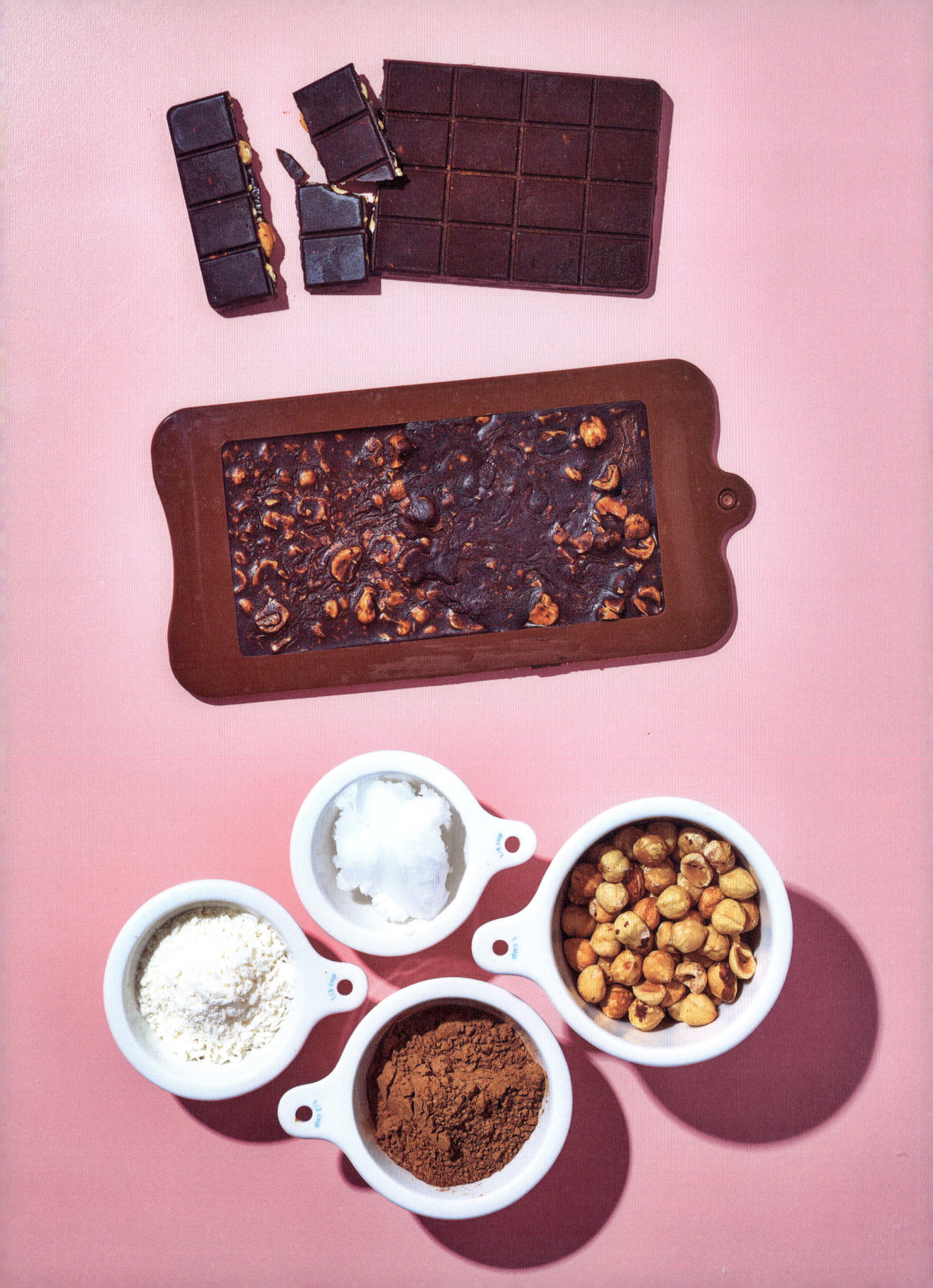

SEED CRACKERS

Each cracker is a powerhouse of omega-3s, minerals and plant-based protein, making them ideal for those seeking a mindful and balanced snack.

Whether you enjoy them plain, as a base for your favourite toppings, or paired with hummus, guacamole or plant-based cheese, these gluten-free crackers provide a nutrient-dense alternative to store-bought options.

Try experimenting with different seeds and spices in the mix, a sprinkle of garlic powder, rosemary or nutritional yeast, for enhanced flavour.

INGREDIENTS

- 14g (½oz) flaxseeds
- 30g (1oz/ ¼ cup) rice flour
- ½ tsp salt
- 44g (1½oz/scant ⅓ cup) sunflower seeds
- 40g (1½oz/¼ cup) pumpkin seeds
- 30g (1oz/scant ¼ cup) hemp seeds
- 1 tbsp chia seeds
- 240ml (8fl oz/1 cup) boiling water

MINDFUL BENEFITS:

- Flax and chia seeds are rich in omega-3 fatty acids, which support brain health.

- Hemp seeds provide complete plant protein, ideal for sustained energy and cognitive function.

COOKING TIP:

- To ensure an even thickness, place another sheet of parchment on top of the mix and roll with a baking pin before baking.

Prepare the Dry Ingredients:
Step 1: In a large bowl, combine the flaxseeds, rice flour, salt, sunflower seeds, pumpkin seeds, hemp seeds and chia seeds. Mix well.

Add Boiling Water:
Step 2: Pour the boiling water over the seed mixture. Stir thoroughly until the mixture thickens and forms a gel-like consistency.

Spread the Mixture:
Step 3: Preheat your oven to 135°C/275°F/Gas 1. Line a baking sheet with baking parchment.

Step 4: Spread the seed mixture evenly on the prepared baking sheet, making sure it is about 3mm/⅛ inch thick. Use a spatula to smooth it out.

Bake:
Step 5: Bake in the preheated oven for 90 minutes or until the crackers are dry and crisp.
Tip: Check halfway through and rotate the baking sheet to ensure even baking.

Cool and Cut:
Step 6: Remove from the oven and let the crackers cool completely on the baking sheet.

Step 7: Once cool, break or cut into desired shapes and sizes.

Storage:
Step 8: Store the seed crackers in a labelled airtight container at room temperature. They will keep for up to 2 weeks.

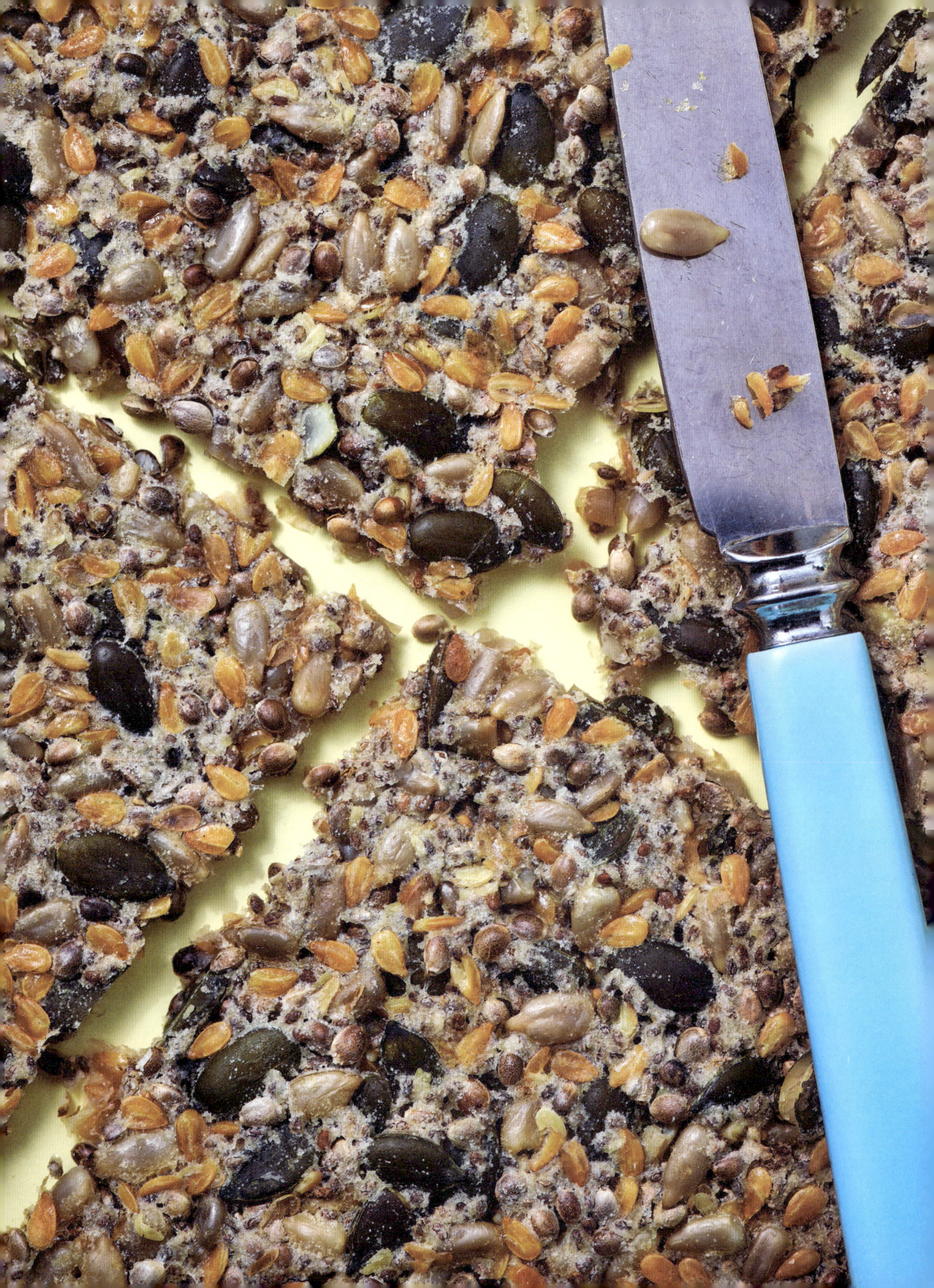

ACTIVATED BUTTERS

"The simplest changes can unlock the greatest benefits."

Nuts and seeds are nutritional powerhouses, but are we really getting the most out of them?

The concept of "activation" in the context of nuts and seeds is inspired by ancient food preparation techniques that recognized the need to make these nutrient-dense foods more digestible and their nutrients more accessible.

It flips the script on how we prepare these everyday staples turning them into health-boosting ingredients.

Activation might sound complicated, but it's anything but. The process begins with soaking nuts or seeds in water, which initiates germination or sprouting.

This simple step reduces phytic acid, a compound that binds to minerals and prevents your body from fully absorbing them. It also deactivates enzyme inhibitors that can make raw nuts and seeds tough on your digestive system. Once soaked, the nuts or seeds are gently dehydrated at a low temperature until they're completely dry. This careful drying process preserves the integrity of the nutrients and the beneficial enzymes that have been activated through soaking.

The result is a product that is much easier on the digestive system, allowing for better absorption of the nuts' and seeds' abundant nutrients.

Activated butters made from peanuts, sunflower seeds and almonds become powerhouse spreads that offer enhanced health benefits.

Peanuts, for example, become a more potent source of protein and biotin, essential for energy production and skin health.

Sunflower seeds, already known for their high vitamin E content, become an even more effective antioxidant when activated.

Almonds, rich in calcium and magnesium, contribute to bone health, and their activated form makes it easier for the body to utilize these minerals.

Making your own activated butters at home is a simple practice that puts you in control of both quality and content. Unlike many store-bought spreads, which often contain added oils, sugars or preservatives, homemade versions retain the purity of the ingredients.

This means you're not just avoiding unnecessary additives – you're preserving the full flavour and nutritional value of the activated nuts and seeds.

Plus, by sourcing organic nuts and seeds, you eliminate the risk of pesticides and contaminants. The result? A spread that's fresher, healthier and aligned with your commitment to mindful eating.

Be very careful because you're likely to experience an improvement in gut health due to the reduction of antinutrients that can cause digestive disturbances.

And the enhanced mineral availability can contribute to a better overall nutrient status – supporting everything from enzyme function and muscle relaxation to nerve transmission and blood sugar control.

So skip this if you do not want a deeper connection to the food that fuels you!

ACTIVATED PEANUT/ ALMOND/ SUNFLOWER BUTTERS

INGREDIENTS

- 300g (10½oz/2 cups) raw peanuts, sunflower seeds or almonds
- Water for soaking
- ½ teaspoon salt (optional)

USAGE:

- Spread on toast, add to smoothies, or pair with fruits and vegetables for a versatile snack.

MINDFUL BENEFITS:

- Nut or seed butter stabilizes blood sugar levels, supporting steady energy and focus through the day, while its nutrient-dense profile helps reduce mental fatigue.

- Peanuts: Rich in protein and biotin, essential for energy and skin health.

- Sunflower Seeds: High in vitamin E, an antioxidant that supports immune health and reduces oxidative stress.

- Almonds: Provide calcium and magnesium, crucial for bone health and muscle relaxation, aiding focus.

Activate the Nuts or Seeds:
Step 1: Place the raw peanuts, sunflower seeds or almonds in a large bowl and cover with water. Soak for at least 12 hours or overnight.

Step 2: Drain and rinse the nuts or seeds thoroughly.

Dehydrate the Nuts or Seeds:
Step 3: Spread the soaked nuts or seeds on a baking sheet in a single layer.

Step 4: Dry in the oven at the lowest temperature setting (50°C/120°F/Gas ½) or use a dehydrator until completely dry (12–24 hours).

Blend into Butter:
Step 5: Place the dried nuts or seeds in a high-powered blender or food processor. Blend until smooth and creamy, scraping down the sides as needed. This may take 5–10 minutes.

Step 6: Add salt to taste, if desired.

Storage:
Step 7: Transfer the butter to a labelled airtight container. Store in the refrigerator for up to 2 weeks.

COOKING TIP:

- For extra creaminess, add 1 tablespoon of coconut oil or another neutral oil during blending.

CREATIVE TIP:

- Customize your butter with added flavours like cinnamon, honey or vanilla extract for a unique twist.

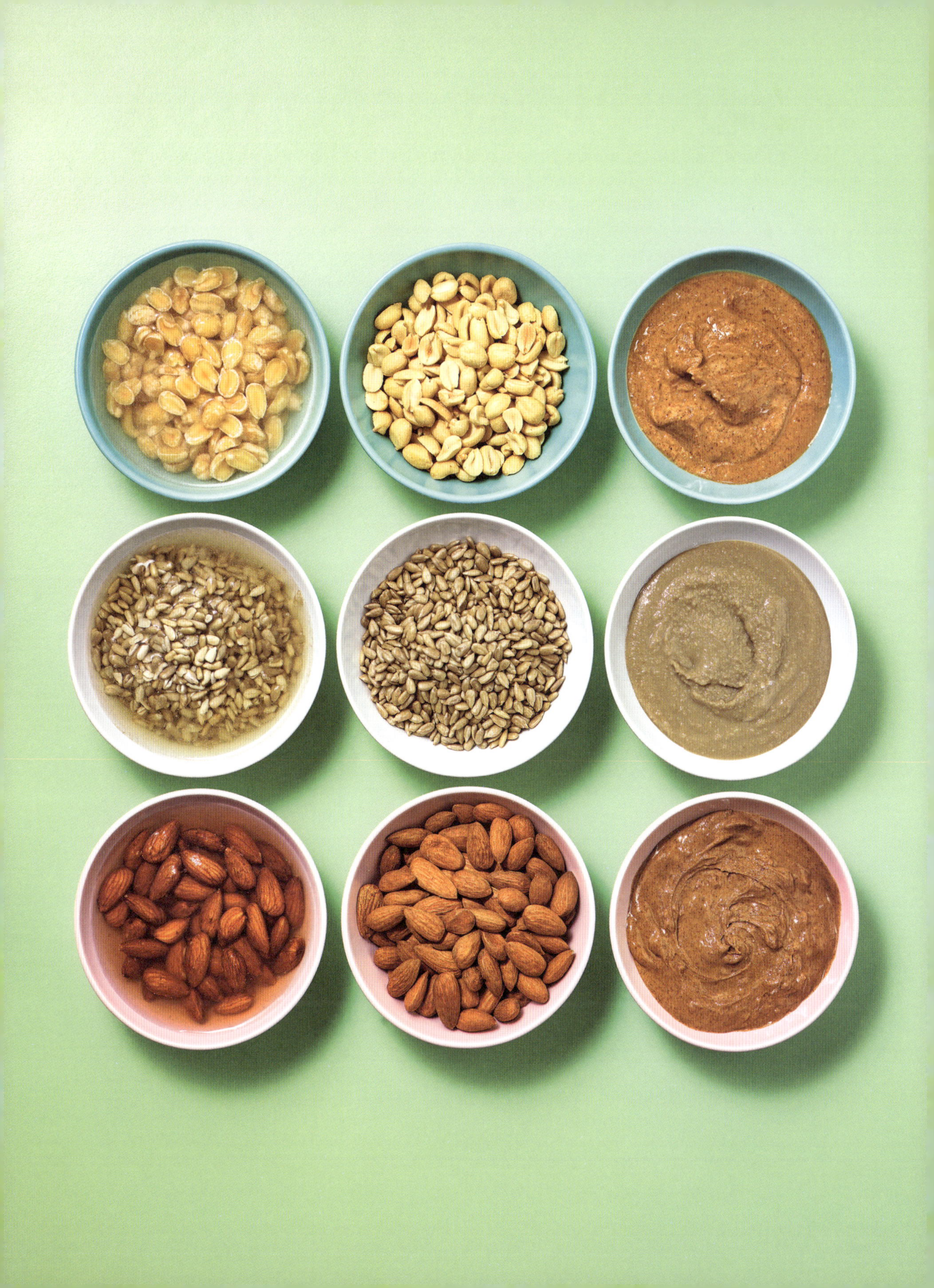

ITALIAN HOT CHOCOLATE

Over a decade ago, when I set foot in London, at the chill of the first winter I started craving the thick, creamy Italian hot chocolate I grew up with.

Surprisingly, the hot chocolate there was nothing like the luscious, dark drink I was used to. Whether it was the pre-made versions on supermarket shelves or those served in cafes and bars, I was always disappointed.

There were a few delightful exceptions, of course. Occasionally, I'd stumble upon a special café or find the classic brands in Italian delis, which brought back a taste of home.

But being new in town and with very few pay checks in the bank, I was very mindful of savings (most of the time, anyway), so I took matters into my own hands.

Over the years, I have perfected my own version of Italian hot chocolate. Here, I share a recipe that is so rich and indulgently chocolatey, it's to die for.

INGREDIENTS

- 100g (3½oz/1¼ cup) alkalized cocoa powder
- 80g (3oz/1 cup) sustainably sourced dark cocoa powder
- 60g (2oz/⅓ cup) light brown soft sugar
- 4 tsp cornflour/cornstarch
- 120ml (4fl oz/½ cup) plant-based milk (such as almond, soy or oat)

COOKING TIP:

- Tailor the cocoa ratios to your liking, ensuring a perfect balance of bold and subtle chocolate notes.

Prepare the Dry Mix:
Step 1: In a medium bowl, combine the alkalized cocoa powder, dark cocoa powder, light brown soft sugar and cornflour/cornstarch. Mix well to ensure an even distribution of ingredients.

Heat the Milk:
Step 2: In a small saucepan, heat the plant-based milk over medium heat until it begins to simmer.

Combine and Cook:
Step 3: Add 2 tablespoons of the prepared cocoa mix to the simmering milk, whisking continuously to prevent lumps.

Step 4: Continue to simmer the mixture, stirring frequently, until it reaches your desired thickness. This should take about 5–7 minutes.

Serve:
Step 5: Pour the hot chocolate into a mug. Serve with a dollop of whipped cream or a sprinkle of chilli for a kick. Store in the refrigerator for up to 2 weeks.

CREATIVE TIP:

- Experiment with toppings or flavourings, such as a pinch of sea salt, a dash of cinnamon or a splash of vanilla extract, to craft your perfect cup.

MINDFUL BENEFITS:

- Winter is an ideal time to slow down and embrace moments of rest. Taking the time to make and savour a cup of rich hot chocolate can be a perfect way to practice self-care.

- Allow yourself to enjoy the simple pleasure of doing nothing while you sip your drink, appreciating the warmth and comfort it brings. This mindful pause can help reduce anxiety, recharge your mind and reinforce the importance of taking breaks during the colder months.

READY MEALS:
Effortless Nourishment for the Modern World

"Good food is the foundation of genuine happiness."
Auguste Escoffier

In a world that demands so much of our attention, food should feel like a solution, not a source of stress.

The kitchen can quickly become overwhelming – a minefield of decisions, steps and distractions.

It's easy to see why prepackaged, shelf-ready meals dominate supermarket aisles. They promise speed, simplicity and relief from the chaos of daily life.

But here's the thing: convenience food isn't designed to help you thrive.

It's designed to keep you dependent. Beneath its glossy packaging is a product engineered for profit, not nourishment.

The result? Food that fills your stomach but leaves your body depleted and your mind dulled.

Supermarket-ready meals are not food in the traditional sense; they are products. Engineered to last longer, be addictive and cost less to produce, these meals are stripped of their vitality long before they reach your plate.

What's left behind is an illusion of sustenance, masking the reality of empty calories, synthetic additives and depleted energy.

The problem runs deeper than the food itself. Processed meals are part of a system designed to keep us disconnected – from the origins of our food, from the act of cooking, and even from our own wellbeing.

It's not just about making food easier; it's about shifting control. The less connected you are to your nourishment, the more you rely on the products they sell.

And it works.

The blood sugar spikes and crashes leave you craving more. The lack of real nutrients creates an endless cycle of fatigue and overconsumption.

All of this isn't just an unfortunate byproduct – it's the point.

Processed meals don't just rob you of energy – they rob you of agency.

By eating food that's been stripped of its essence, you're less likely to feel alive, present or capable of making intentional choices. It's hard to focus, let alone thrive, when the very thing meant to fuel you is designed to keep you numb.

For neurodivergent individuals, the stakes are even higher.

Overwhelm from decision-making and preparation is a daily reality, and prepackaged meals might seem like a quick fix.

But they often exacerbate the very problems they claim to solve, creating a fog of lethargy and disconnection that makes it harder to break free.

What if convenience didn't have to come at the cost of vitality?

Ready meals, when made with intention, are the antidote to this manufactured dependency. With a little preparation, you can create meals that are as quick and easy as their store-bought counterparts but are designed to nourish your body and clear your mind.

Imagine having a jar of instant risotto or a dashi base ready for action. A homemade frozen pizza prepped for the oven. These aren't just meals; they're tools.

Each one is a small act of care, a future-proofed solution that meets you where you are, whether you're in the middle of a busy workweek or navigating a low-energy day.

The difference is in the control.

When you make your own ready meals, you're both cooking and reclaiming your relationship with food.

Every jar, every container, every thoughtfully-prepared dish is a step toward breaking free from a system that thrives on your disconnection.

Bear in mind, though, that homemade ready meals aren't about perfection. They're about balance. They let you plan ahead so that, on the hard days, you don't have to start from scratch.

This isn't about cutting corners – it's about creating a kitchen that works for you, not against you.

For those navigating neurodivergence, this approach is transformative. The overwhelming cycle of decision-making and execution becomes simpler. The act of preparing meals in advance is a way of showing up for your future self, reducing the mental load when energy or focus is in short supply.

By reclaiming convenience on your own terms, you create space for creativity, calm and clarity. Cooking becomes less about getting through the day and more about creating moments of mindfulness and nourishment, even in chaos.

Saving time is great, but this is about shifting your mindset. It is about choosing balance over burnout and breaking free from systems that don't serve you.

In a world that often uses convenience to keep you passive, taking control of your food is an act of rebellion.

It's a declaration that your health, your energy and your choices matter.

So, take a breath. Plan ahead. Prepare meals that make your life easier, your body stronger and your mind clearer.

INSTANT GARDEN RISOTTO

If you are a risotto lover like me, this ready meal is a must!

But let's be honest – traditional risotto requires time, patience and precision. Making a classic risotto from scratch usually takes about 18–20 minutes of constant stirring, provided your stock and garnishes are prepped and ready to go.

It's not always practical, especially when life gets busy. That's where this ready meal steps in. With just a bit of preparation, you can create a dehydrated risotto mix that transforms into a comforting meal – all by simply adding water.

The best part of this? It's an accessible skill for home cooks to learn and personalize in as many ways as you feel.

I said it before: investing in a dehydrator might sound intimidating, but it's surprisingly affordable and easy to maintain (see page 47).
Even with rising energy costs, using a dehydrator is cost-effective.

My dehydrator, for example, consumes about 0.8 to 1 kW per hour. With energy costs of 36p/$0.46 per kW, running it for 20 hours a month costs roughly £7.20/$9.12 – a small price to pay for the convenience, flavour and sustainability it adds to my kitchen.

Here I am using freshly harvested ingredients from the garden, but you can replicate the recipe with other veggies. Not into broccoli or kale? Swap in your favourite vegetables! Just remember to blanch those that need it before dehydrating to retain their nutrients and colour, which can go straight into the pan once cooking the mix.

INGREDIENTS

- 500g (17½oz/2½ cups) parboiled rice
- 1 broccoflower (green cauliflower)
- 1 cluster of oyster mushrooms
- 150g (5oz/6 cups) curly kale
- ½ tsp chopped fresh rosemary
- ½ tsp chopped fresh mint
- 100g (3½oz/½ cup) milled activated peas
- 4 tbsp homemade vegetable bouillon

Prepare the Rice:

Step 1: Cook the parboiled rice in salted boiling water for 15 minutes.

Step 2: Dehydrate the cooked rice until completely dry and crisp.

Prepare the Vegetables:

Step 3: Blanch the broccoflower, oyster mushrooms, and curly kale and refresh.

Step 4: Dehydrate the vegetables using a dehydrator or oven until they are completely dry and crisp.

Mix the Ingredients:

Step 5: In a large bowl, combine the dehydrated rice, dehydrated vegetables, fresh rosemary, fresh mint, milled activated peas, and vegetable bouillon.

Recipe continued on the next page …

THE CABINETS

MINDFUL BENEFITS:

• Using fresh and high-quality vegetables ensures a nutrient-rich meal. Dehydration preserves vitamins and minerals, making this dish a wholesome and vibrant option for busy days.

• The structure of this ready meal simplifies cooking, reducing the stress and overwhelm of meal preparation. Knowing you have a nutritious meal prepped can help maintain focus and create a sense of control.

Storage:
Step 6: Store the mixture in a labelled airtight container in a cool, dry place until ready to use. It will last up to 1 year.

Cook the Risotto:
Step 7: When ready to cook, add the risotto mix to a pot.

Step 8: Add double the weight of water (about 1 litre/35fl oz/4¼ cups for 500g/17½oz/2½ cups of mix) to the pot.

Step 9: Bring to a boil, then simmer for 8 minutes, stirring occasionally.

Finish and Serve:
Step 10: Remove from heat and add a knob of butter or oil and some cheese. Stir until combined.

CREATIVE TIP:

• Experiment with spices or herbs to vary the flavour. A pinch of saffron or turmeric can add colour and depth to your risotto.

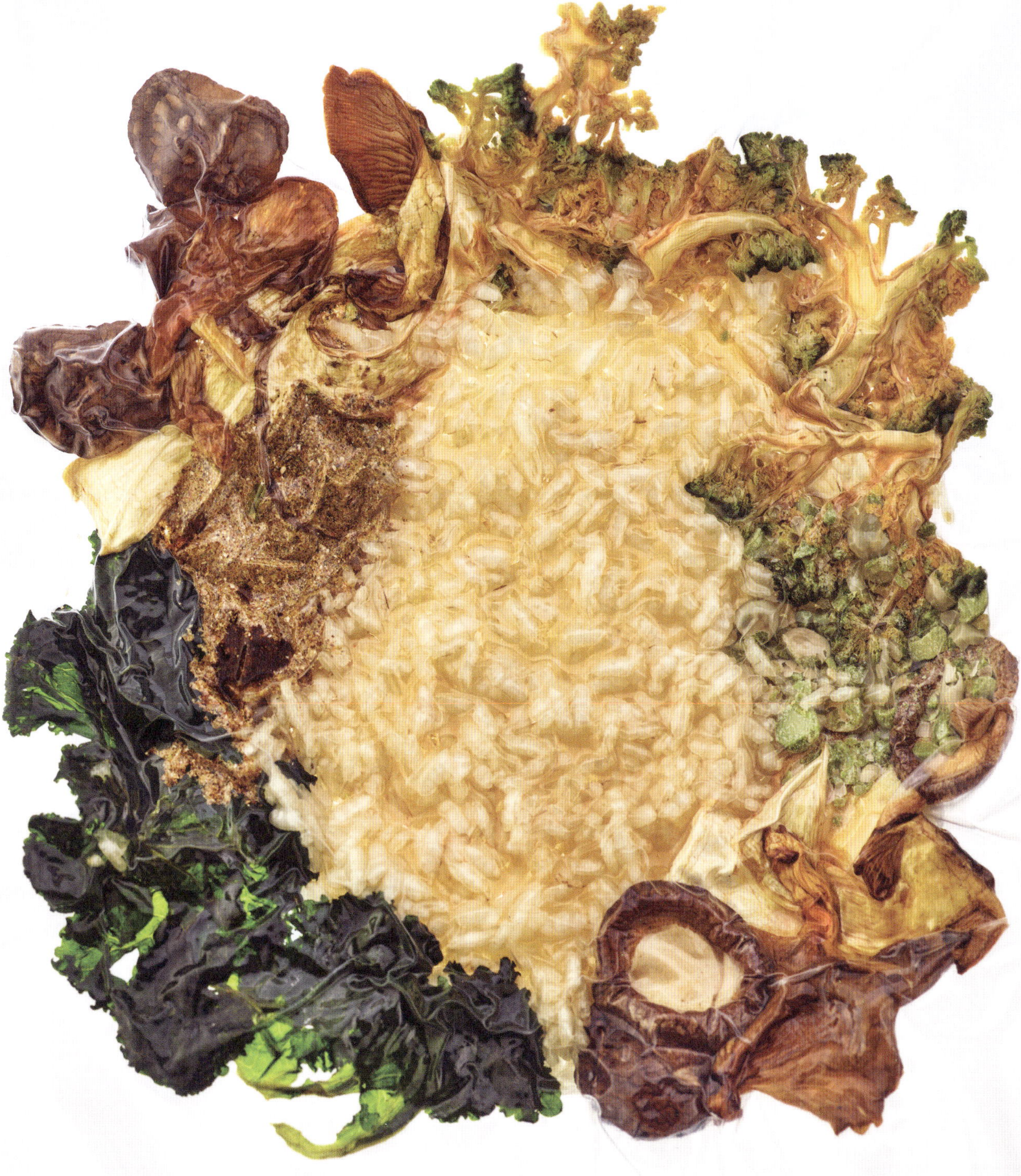

INSTANT TOMATO SOUP

For busy bees craving a comforting meal, this homemade instant tomato soup is a game-changer! Packed with flavour and nutrients, it's the perfect solution for those swamped with meetings or simply seeking a quick, delicious bite.

This recipe yields about six portions, with a shelf life of 6 months in jars or bags – and up to a year if vacuum-packed. Trust me, though, it's so good they won't last that long! To make a serving, simply add hot water to a portion of the powdered soup, stir well and let it rehydrate for a few minutes.

INGREDIENTS

- 1 garlic clove
- 1 onion
- Extra virgin olive oil, to fry
- 650g/23oz/2¾ cups pelati (see page 92)
- A few basil leaves
- 3 tbsp homemade bouillon (see page 118)
- 3 tbsp homemade potato flour (see page 39)
- 2 tsp dried oregano

COOKING TIP:

- **No dehydrator?** Use an oven set to its lowest temperature. Check the mixture every 30 minutes to prevent burning. Spread the mixture evenly (1/8 inch) on trays to ensure consistent drying times.

CREATIVE TIP:

- **Experiment with spices** like smoked paprika, thyme or chilli flakes for added depth and heat. Incorporate other herbs like parsley or sage to create your signature blend.

Prepare the Aromatics:
Step 1: Finely chop the garlic and onion.

Step 2: In a large pan, heat a little oil over medium heat. Add the chopped garlic and onion, and sauté for about 3–4 minutes until softened and fragrant.

Add Tomatoes:
Step 3: Add the peeled tomatoes (pelati) to the pan.

Step 4: Cook over medium heat for about 25 minutes, stirring occasionally, until the tomatoes are broken down and the flavours are well combined.

Infuse with Basil:
Step 5: Allow the mixture to cool slightly, then add the basil to the mix and let it infuse for 15 minutes. Remove the basil before dehydrating.

Dehydrate the Infused Mixture:
Step 6: Spread the mixture thinly across dehydrator trays.

Step 7: Dehydrate at 60°C/140°F until fully dried (duration varies based on thickness).

Powder the Soup:
Step 8: Break the dried soup into pieces and blend it. Add the bouillon and potato flour. Blend on high speed until finely powdered.

Storage:
Step 9: Store the powdered soup in labelled airtight jars for up to 6 months, or vacuum-packed for up to a year.

CREATIVE TIP:

• Enhance the soup with spices or herbs like cumin, smoked paprika, thyme or parsley for added flavour and depth.

INSTANT VEG & LEGUMES SOUP

How many people have told you that they are unable to digest or feel bloated after eating legumes? Does this apply to you, too? Well, in most cases, this is brought on by antinutritional elements such as enzyme inhibitors and phytic acid when legumes are in their dry form. This stops them from sprouting and keeps them well preserved in our pantry or cupboards.

This recipe starts with the activation of legumes, a concept that we already explored when making nut butters (see page 74) and to take things a step further, then mills the legumes (remember this technique? See page 43) to make them lighter and to begin breaking down the starches, avoiding as many potential fermentations in our gut as we can. This soup is ideal for quick, nutritious meals. Just add hot water and cook for a few minutes.

INGREDIENTS

- 1 onion
- 1 courgette/zucchini
- 2 carrots
- 1 leek
- 100g/3½oz/2 cups curly kale from the garden
- 100g/3½oz/⅔ cup potato flour (see page 39)
- 4 tbsp vegetable bouillon (see page 118)
- 100g/3½oz/ ¾ cup milled activated lentils
- 100g /3½oz/ ¾ cup milled activated peas
- 100g/3½oz/ ¾ cup milled activated chickpeas/garbanzo beans
- 1 tbsp extra virgin olive oil
- Salt as needed

TO PREPARE:

- To make a serving, mix about 5 tbsp of powdered soup with 750ml (25fl oz) of hot water. Boil gently for 3 minutes and serve.

Activate the Legumes:
Step 1: Soak the lentils, peas and chickpeas/garbanzo beans in water with a splash of lemon juice or vinegar for 12 hours.

Step 2: Drain and rinse the legumes thoroughly.

Cook the Vegetables:
Step 3: Chop the onion, courgette/zucchini, carrots and leek. Sauté in a large pot with the olive oil until softened.

Step 4: Add the kale and cook until wilted.

Add the Activated Legumes:
Step 5: Add the activated legumes to the pot.

Cook the Soup:
Step 6: Add enough water to cover the ingredients and simmer until everything is tender, about 30 minutes.

Step 7: Stir in the potato flour, vegetable bouillon and salt.

Dry the Soup:
Step 8: Spread the cooked mix thinly on dehydrator trays or baking sheets and dehydrate at 60°C (140°F) until dry.

Powder the Soup:
Step 9: Once dried, blitz the mixture into a fine powder using a blender or food processor.

Storage:
Step 10: Store the powdered soup in labelled airtight jars for up to 6 months or vacuum-packed for up to a year.

HIGH PROTEIN PASTA

"Good food is not only what you eat; it's how you connect with it."

This pasta is a celebration of how simple ingredients can transform into something extraordinary. A culinary innovation that marries nutrition with convenience, these recipes are a testament to the power of legumes to nourish both body and mind. Each bean and pulse brings unique qualities: the earthy flavour of lentils, the nutty richness of mung beans, and the versatility of chickpeas/garbanzo beans, packed with protein, fiber and essential minerals.

This pasta is more than a wholesome, gluten-free alternative to traditional Italian gold. It's a therapeutic experience, blending the mindful rhythm of mixing and kneading with the creative joy of shaping.

INGREDIENTS

Red Lentil & Chickpea/Garbanzo Bean Pasta:
- 120g (4oz/1 cup) red lentil flour (see page 37)
- 120g (4oz/1 cup) chickpea/garbanzo bean flour (see page 36)
- 120ml (4fl oz/½ cup) water

Mung Bean & Marrowfat Pea Pasta:
- 120g (4oz/1 cup) mung bean flour
- 120g (4oz/1 cup) marrowfat pea flour
- 120ml (4fl oz/½ cup) water

Black-Eyed Bean, Black Turtle Bean and Soy Bean Pasta:
- 80g (3oz/ ⅔ cup) black-eyed bean/black-eyed pea flour
- 80g (3oz/⅔ cup) black turtle bean/black bean flour
- 80g (3oz/⅔ cup) soy bean flour
- 120ml (4fl oz/½ cup) water

Mix the Flours:
Step 1: Combine the chosen flours in a large mixing bowl.

Add Water:
Step 2: Gradually add the water to the flour mix, stirring constantly until a dough forms. You may need to adjust the water to achieve the right consistency: a slightly sticky, shaggy dough that holds together without crumbling.

Knead the Dough:
Step 3: Knead the dough on a lightly floured surface for about 5–7 minutes, until smooth and elastic.

Rest the Dough:
Step 4: Cover the dough with a damp cloth and let it rest for 20–30 minutes.

Shape the Pasta:
Step 5: Roll out the dough using a pasta machine or a rolling pin until it reaches your desired thickness. Cut into your preferred pasta shapes.

Dry the Pasta:
Step 6: Lay the pasta out on a drying rack or a cloth and let dry before cooking or storing. This can take several hours.

Cook the Pasta:
Step 7: To cook, bring a large pot of salted water to a boil. Add the pasta and cook for 2–5 minutes or until al dente. Drain and serve with your favourite sauce.

Recipe continued on the next page …

MINDFUL BENEFITS:

• The tactile process of mixing, kneading and shaping pasta dough can be meditative and calming. It's a focused, repetitive activity that encourages mindfulness and reduces stress.

Storage:
Step 8: Store the pasta in airtight jars for 12 months.

COOKING TIP:

• Knead thoroughly to ensure the dough develops elasticity for a superior pasta texture.
• If you don't have a pasta machine, you can see my YouTube for a tutorial on how to shape pasta by hand.

CREATIVE TIP:

• Add herbs or spices like garlic powder, paprika or dried basil to the dough for a flavour twist. This simple step customizes your pasta and complements your sauces beautifully.

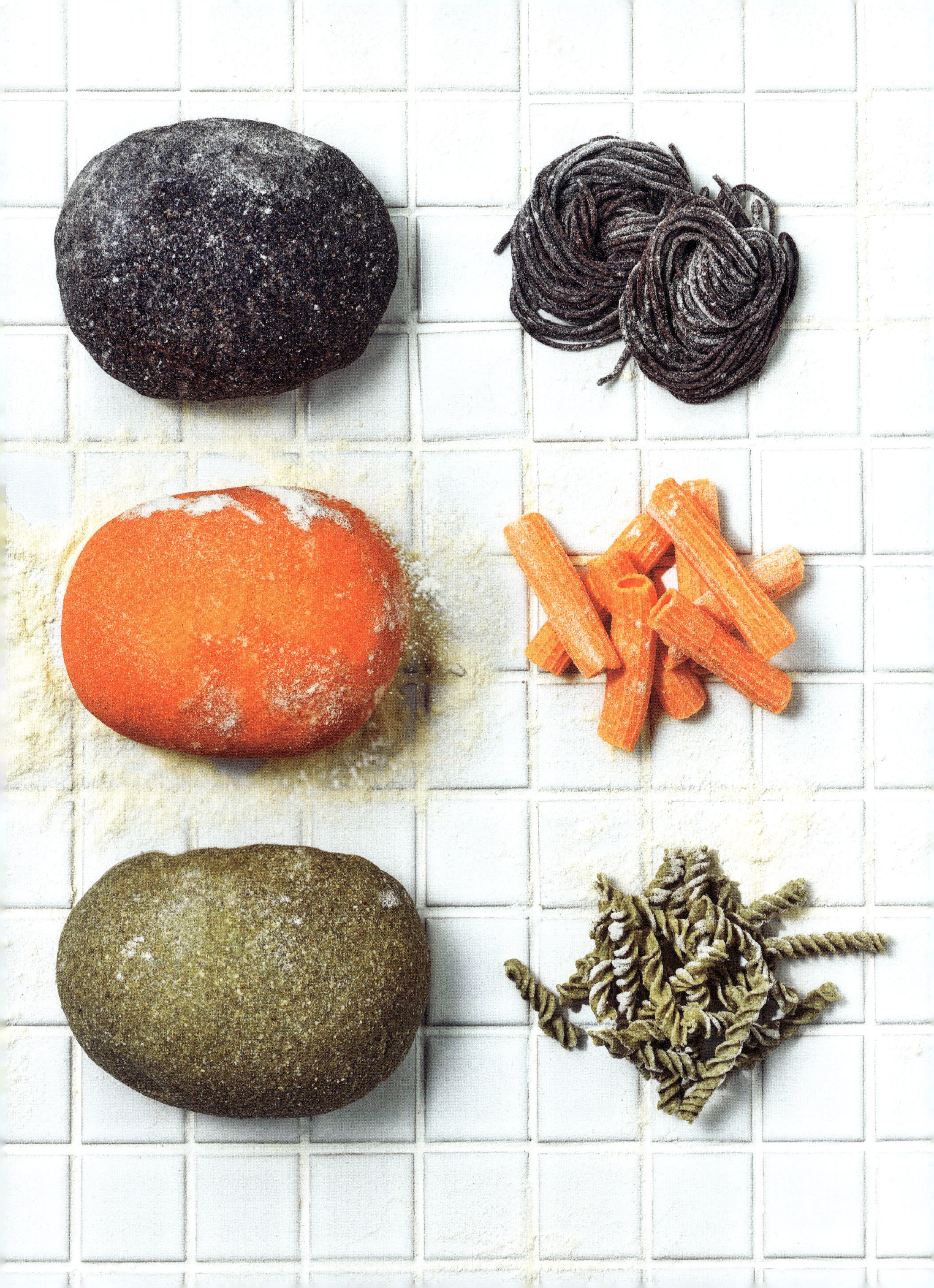

STOCKS AND SAUCES: The Foundation of Flavor

"A kitchen without stock is like a painter without paint."

A good stock or sauce is like the secret handshake of a great dish – it ties everything together, elevating even the simplest ingredients into something remarkable.

Where pasta brings texture and substance, stocks and sauces bring depth and character. They're the unsung heroes of every kitchen, the foundation upon which unforgettable meals are built, the tools for flavour, nourishment and creativity.

Whether it's a rich gravy, a delicate dashi or a robust vegetable stock, these essentials are your kitchen's most versatile assets.

The beauty of homemade stocks and sauces is in their simplicity and intention.

Each one is a chance to reduce waste, repurpose ingredients and create something greater than the sum of its parts. And for those navigating the complexities of modern life – or neurodivergent challenges – these kitchen staples offer grounding rituals and easy solutions.

With just a bit of preparation, you can create a pantry of ready-to-use stocks that bring ease, mindfulness and vitality to your meals.

It's the next step in your journey toward a kitchen that works with you ...

• Recipes on the next page

PELATI

Pelati and passata (see page 93) are quintessential Italian staples, capturing the essence of ripe tomatoes in two distinct and cherished forms.

Homemade pelati are sun-ripened tomatoes that have been blanched and peeled with loving care. This traditional method locks in the tomatoes' fresh, garden-picked taste and natural sweetness, making them a superior choice for enhancing the flavour of stews, soups and sauces.

The absence of industrial processing means each batch of homemade pelati is as wholesome as it is delicious.

For the best results, the ideal tomatoes for this process are meaty varieties such as Roma, San Marzano or plum tomatoes. Their firm flesh and low water content ensure a rich, concentrated flavour that holds up beautifully in cooking.

Avoid using shop-bought salad tomatoes, which are often too watery and lack the intensity needed to create truly exceptional pelati.

Use homemade pelati in stews, soups, sauces and any dish that calls for whole or crushed tomatoes.

INGREDIENTS

- 5kg (11lb) fresh, ripe, undamaged tomatoes
- Water (for boiling)
- Ice water (for cooling)

MINDFUL BENEFITS:

- Tomatoes provide folate and vitamin B6, essential for mood regulation and reducing symptoms of anxiety. Potassium promotes better blood flow to the brain, enhancing focus and concentration.

CREATIVE TIP:

- Try roasting the tomatoes before peeling to add a deeper, smoky flavour to your pelati.

Blanch the Tomatoes:

Step 1: Bring a large pot of water to a boil.

Step 2: Make a small 'X' incision at the bottom of each tomato.

Step 3: Prepare a bowl of ice water.

Blanch and Peel:

Step 4: Place the tomatoes in the boiling water for 30–60 seconds or until the skins start to peel back.

Step 5: Immediately transfer the tomatoes to the ice water to cool.

Step 6: Once cooled, peel off the skins starting from the "X" incision.

Storage:

Step 7: Transfer the peeled tomatoes to a labelled sterilized jar or container. Store in the refrigerator for up to a week or freeze for longer storage.

COOKING TIP:

- To enhance the flavour, add a pinch of salt and a few basil leaves to the jar before sealing.

PASSATA

Passata is a smooth, velvety tomato puree and a staple of Italian cuisine. Its origins lie in the tradition of preserving the fresh, robust flavours of sun-ripened tomatoes for year-round use. Making passata at home captures the essence of ripe tomatoes – whether you use it as the foundation for a marinara sauce or the heart of a hearty minestrone, homemade passata is a versatile and vibrant addition to any dish.

Use homemade passata as a base for sauces, soups and stews. It's perfect for pasta sauces, pizza sauce, and more.

INGREDIENTS

- Fresh ripe tomatoes
- Salt (optional)
- Fresh basil (optional)

COOKING TIP:

- To intensify the flavour, simmer the passata on a low heat until it reduces to your desired consistency.

MINDFUL BENEFITS:

- Passata's vibrant colour and fresh aroma can engage the senses, promoting mindfulness and relaxation. Check some videos on Youtube and you'll see the nonnas smiling throughout the whole process!

Prepare the Tomatoes:
Step 1: Wash and chop the tomatoes into quarters.

Cook the Tomatoes:
Step 2: Place the tomatoes in a large pot and cook over medium heat until they break down and release their juices, about 10–15 minutes.

Puree the Tomatoes:
Step 3: Pass the cooked tomatoes through a food mill or sieve to remove the skins and seeds, resulting in a smooth puree.

Season:
Step 4: Add a pinch of salt and a few basil leaves to the puree (optional).

Storage:
Step 5: Transfer the passata to labelled sterilized jars or containers. Store in the refrigerator for up to a week or freeze for longer storage.

CREATIVE TIP:

- Add garlic, onions or chilli peppers to the tomatoes while cooking for a flavoured passata with an extra kick.

SUPER CONCENTRATED TOMATO PURÉE

Super concentrated tomato purée is a rich, robust culinary treasure that transforms dishes with its deep, natural flavour.

This method reduces them into a thick, potent form – a fresher and tastier alternative to store-bought varieties.

Use this concentrated purée as a base for sauces, soups or condiments. Dilute as needed to suit your dish.

INGREDIENTS

- 5kg/11lb ripe, unblemished tomatoes
- Boiling water (enough to cover)

COOKING TIP:

- Experiment with different types of tomatoes to discover unique flavour profiles. For more depth, try adding herbs like basil, oregano or thyme before dehydrating.

CREATIVE TIP:

- Blend dehydrated tomato skins into a powder to use as a seasoning for soups, stews or roasted vegetables.

Prepare the Tomatoes:

Step 1: Wash the tomatoes thoroughly. Score the skin of each tomato with a cross.

Step 2: Blanch the tomatoes in boiling water for a few minutes until the skins start to peel away.

Step 3: Remove the skins and cut the tomatoes in half (or quarters if large). Save the tomato water and skin for recipes like stock cubes (page 119) or DIY gravy (page 96).

Dehydrate:

Step 4: Place the tomato pieces on dehydrator trays or baking sheets lined with parchment paper. Spread them evenly without overlapping.

Step 5: Set the dehydrator or oven to 50–60°C. Dehydrate the tomatoes for about 8 hours until they lose most of their water content without completely drying out.

Blend into a Purée:

Step 6: Allow the tomatoes to cool slightly. Transfer them to a blender or food processor and blend until smooth, creating a thick tomato purée.

Storage:

Option 1: Freezing: Spread the purée on a parchment-lined sheet, cover with another layer of parchment, and use a rolling pin to create an even layer. Freeze, then break into squares and store in a freezer bag for up to 1 year.

Option 2: Canning: Spoon the purée into small, sterilized jars. Close the lids and place the jars in a pot covered with cold water. Simmer for 2 hours. Turn off the heat and let the jars cool. Dry and store in a pantry for up to 1 year.

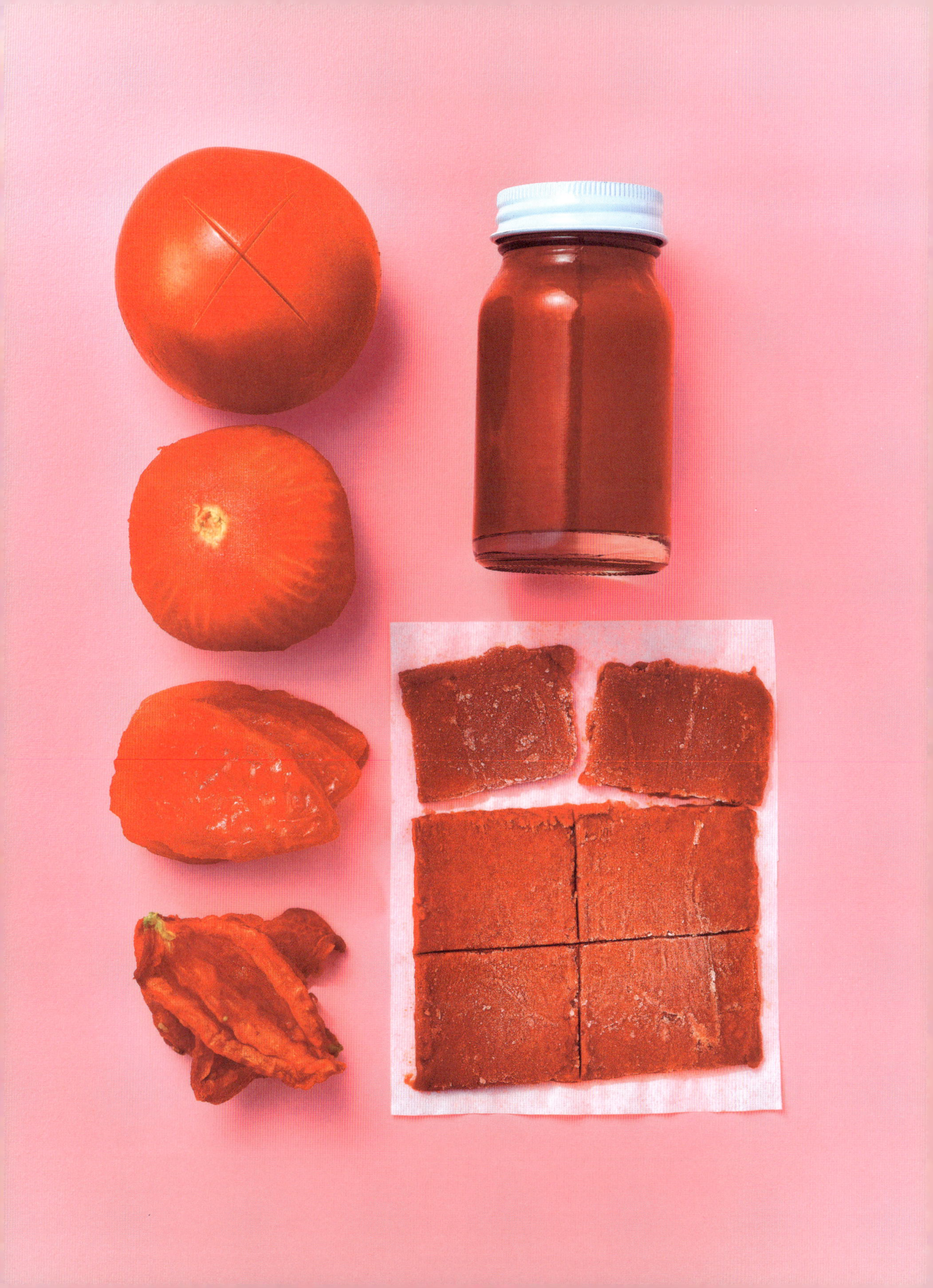

DIY GRAVY POWDER

DIY Gravy Powder is a healthier, gluten-free and lower-sodium alternative to store-bought options.

Unlike commercial varieties filled with preservatives and artificial flavours, this homemade blend features wholefood ingredients for a naturally flavourful and nourishing addition to your meals.

Packed with protein and fiber from red lentils and an array of complementary spices, this powder transforms simple dishes into comforting, satisfying meals.

INGREDIENTS

- 100g (3½oz) red lentils (½ cup, cooked or dry)
- 3 tbsp potato starch (or 2½ tbsp cornflour/cornstarch)
- 2 tbsp homemade dashi (see page 98) or mushroom powder
- 2 tbsp instant homemade tomato soup powder (see page 84) or tomato powder
- 2 tsp black pepper
- 1 tbsp onion powder
- 2½ tsp Himalayan salt
- 1 tsp garlic powder
- 1 tsp smoked paprika
- ½ tsp coffee powder (or black cacao, caffeine-free option)
- ½ tsp cumin powder
- ¼ tsp nutmeg powder

Using Cooked Lentils:

Step 1: Prepare the Lentils: Rinse lentils thoroughly and cook until tender. Drain and allow to cool completely.

Step 2: Dehydrate the Lentils: Spread cooked lentils on a dehydrator tray or baking sheet. Dehydrate at 60°C/140°F until fully dry, which may take several hours.

Using Dry Lentils:

Step 1: Prepare Red Lentil Flour: see page 37.

Combine All Ingredients:

Step 2: Mix the Powder: In a large mixing bowl, combine lentil powder (from cooked or dry lentils) with potato starch (or cornflour/cornstarch), dashi (or mushroom powder), tomato soup powder (or tomato powder), black pepper, onion powder, Himalayan salt, garlic powder, paprika, coffee powder (or black cacao), cumin powder, and nutmeg powder. Mix thoroughly for even distribution.

Storage:

Step 3: Store the Gravy Powder: Transfer to a labeled, airtight container and store in a cool, dry place for up to 6 months.

TO PREPARE:

- To make the gravy, mix 2-3 tbsp of the powder with 240ml (9fl oz/1cup) of boiling water. Stir continuously until it thickens to your desired consistency.

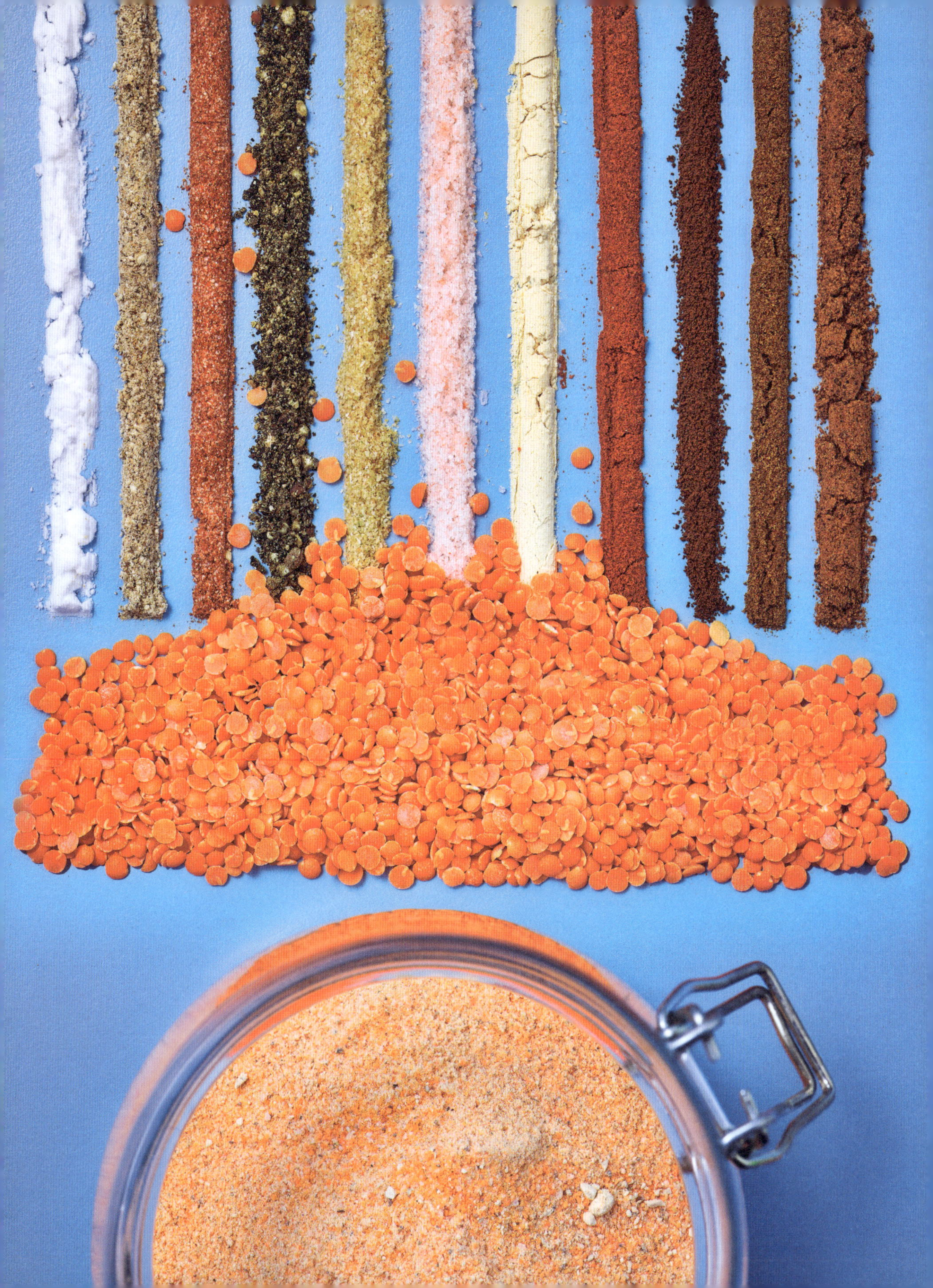

INSTANT DASHI POWDER

Dashi is the soul of Japanese cuisine – a versatile, umami-packed broth that elevates every dish it touches. From miso soup to delicate simmered vegetables, it's the foundation upon which traditional Japanese flavours are built. Historically, dashi has been crafted using kombu (dried kelp) and katsuobushi (fermented skipjack tuna flakes), using techniques refined over centuries. Its simplicity belies its power: a clear, golden broth that transforms the ordinary into astonishing dishes.

The origins of dashi go beyond technique. It embodies the Japanese principle of umami, a flavour profile celebrated long before umami entered Western culinary vocabulary. This elusive "fifth taste" is what makes dashi a cornerstone of traditional cooking. By combining carefully dried mushrooms like shiitake and king oysters with miso, this recipe delivers all the rich, savoury complexity of classic dashi without the need for fish.

INGREDIENTS

- 450g (16oz) dry king oyster mushrooms
- 400g (14oz) dry shiitake mushrooms
- 250g (9oz/1 cup) miso (before drying)
- 1½ sheets kombu algae

MINDFUL BENEFITS:

- **Kombu:** Rich in iodine and essential minerals that support thyroid health and overall wellness.

- **Miso:** The fermentation in miso adds probiotics, which enhance gut health and mental well-being by supporting the gut-brain connection.

Dry the Miso:
Step 1: Spread the miso thinly on a dehydrator tray or a baking tray if using an oven.

Step 2: Dehydrate at 60°C/140°F until completely dry. This can take several hours.

Prepare the Mushrooms:
Step 3: Ensure the king oyster and shiitake mushrooms are thoroughly dried.

Combine Ingredients:
Step 4: Break the dried miso into small pieces.

Step 5: In a blender or food processor, combine the dried miso pieces, dry king oyster mushrooms, dry shiitake mushrooms and kombu algae.

Blend to a Powder:
Step 6: Blend until you achieve a fine powder. This may take a few minutes to ensure all ingredients are thoroughly ground.

Storage:
Step 7: Transfer the dashi powder to a labeled airtight container. Store in a cool, dry place for up to 6 months.

TO PREPARE:

Dissolve 1-2 tsp of dashi powder in 1 cup of hot water to make instant dashi stock.

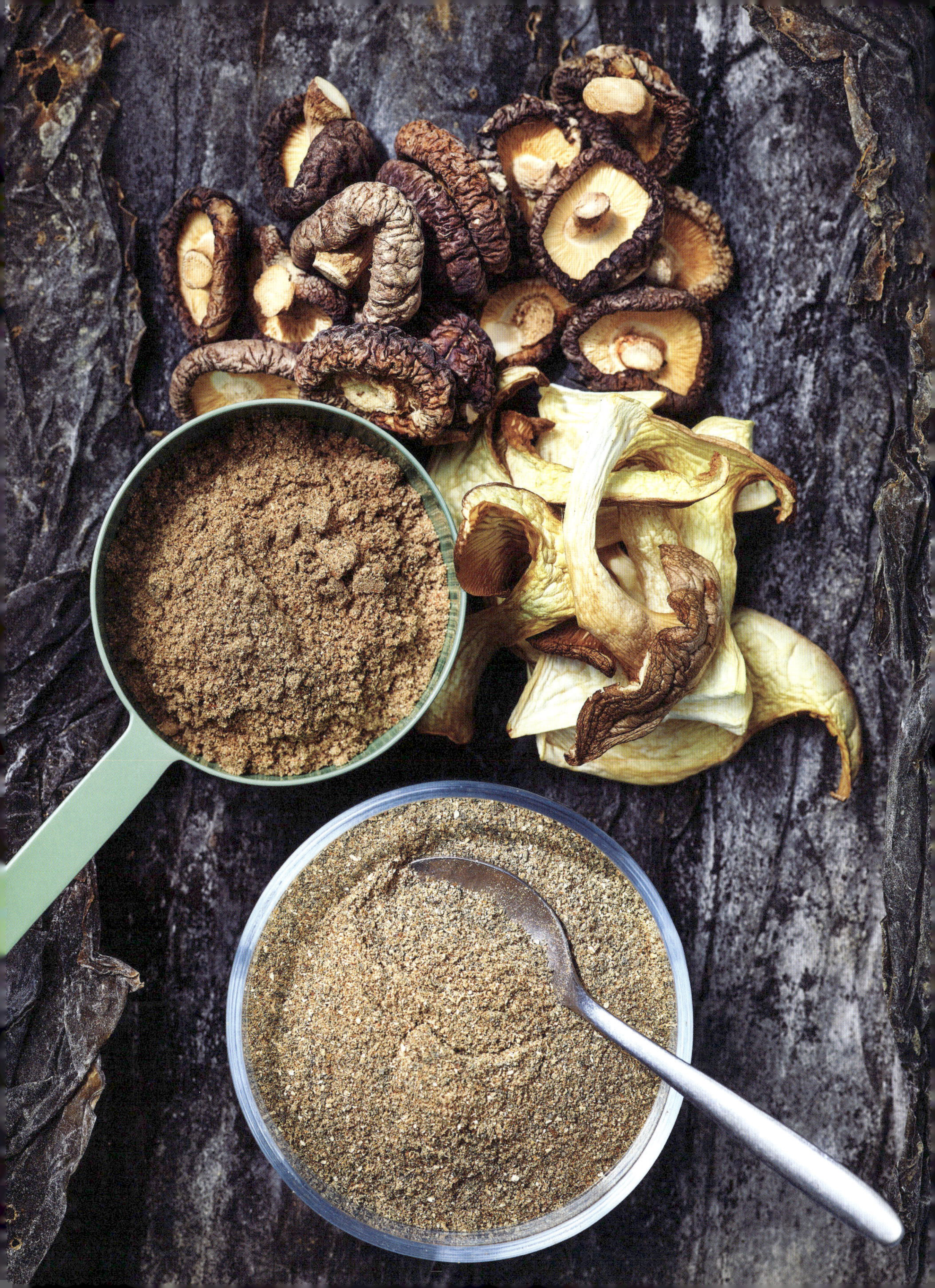

VEGAN WORCESTER SAUCE

Worcester sauce, often referred to as Worcestershire sauce, is a beloved condiment with a fascinating history that dates back to 19th-century England. Originally crafted by chemists John Lea and William Perrins in Worcester, England, this fermented sauce was inspired by Indian spices and adapted to suit Western palates.

The resulting blend became an international sensation, known for its sweet, tangy and umami-rich flavour profile.

Traditional Worcester sauce contains anchovies, making it unsuitable for vegans or those seeking a plant-based lifestyle.

However, this vegan alternative preserves the bold and intricate flavour profile of the original while embracing natural, wholesome ingredients.

With tamarind, molasses and a medley of spices, this homemade version offers a depth of flavour that enhances everything from stews to dressings, marinades and more.

INGREDIENTS

- 240ml/8fl oz/1 cup apple cider vinegar (see page 122)
- ¼ cup soy sauce or tamari (for gluten-free)
- 2 tbsp molasses
- 1 tbsp Dijon mustard
- 1 tbsp tamarind paste
- 1 tsp garlic powder
- 1 tsp onion powder
- ½ tsp ground ginger
- ½ tsp ground cloves
- ¼ tsp ground cinnamon
- ¼ tsp black pepper
- ¼ tsp smoked paprika
- ¼ tsp cayenne pepper (optional for heat)

Combine Ingredients:
Step 1: In a saucepan, combine the apple cider vinegar, soy sauce or tamari, molasses, Dijon mustard, tamarind paste, garlic powder, onion powder, ground ginger, ground cloves, ground cinnamon, black pepper, smoked paprika and cayenne pepper (if using).

Simmer:
Step 2: Bring the mixture to a simmer over medium heat. Let it simmer for 10–15 minutes, stirring occasionally to combine the flavors.

Cool and Strain:
Step 3: Remove from heat and allow the mixture to cool completely. Strain through a sieve or fine-mesh strainer to achieve a smooth sauce.

Storage:
Step 4: Transfer the sauce to a labeled airtight container. Store in the refrigerator for up to 4 weeks.

COOKING TIP:

- Adjust the sweetness with more molasses or tweak the heat level by increasing or reducing cayenne pepper to suit your taste.

MINDFUL BENEFITS:

• **Apple Cider Vinegar:** Known for supporting digestion and stabilizing blood sugar, which can help with focus and mood stability. It also has antimicrobial and antioxidant properties.

• **Tamarind Paste:** A rich source of magnesium and potassium, which aids in stress reduction and muscle function.

NO-FISH SAUCE

No-fish sauce is a vegan alternative to traditional fish sauce, which is a staple in Southeast Asian cuisine. It brings the same umami-rich profile to dishes through a blend of savoury ingredients such as seaweed, soy sauce and fermented beans. Making this sauce at home allows vegans and vegetarians to achieve the deep flavours of fish sauce without compromising their dietary choices, using all-natural ingredients.

Use as a 1:1 substitute for traditional fish sauce in soups, stews, stir-fries, marinades and salad dressings.

INGREDIENTS

Quick No-Fuss Version:
- 1 mug light soy sauce or tamari (gluten-free soy sauce)
- 1 sheet nori seaweed
- ½ tsp salt

I-Have-People-to-Dinner Version:
- 1 mug light soy sauce or tamari (gluten-free soy sauce)
- 1 sheet nori seaweed
- ½ tsp salt
- 1 tbsp dried shiitake mushroom powder
- 1 clove garlic, minced
- 1 tsp molasses or brown sugar
- 1 tbsp apple cider vinegar (see page 122)
- 1 tsp miso paste (optional for extra depth)

QUICK NO-FUSS METHOD

Combine Ingredients:
Step 1: In a blender, combine the light soy sauce or tamari, nori seaweed and salt.

Blend:
Step 2: Blend all the ingredients together for 30–50 seconds until the nori seaweed is finely processed.

Strain:
Step 3: Strain the mixture through a sieve or fine-mesh strainer to remove any solids, ensuring a smooth sauce.

Storage:
Step 4: Transfer the vegan fish sauce to a labeled airtight container. Store in the refrigerator for up to 4 weeks.

I-HAVE-PEOPLE-TO-DINNER METHOD

Combine Ingredients:
Step 1: In a blender, combine all the ingredients.

Blend:
Step 2: Blend all the ingredients together for 30–50 seconds until all the ingredients are finely processed.

Strain:
Step 3: Strain the mixture through a sieve or fine-mesh strainer to remove any solids, ensuring a smooth sauce.

Storage:
Step 4: Transfer to a labelled airtight container. Store in the refrigerator for up to 4 weeks.

MINDFUL BENEFITS:

- **Nori:** High in iodine and minerals, nori supports thyroid health, helping to stabilize energy levels, a key factor for managing focus and attention.

- **Soy Sauce or Tamari:** Provides essential amino acids that aid neurotransmitter production, supporting cognitive function and mood regulation.

- **Dried Shiitake Mushrooms:** Contain antioxidants and compounds that reduce inflammation, positively affecting brain health and mental clarity.

- **Garlic:** Known for its antibacterial and heart health benefits, it also supports brain function by improving circulation.

COOKING TIP:

- Add a splash of lime juice for brightness and acidity to balance the sauce's richness.

CREATIVE TIP:

- Enhance the umami profile with a small piece of kombu or experiment with different types of miso for varied depth and flavour.

CANNED/JARRED LEGUMES, BEANS, CHICKPEAS, LENTILS, PEAS

"The quality of our food reflects the quality of our care."
Alice Waters

Canned legumes are a staple in pantries around the world, celebrated for their convenience and nutritional value. Opting to can your own legumes at home elevates this everyday convenience to a new level of freshness and quality.

When you can legumes yourself, you have the freedom to choose from a vast array of varieties – beyond what is typically offered on grocery shelves – from heirloom beans to exotic lentils, each with its own unique flavour and texture. Canning at home also allows you to control the canning process, ensuring there are no added salts, sugars or preservatives that often accompany store-bought cans. You can adjust seasonings to your preference, and by canning in batches that suit your consumption, you can avoid the waste and overstocking that can occur with store-bought legumes.

Moreover, there's a certain beauty in the rows of jars filled with home-canned legumes, lined up in your cabinets, ready to be opened at a moment's notice. They represent not just a practical choice, but a commitment to the quality of the food you serve.

Each jar is a self-contained promise of a nutritious addition to meals, embodying both the foresight of preparation and the pleasure of enjoying a variety of legumes year-round. Canning legumes at home is an investment in your culinary freedom, sustainability and the joy of eating well.

INGREDIENTS

- 2 kg/70 ½ oz dry legumes (beans, chickpeas/garbanzo beans, lentils, peas, broad beans, etc.)
- 2 tbsp salt

Soak the Legumes:

Step 1: Place the legumes in a large bowl and cover with cold water. Soak for the appropriate time:
- Lentils and peas: 12 hours
- Chickpeas/garbanzo beans: 48 hours
- Other beans: 24 hours

Step 2: Change the water at least once a day during the soaking period.

Recipe continued on the next page …

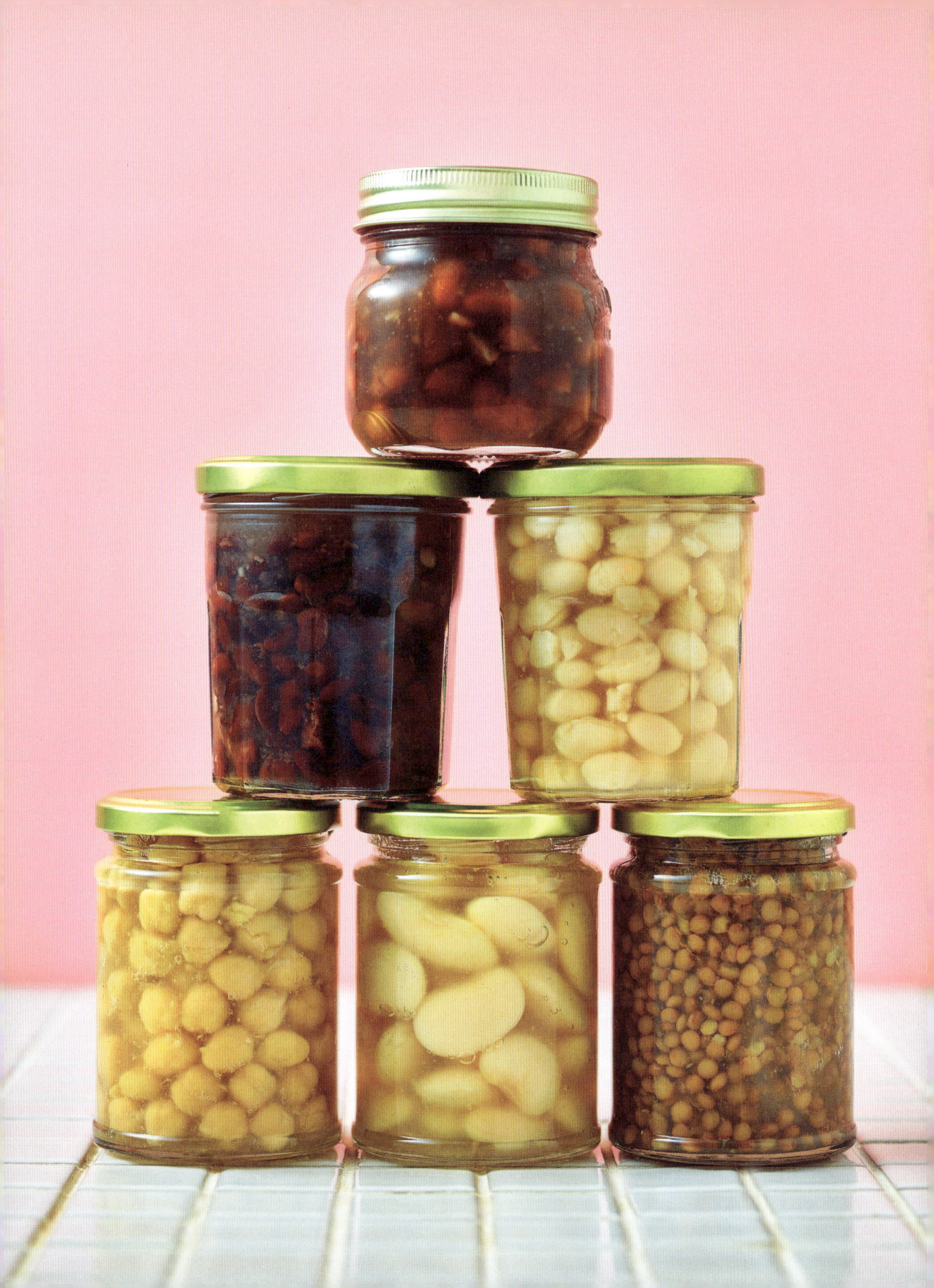

COOKING TIP:

• Ensure all jars are properly sealed and sterilized to prevent spoilage and contamination.

MINDFUL BENEFITS:

• Legumes' high magnesium and folate content can help reduce stress and improve cognitive function, enhancing focus and attention.

CREATIVE TIP:

• Add aromatic herbs, spices, garlic or onion directly to the jars before sealing to create unique flavour profiles for your legumes.

Cook the Legumes:

Step 3: After soaking, drain the legumes and transfer them to a large pot or pressure cooker. Cover with plenty of water and cook until just tender but still firm:
• Lentils: 30 minutes, or 12 minutes in a pressure cooker
• Peas: 40 minutes, or 18 minutes in a pressure cooker
• Chickpeas/garbanzo beans, beans, broad beans: 60 minutes, or 30 minutes in a pressure cooker

Step 4: Avoid stirring during cooking to prevent the legumes from breaking.

Step 5: Add the salt toward the end of the cooking time. Allow the legumes to rest in the salted water for a few minutes before draining.

Prepare the Jars:

Step 6: Sterilize jars by boiling them in water for 30 minutes.

Step 7: Divide the cooked legumes among the jars, pressing gently to pack them in. Pour in the cooking broth to cover the legumes.

Step 8: Seal the jars with airtight lids. Wrap each jar in a cloth, place them in a large pot, cover with cold water, and bring to a boil. Simmer on low heat for 30 minutes.

Cool and Check Seals:

Step 9: Allow the jars to cool in the pot. Check that a vacuum seal has formed. If not, repeat the boiling process.

Storage:

Store the jarred legumes in a cool, dark place for up to a year. Once opened, consume within a week.

THE ART OF PRESERVATION – PICKLING, FERMENTING AND THE SLOW FOOD JOURNEY

"Every jar holds a story – a celebration of time, flavour and connection."

In the rhythmic dance of the seasons, nature offers a bounty that insists on being celebrated.

Preserving at home is our way of honouring this abundance.

This part of the book is dedicated to the mindful practices of pickling and fermenting – cornerstones of the Slow Food movement.

As we navigate the cycles of growth and harvest, "Reasoning with the Season" becomes our mantra.

It's a conscious approach that respects the natural timing of crops, capturing their peak freshness and nutritional zenith.

Here we delve into the ancient traditions that have allowed generations to extend the life of their food, turning the ephemeral into the enduring.

Pickling is a preservation method steeped in history, an alchemy where vinegar, salt and spices come together to safeguard the harvest. It's a craft that transforms cucumbers into crisp dill pickles, beets/beetroots into tangy delights and cabbage into the beloved sauerkraut.

Through pickling, we create zesty condiments and side dishes that can brighten any meal, infusing them with flavours that are as intense as they are enduring.

Fermentation, on the other hand, is a silent and mysterious process where microorganisms play the leading role.

This transformative journey not only preserves our food but also enhances its health benefits, giving us probiotic-rich foods like kimchi, kefir and kombucha.

It's a natural process that heightens nutritional value and gives birth to complex flavours from the simplest of ingredients.

Engaging in the practice of preserving at home is to participate in the Slow Food ethos – it's to choose quality over convenience, tradition over trend, and wholesomeness over haste.

It's about slowing down to appreciate the process, from the initial preparation to the final enjoyment of opening a jar of home-crafted goodness.

Each jar you seal is a time capsule, a celebration of the season it was made, waiting patiently to be reopened and relished. With every pop of a lid, we're reminded of the summer's heat, the autumn's transition or the spring's awakening – we're uncorking memories, unleashing flavours and connecting with a time and place that, thanks to our efforts, can be revisited with each taste.

This section is a guide to living a more harmonious, sustainable life. It's an invitation to become artisans of time, to engage with our food in a way that nourishes not just our bodies but also our connection to the earth and its cycles.

Through pickling and fermenting, we become custodians of tradition and advocates for a future where every meal reflects mindfulness and every jar a celebration of time itself.

COOKING TIP:

- With all pickles, make sure the vegetables or fruit stays submerged under the liquid to prevent mould. If necessary, use a clean weight to keep them submerged.

• Recipes on the next page

SAUERKRAUT

Sauerkraut is a celebration of simplicity and time. Originating from Central Europe, this fermented cabbage has become synonymous with health and longevity.

The lactic acid bacteria that thrive during fermentation not only preserve the cabbage but also enrich it with probiotics that support gut health, enhance digestion, and boost the immune system.

Use sauerkraut as a topping for sandwiches, salads, or as a side dish to enhance your meals with a tangy, probiotic-rich boost.

INGREDIENTS

- 1 medium green cabbage (about 1kg/35oz)
- 1 tbsp sea salt
- 1 tsp caraway seeds (optional)

MINDFUL BENEFITS:

- Sauerkraut's probiotics support gut health, which is deeply connected to mood regulation and cognitive function, aiding in mental clarity and reducing stress.

- High in vitamin C, it enhances immunity and skin health while contributing to vitality.

Prepare the Cabbage:
Step 1: Remove the outer leaves of the cabbage. Cut the cabbage into quarters and remove the core. Slice the cabbage thinly.

Massage the Cabbage:
Step 2: Place the sliced cabbage in a large bowl. Sprinkle the sea salt over the cabbage. Using your hands, massage the salt into the cabbage until it begins to release liquid and become limp, about 5–10 minutes.

Pack the Cabbage:
Step 3: Pack the cabbage tightly into a clean, sterilized jar. Press it down firmly so that the liquid rises above the cabbage. Add the caraway seeds, if using.

Ferment:
Step 4: Cover the jar with a cloth or lid loosely to allow gases to escape. Place the jar in a cool, dark place at room temperature. Ferment for 1–4 weeks, checking daily to ensure the cabbage is submerged under the liquid.

Storage:
Step 5: Once the sauerkraut has reached your desired flavour and texture, seal the jar with a lid and store it in the refrigerator. It will keep for several months.

CREATIVE TIP:

- Experiment with adding other vegetables like carrots, beets/beetroots, or radishes to your sauerkraut for added flavour and nutrition.

PRESERVED LEMONS

In the warm Mediterranean sun, preserved lemons come to life, imbuing the citrus with an intense lemony essence.

This North African and Middle Eastern staple involves curing lemons in salt and their own juice, transforming them into a condiment with a mellow yet complex flavour. Homemade preserved lemons offer a fresher, more nuanced tartness than store-bought varieties and can elevate the simplest of recipes with a burst of umami.

Use preserved lemons to add a burst of flavour to stews, salads, marinades and tagines. Rinse the lemon before use to remove excess salt, and use the peel as well as the pulp.

INGREDIENTS

- 4–6 organic lemons
- 72g/2½oz/¼ cup sea salt (plus more as needed)
- Freshly squeezed lemon juice (from about 2 lemons)
- Bay leaves, cinnamon sticks or peppercorns (optional)

MINDFUL BENEFITS:

- Lemons are high in vitamin C, which supports the immune system, skin health, and collagen production.

- The fermentation process enhances the lemons' probiotic content, aiding in digestion and gut health. The high vitamin C content can support adrenal function, helping to reduce stress and improve mood.

Prepare the Lemons:
Step 1: Wash the lemons thoroughly. Cut each lemon into quarters lengthwise, but do not cut all the way through, leaving the quarters attached at the base.

Massage the Lemons:
Step 2: Sprinkle a generous amount of sea salt into the interior of each lemon, then press the quarters back together.

Pack the Lemons:
Step 3: Place the salted lemons into a sterilized jar, pressing them down to release their juices and fit as many lemons as possible. Add additional salt between layers if needed.

Add Lemon Juice:
Step 4: Pour the freshly squeezed lemon juice over the lemons in the jar until they are completely submerged. Add bay leaves, cinnamon sticks or peppercorns for extra flavour if desired.

Ferment:
Step 5: Seal the jar and leave it at room temperature to ferment for about 3–4 weeks, shaking the jar occasionally to distribute the salt and juices.

Storage:
Step 6: After fermentation, store the preserved lemons in a cool dark place. They can last up to a year. Once opened, they go in the fridge and last up to 6 months if under brine.

PICKLES

The humble pickle is a cornerstone of preservation, known for its crisp bite and sour punch.

This method of immersing vegetables in a brine or vinegar solution is loved worldwide, with each culture adding its signature twist.

Homemade pickles not only bypass the additives found in commercial versions but also allow for full flavour customization.

Enjoy pickles as a crunchy, tangy snack, or add them to sandwiches, salads and charcuterie boards.

INGREDIENTS

- 1kg/35oz fresh cucumbers (or your choice of vegetables)
- 480ml/16fl oz/2 cups white vinegar
- 480ml/16fl oz/2 cups water
- 4 tbsp sea salt
- 2 tbsp sugar (optional)
- 1 tbsp pickling spice (such as mustard seeds, coriander seeds, dill seeds and peppercorns)
- 4 cloves garlic, peeled
- Fresh dill (optional)

Prepare the Vegetables:
Step 1: Wash and cut the cucumbers (or other vegetables) into desired shapes (slices, spears or leave them whole, just as I did here).

Make the Base:
Step 2: In a saucepan, combine the vinegar, water, sea salt and sugar (if using). Bring to a boil, stirring until the salt and sugar dissolve.

Pack the Jars:
Step 3: Place the garlic cloves, fresh dill and pickling spices into sterilized jars. Pack the prepared vegetables tightly into the jars.

Add the Brine:
Step 4: Pour the hot brine over the vegetables, making sure they are completely submerged. Leave about 1cm/½ inch of headspace at the top of the jar.

Seal:
Step 5: Seal the jars with lids and follow the canning method on page XXX (step 8 onwards).

Storage:

Store in a cool, dark place for up to 1 year. Once opened, the pickles should be stored in a refrigerator and consumed within 4-6 weeks for the best quality.

CREATIVE TIP:

- Experiment with different vegetables and spices to create unique flavour combinations. Try adding chilli flakes for a spicy kick or ginger for a zesty twist.

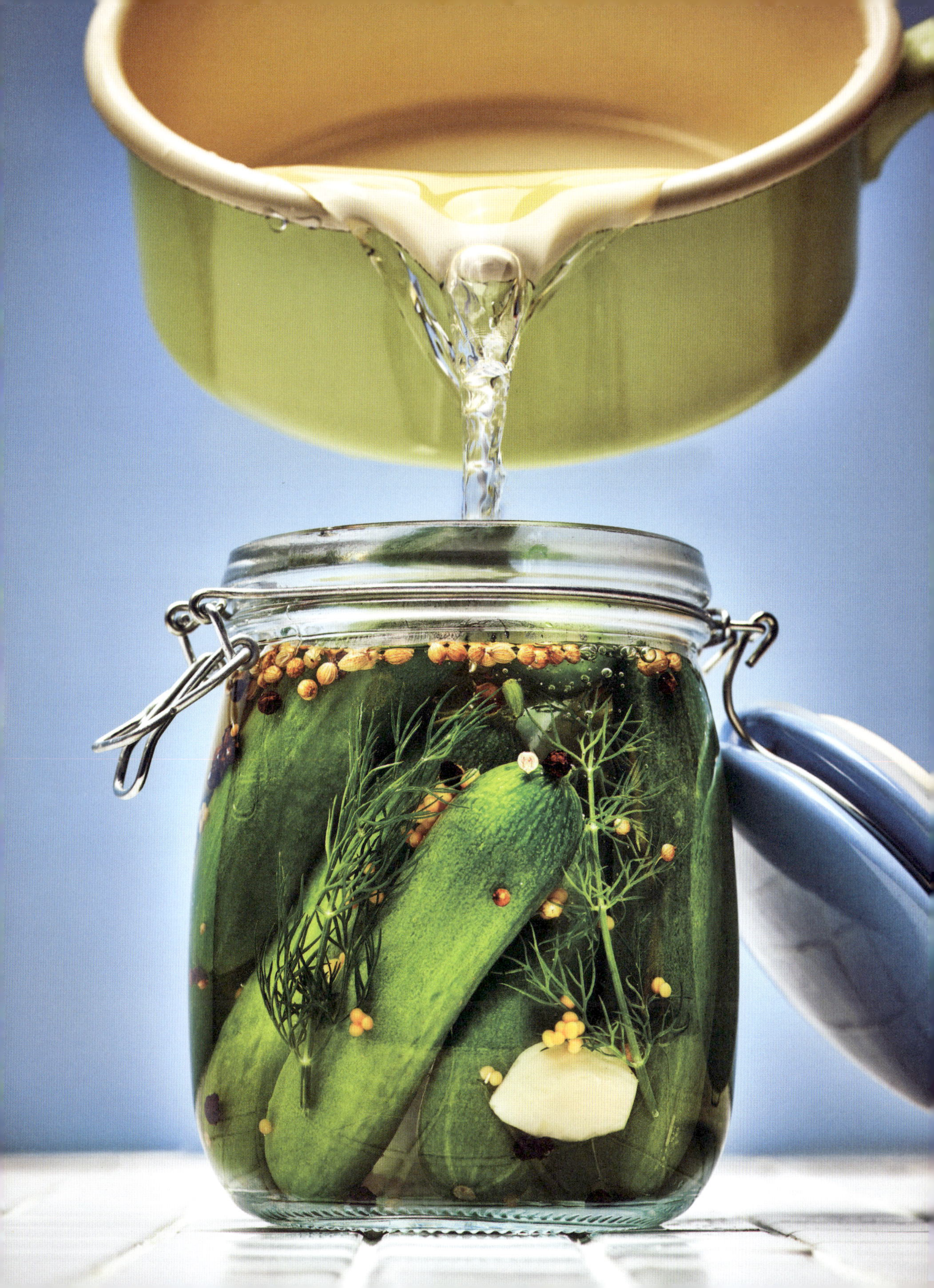

3 THE BIN:
The Resource Recovery Centre

"Waste is not waste until we waste it."
– Will.i.am

This chapter is a pivotal movement in our culinary concerto. Here, we reimagine the traditional bin, transforming it from a final resting place for kitchen waste into a dynamic centre of resourcefulness and regeneration.

This is a place where scraps are not seen as the end of the line but as the beginning of something new, something inventive.

We embark on a journey through the zero-waste philosophy, a path that leads us away from the throwaway culture and into the embrace of mindful consumption.

It's about seeing potential in every peel, every seed, every core and every leftover.

This chapter is not just about minimizing waste – it's about maximizing the utility of each ingredient that passes through your kitchen.

Through creative upcycling techniques, we'll look at commonly discarded food as amazing by-products to craft homemade stocks, coffee, gelling agents, vinegars and much more.

Every recipe is a guide to making the most out of what you already have. It's a testament to the fact that with a little ingenuity, the journey of our food can be extended far beyond the plate.

"The Bin: The Resource Recovery Centre" is a call to action, urging us to rethink our relationship with food and its lifecycle. It provides practical tips and highlights the importance of a zero-waste approach in the kitchen.

A chance to give back to the earth, to nourish it as it nourishes us, and to create a sustainable cycle that benefits our households and the global community.

STOCK CUBES AND BOUILLON

Building on the concept of Stock and Sauces from the previous section, Stock Cubes and Bouillon continues the journey toward flavour development, efficiency and resourcefulness.

Where powders bring the essence of ingredients into compact, shelf-stable formats, we are focusing on creating liquid gold from what might otherwise be discarded.

With these two recipes, every scrap from your kitchen becomes an opportunity.

Vegetable peels, herb stems and other kitchen leftovers transform into flavourful bases for soups, stews and sauces, reducing waste and bringing unparalleled depth to your cooking.

By crafting these staples at home, you ensure a cleaner product – free from preservatives and excessive sodium – all while celebrating a zero-waste philosophy.

CREATIVE TIP:

• Experiment with herbs like thyme, rosemary or additional seaweed varieties for unique flavour profiles.

• Recipes on the next page

VEGETABLE STOCK POWDER

Also known as bouillon, stock powder can trace its roots back to the 18th century when the concept of condensed stocks began to take shape. Traditionally, bouillon cubes were created to provide soldiers and explorers with portable, long-lasting nourishment.

As industrialization grew, the bouillon cube or powder became a pantry staple, offering convenience to busy households. Homemade bouillon, however, predates this industrial era.

In kitchens around the world, cooks simmered bones, vegetables and herbs to create broths for later use. This process not only extended the shelf life of precious ingredients but also maximized their flavour and nutrition – a vital skill in times when waste was not an option. Here we return to these roots of sustainability. It's a simple, waste-conscious method, repurposing leftover vegetables or juicing pulp into a rich, flavour-packed base. Unlike commercial alternatives, homemade bouillon offers purity, depth of flavour and the satisfaction of knowing every ingredient contributes to your mindful ethos.

INGREDIENTS

- 600g/21oz leftover vegetables (carrots, celery, onion, garlic and juicing pulp)
- 300g/10½oz salt (pink Himalayan or any available salt)
- 30g/1oz Icelandic moss (optional, but recommended for added minerals)

TO PREPARE:

- Use 1-2 tsp of powder per cup of boiling water for a quick broth, or add directly to recipes for seasoning.

Prepare the Vegetables:
Step 1: Gather all leftover vegetables and juicing pulp. Chop larger pieces into uniform sizes.

Sweat the Vegetables:
Step 2: Combine the vegetables and salt in a large pot. Cook over low heat, stirring occasionally, until the vegetables soften and release liquid (about 15–20 minutes).

Dehydrate the Mixture:
Step 3: Spread the cooked vegetable mixture onto dehydrator trays or a lined baking sheet. Dehydrate at the lowest oven setting or in a dehydrator until completely dry and brittle (this may take several hours).

Blend to a Powder:
Step 4: Break the dried mixture into smaller pieces and blend in a high-powered blender or food processor until fine.

Storage:
Step 5: Transfer the vegetable stock powder to a labelled airtight container. Store in a cool, dry place for up to 1 year.

STOCK CUBES

Use scraps that are clean and free from mould to ensure a fresh, flavourful stock. Drop a cube into soups, stews or sauces for an instant flavour boost.

INGREDIENTS

- Vegetable scraps (onion ends, carrot peels, celery leaves, herb stems, mushroom stems, etc.)
- Older vegetables from the fridge (wilted but not spoiled)
- 1–2 tbsp quality salt
- Peppercorns, bay leaves or other aromatics (optional)

MINDFUL BENEFITS:

- **Retains nutrients from vegetables that are often lost in traditional cooking methods.**

- **Allows for controlled sodium levels compared to commercial stock cubes.**

CREATIVE TIP:

- Add spices like turmeric or paprika to your stock paste for customized flavours.

Collect and Prepare Scraps:

Step 1: Keep a container in the freezer to collect vegetable and fruit scraps.

Step 2: Roughly chop large pieces to ensure even cooking.

Cook the Scraps:

Step 3: Combine the scraps in a large pot and add just enough water to cover.

Step 4: Add salt and optional aromatics. Simmer for 1–2 hours, allowing the vegetables to soften and release their flavours.

Blend into a Paste:

Step 5: Remove large aromatics (like bay leaves), then transfer the mixture to a blender. Blitz until smooth, adding water sparingly for a thick paste.

Form the Cubes:

Step 6: Spoon the paste into ice-cube trays or spread onto a lined baking sheet. Freeze until solid.

Step 7: Transfer the frozen cubes to a labelled freezer-safe container. Store for up to 6 months.

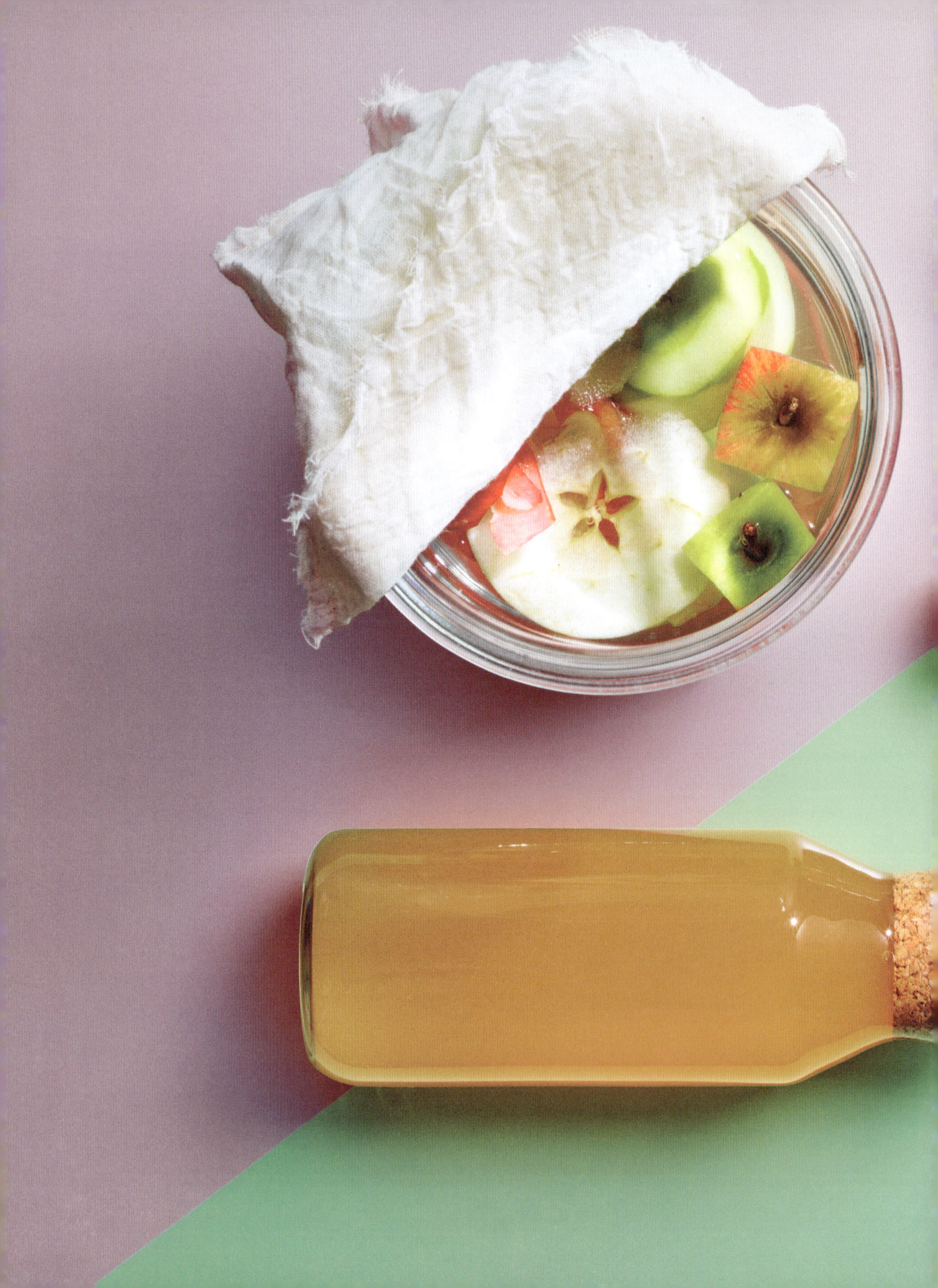

• Recipe on the next page

APPLE CIDER VINEGAR

Apple cider vinegar, or ACV, is a timeless example of resourcefulness meeting wellness in the kitchen. With origins dating back thousands of years, ACV has been revered as both a culinary staple and a natural remedy across cultures. From ancient Babylonians fermenting fruits for vinegar to Hippocrates recommending it, this liquid has stood the test of time – it epitomizes the principles of sustainability and holistic health.

Celebrated for its health-promoting properties, it's a natural probiotic that supports gut health, aids digestion, and helps regulate blood sugar levels. Crafted from humble apple scraps – peels, cores or juicing pulp – ACV transforms effortlessly into a nutrient-rich elixir.

Use apple cider vinegar in salad dressings, marinades, sauces, or even as a natural cleaning agent. It's great diluted in water as a refreshing, tangy drink.

INGREDIENTS

- Apple scraps (cores, peels and any remaining fruit)
- Water
- Specialized wine-making yeast or a mother from another vinegar (optional)

COOKING TIP:

- Ensure apple scraps are completely clean to prevent contamination during fermentation.

CREATIVE TIP:

- Experiment with adding aromatics such as cinnamon sticks, cloves or fresh ginger to infuse the vinegar with additional flavour.

Prepare Apple Scraps:
Step 1: Gather apple scraps such as cores, peels and any remaining fruit. Ensure they are clean and free from mould or rot.

Fill the Jar:
Step 2: Place the apple scraps into a clean container or jar until it's about three-quarters full.

Initiate Fermentation:
Step 3: If desired, add specialized wine-making yeast or a mother from another vinegar to expedite fermentation. Natural sugars in the apple skins also initiate fermentation, so do not worry.

Step 4: Cover the jar with a muslin cloth/cheesecloth secured with a rubber band or string to allow airflow while keeping insects out.

Fermentation Process:
Step 5: Store the jar away from direct sunlight at a temperature between 15–27°C/60–80°F.

Step 6: Stir the mixture daily and leave the jar partially open to allow gas to escape. This stage converts sugars into alcohol over approximately 3–4 weeks.

Acetic Acid Fermentation:
Step 7: After alcoholic fermentation, strain the mixture to remove solids and return the liquid to the jar.

Step 8: Cover the jar again with a cheesecloth and ferment for another 2–4 weeks. During this stage, bacteria convert alcohol into acetic acid, creating vinegar's signature tang.

Check for Readiness:
Step 9: Taste the vinegar periodically or use a pH probe to measure acidity, aiming for a pH between 2 and 3.

Clarify and Filter:
Step 10: Once fully fermented, filter the vinegar through a cheesecloth or coffee filter to remove remaining solids.

Storage:
Step 11: Transfer the vinegar into a clean bottle, label it with the date of production, and store it in a cool, dark place.

MINDFUL BENEFITS:

• ACV contains probiotics that promote gut health and digestion, supporting overall mental clarity and emotional balance.

• Its role in regulating blood sugar levels can prevent energy spikes and crashes, fostering sustained focus and calm.

DATE SEED COFFEE

For those navigating the challenges of fluctuating energy levels, particularly individuals with neurodivergences, caffeine can be both a friend and a foe. While it offers a temporary energy boost, it often comes with a crash that can disrupt focus and increase anxiety.

Date Seed Coffee is a gentle and nourishing alternative that delivers the rich experience of coffee, minus the caffeine. It mirrors the robust, full-bodied flavour making it an ideal choice for those sensitive to stimulants or seeking a more balanced approach to energy management.

An uplifting yet calming ritual.

What sets Date Seed Coffee apart is its nutritional value. Rich in antioxidants and dietary fiber, it supports gut health, which has been shown to play a vital role in mental wellbeing.

A mindful way to start the day or recharge during a busy afternoon. Enjoy Date Seed Coffee hot or iced. It pairs well with honey, maple syrup or your preferred sweetener and favorite plant-based milk.

INGREDIENTS

- 160g/5½oz/1 cup date seeds
- Spices such as cinnamon, cardamom or nutmeg for added flavour (optional)

MINDFUL BENEFITS:

- Date seeds are rich in antioxidants, combating oxidative stress to support brain health.

- The dietary fiber in date seeds promotes gut health.

COOKING TIP:

- Ensure the seeds are completely dry before grinding to prevent spoilage and ensure an even grind.

Prepare the Seeds:
Step 1: Collect the seeds from fresh dates. Wash them thoroughly to remove any remaining fruit.

Roast the Seeds:
Step 2: Spread the date seeds on a baking sheet in a single layer. Roast in the oven at 180°C/350°F for 45–60 minutes, stirring occasionally, until the seeds are dark and aromatic.

Cool and Grind:
Step 3: Allow the roasted seeds to cool completely. Once cooled, grind them into a fine powder using a coffee grinder or high-powered blender.

Brew the Coffee:
Step 4: Use the ground date seeds as you would regular coffee grounds. For each cup of coffee, use 1–2 tablespoons of the date seed powder. Brew using a French press, drip coffee maker or espresso machine.

Optional Flavouring:
Step 5: Add spices such as cinnamon, cardamom or nutmeg to the ground date seeds before brewing for an extra layer of flavour.

CREATIVE TIP:

• Blend date seed coffee with roasted barley, chicory or nuts to craft your own signature coffee blend with unique depth and flavour.

COCONUT FLOUR

Coconut flour is a sustainable and gluten-free ingredient made by repurposing the pulp left over from homemade coconut milk (see page 148).

With minimal effort, this by-product transforms into a nutrient-dense pantry staple, perfect for baking and desserts, all while supporting a zero-waste lifestyle.

You can use it as a gluten-free alternative to wheat flour and it works well in pancakes, muffins and cakes. Coconut flour absorbs significantly more liquid than other flours, so adjust the liquid quantities in your recipes accordingly. Start with small amounts of flour and add more gradually to achieve the desired consistency.

INGREDIENTS

- Leftover coconut pulp from homemade coconut milk

MINDFUL BENEFITS:

- Coconut flour is rich in dietary fibre, which promotes digestive health and helps maintain steady energy levels, supporting focus and mental clarity.

- Its plant-based protein content contributes to sustained energy and muscle repair.

CREATIVE TIP:

- Incorporate coconut flour into smoothies, energy bars, or as a breading for roasted vegetables and tofu to add a unique, tropical twist.

Prepare the Pulp:
Step 1: After making coconut milk, gather the leftover coconut pulp. Squeeze out as much remaining liquid as possible using a nut milk bag or muslin cloth/cheesecloth.

Dry the Pulp:
Step 2: Spread the coconut pulp in a thin layer on a baking sheet.

Step 3: Dry the pulp in the oven at a low temperature (around 90°C/200°F) for 2–3 hours, or until completely dry and crisp. Alternatively, use a dehydrator if you have one.

Blend to a Flour:
Step 4: Once the pulp is thoroughly dried, blend it in a high-powered blender or food processor until it becomes a fine powder.

Storage:
Step 5: Transfer the coconut flour to a labelled airtight container. Store in a cool, dry place. It can last for several months if stored properly.

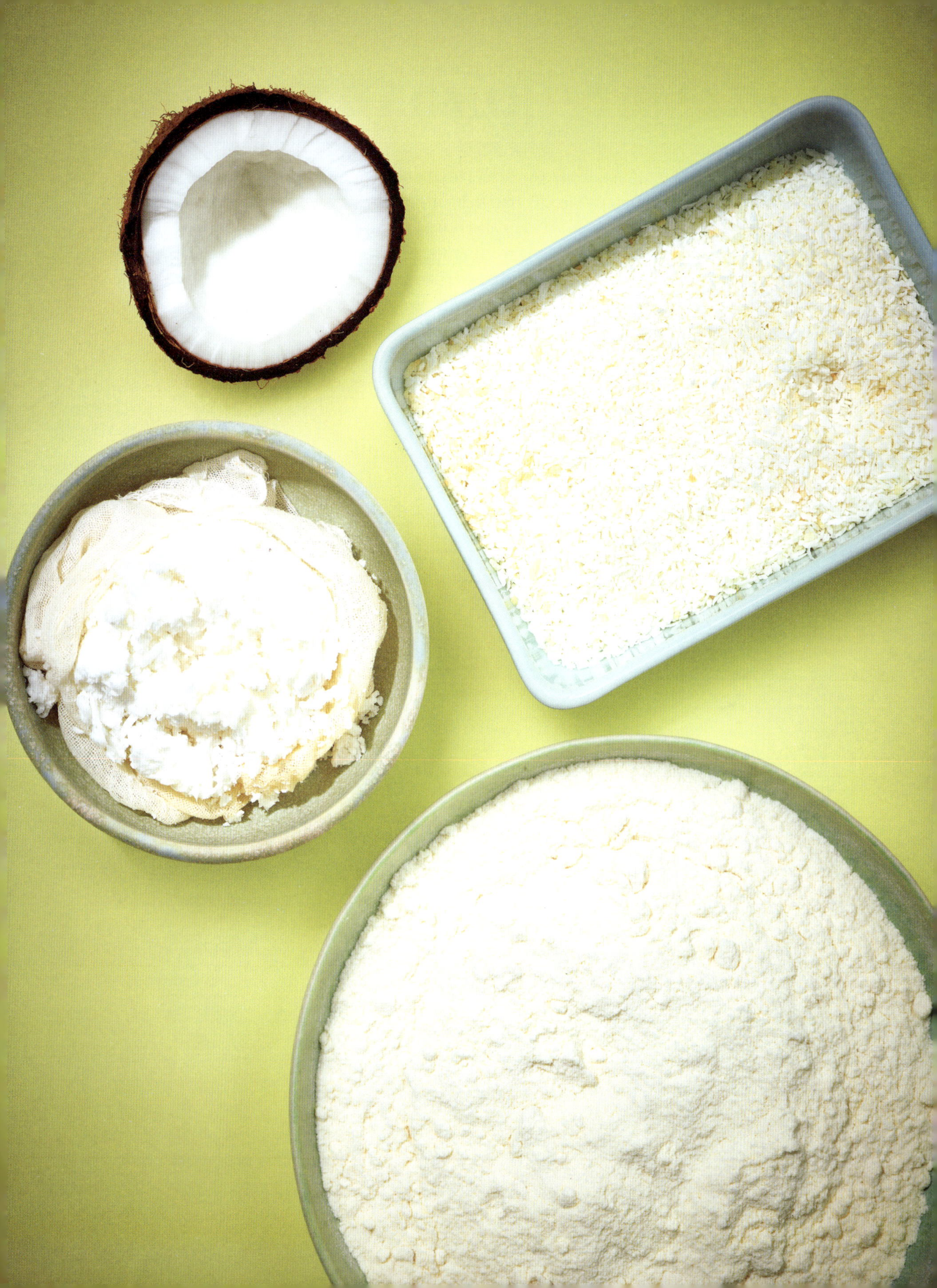

HOMEMADE KETCHUP

Ketchup is a universal favourite, but the store-bought versions often come with hidden additives, excessive sugar and single-use packaging.

A zero-waste homemade ketchup changes the game, offering a cleaner, more sustainable alternative that doesn't sacrifice taste.

By rethinking food scraps like carrot pulp and onion peels, this recipe takes a new approach to creating a rich, flavourful condiment.

Infused with spices like turmeric and ginger, this ketchup offers health benefits that traditional versions can't match.

Use this homemade ketchup as a delicious condiment for burgers, fries and sandwiches, or as a base for sauces and marinades.

INGREDIENTS

- 2 onion peels (first white layer)
- Pulp from 4 juiced carrots
- 900g/32oz/4 cups pelati (see page 92)
- 2 garlic heads
- 1 small thumb of ginger
- 1 tbsp bouillon (see page 118)
- 4 cloves
- 1 tsp chilli powder
- 1 tsp turmeric
- 1 tsp cumin

COOKING TIP:

- Adjust the seasoning to your taste. For a sweeter ketchup, add a small amount of agave or maple syrup.

Prepare the Ingredients:
Step 1: Roughly chop the onion peels, garlic and ginger.

Cook the Base:
Step 2: In a large pot, combine the onion peels, carrot pulp, pelati, garlic and ginger. Bring to a simmer over medium heat.

Step 3: Add the bouillon, cloves, chilli powder, turmeric and cumin. Stir well to combine.

Simmer and Blend:
Step 4: Simmer the mixture for about 30–45 minutes, stirring occasionally, until the vegetables are soft and the flavours have melded together.

Step 5: Remove from the heat and allow to cool slightly. Blend the mixture until smooth using a blender or immersion blender.

Strain:
Step 6: Strain the blended mixture through a sieve or fine-mesh strainer to remove any solids and achieve a smooth ketchup consistency.

Storage:
Step 7: Transfer the ketchup to labeled sterilized jars or bottles. Store in the refrigerator for up to 3 months.

CREATIVE TIP:

- Experiment with additional spices like smoked paprika or allspice to create a unique flavour profile tailored to your dishes.

CANDIED GINGER, LEMON & ORANGE

Every peel, every slice and every forgotten piece of fruit has potential.
   Candying is a ritual of care and creativity where you take the time to honour the whole fruit and its flavours.
Candied ginger and citrus peels make delightful snacks, garnishes for desserts and cocktails, or flavourful additions to baked goods.

INGREDIENTS

- 200g/7oz/1½ cups ginger root, peeled and sliced
- Peels from 3 lemons
- Peels from 2 oranges
- 400g/14oz/2 cups sugar (plus extra for rolling, optional)
- 240ml/9fl oz/1 cup water

COOKING TIP:

- Blanching the peels thoroughly is essential for removing bitterness and achieving a balanced flavour.

CREATIVE TIP:

- Try candying other peels like lime, grapefruit, or even unconventional options like carrot for a colourful twist.

Prepare the Peels:
Step 1: Remove as much of the white pith as possible from your leftover peels. Slice the peels into thin strips. Now slice your leftover ginger into thin strips too (I know you never use the whole thumb when cooking!).

Blanch the Peels and Ginger:
Step 2: Blanch the ginger slices, lemon peels and orange peels. Start from cold water, bring it to the boil and refresh. Repeat this process 2 more times for the peels to further reduce bitterness.

Simmer in Syrup:
Step 3: After the final blanching, drain the water and immediately add fresh water and sugar directly into each pot with the peels or ginger. Stir to dissolve, then bring to a gentle simmer over low heat.

Candy the Peels and Ginger:
Step 4: Simmer on low heat, stirring occasionally. The peels and ginger should become translucent, and the syrup should thicken and coat them homogenously.

Dry the Candied Peels and Ginger:
Step 5: Using a slotted spoon, transfer the candied ginger and peels to a cooling rack set over a baking sheet to dry. Allow to dry for several hours or overnight.

Storage:
Step 6: Store the candied ginger and peels in an airtight container in a cool, dry place. Properly dried and stored, they can last up to 2 months.

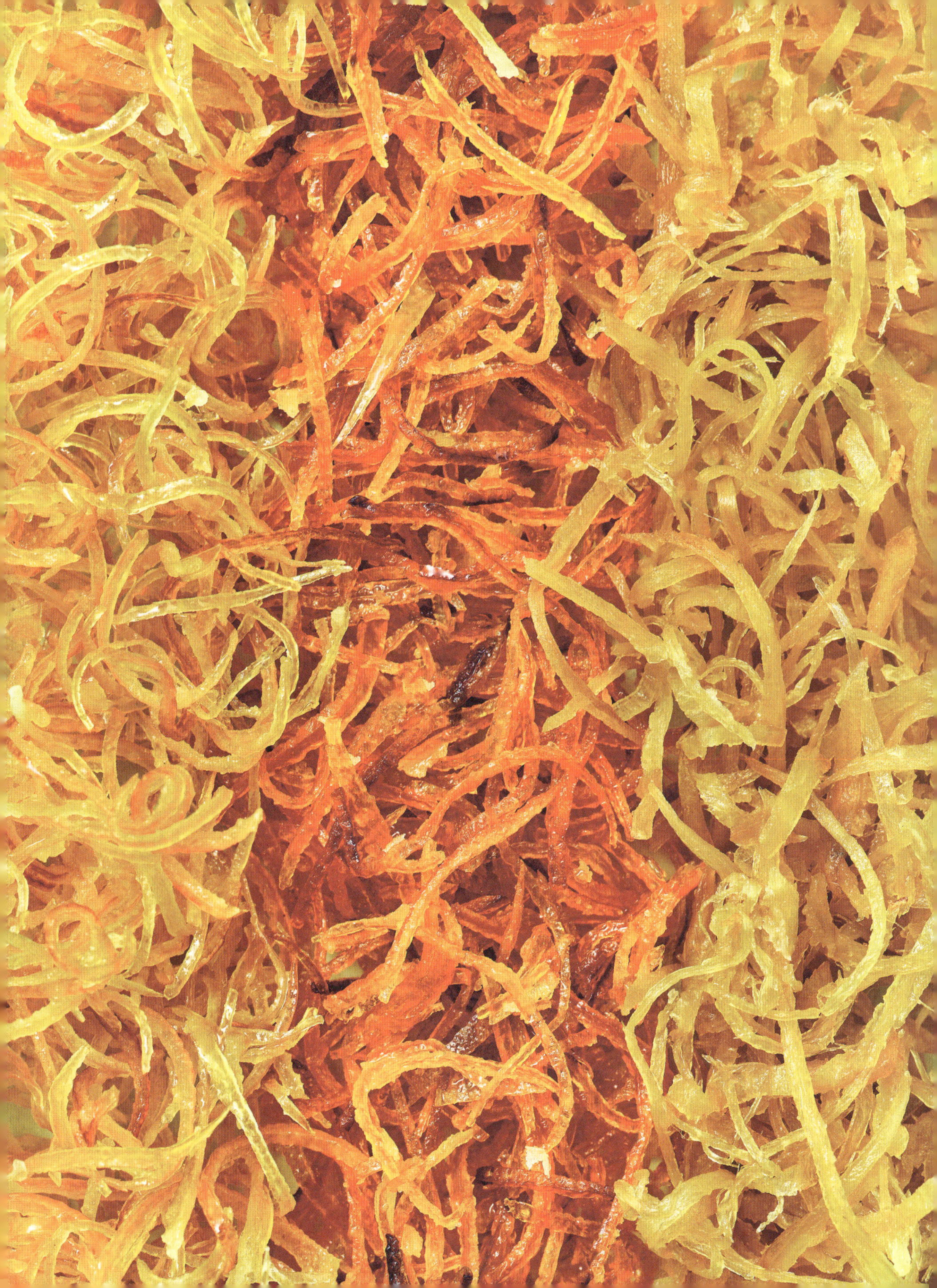

ZERO-WASTE CROSTATINA

The Italian crostatina is a dessert beloved for its simplicity, elegance and perfect balance of sweetness and crunch.

In this version, we are taking a timeless classic and giving it a zero-waste makeover. By incorporating okara – a nutrient-rich by-product of homemade soy milk – into the shortcrust pastry, this recipe proves that indulgence and sustainability can go hand in hand.

Okara is often overlooked and discarded, but it's a nutritional powerhouse, rich in fiber, protein and minerals. Using it in the crust adds a unique tenderness and depth to the pastry.

Each crostatina becomes a symbol of thoughtful, ethical cooking – a dessert that satisfies both your palate and the principle of the journey through this mindful kitchen map.

INGREDIENTS

- 250g/8¾oz/2 cups plain/all-purpose flour (or a gluten-free alternative, if preferred)
- 50g/1¾oz/¼ cup sugar (can be adjusted based on the sweetness of your okara)
- A pinch of salt
- Zest of 1 lemon (optional, for a citrus note)
- 180g/6 ⅓ oz/2½ cups okara, thoroughly dried (see page 168)
- 100g/3½oz/½ cup vegan butter, chilled and cubed (see page 156)
- 2–4 tbsp cold water (as needed)
- 350g/12 ⅓ oz jam (see page 141)

Make the crust dough:

Step 1: In a large bowl, whisk together the flour, sugar, salt and lemon zest for even distribution.

Step 2: Add the okara to the bowl and mix until it's well combined with the dry ingredients.

Step 3: Work in the vegan butter using your fingertips or a pastry blender until the mixture resembles coarse sand.

Step 4: Gradually drizzle in cold water, one tablespoon at a time, and mix until the dough comes together into a ball. Avoid overworking to maintain tenderness.

Step 5: Wrap the dough in wrap or place it in a covered bowl. Chill in the refrigerator for at least 30 minutes to firm up.

Assemble the crostatina:

Step 6: Preheat the oven to 180°C/350°F/Gas 4.

Step 7: Roll out the chilled dough on a lightly-floured surface to about 3mm thickness.

Step 8: Cut out circles to fit into tart tins, pressing the dough gently into the tins. Trim any excess dough.

Step 9: Prick the bottom of the pastry with a fork to prevent puffing during baking.

Recipe continued on the next page ...

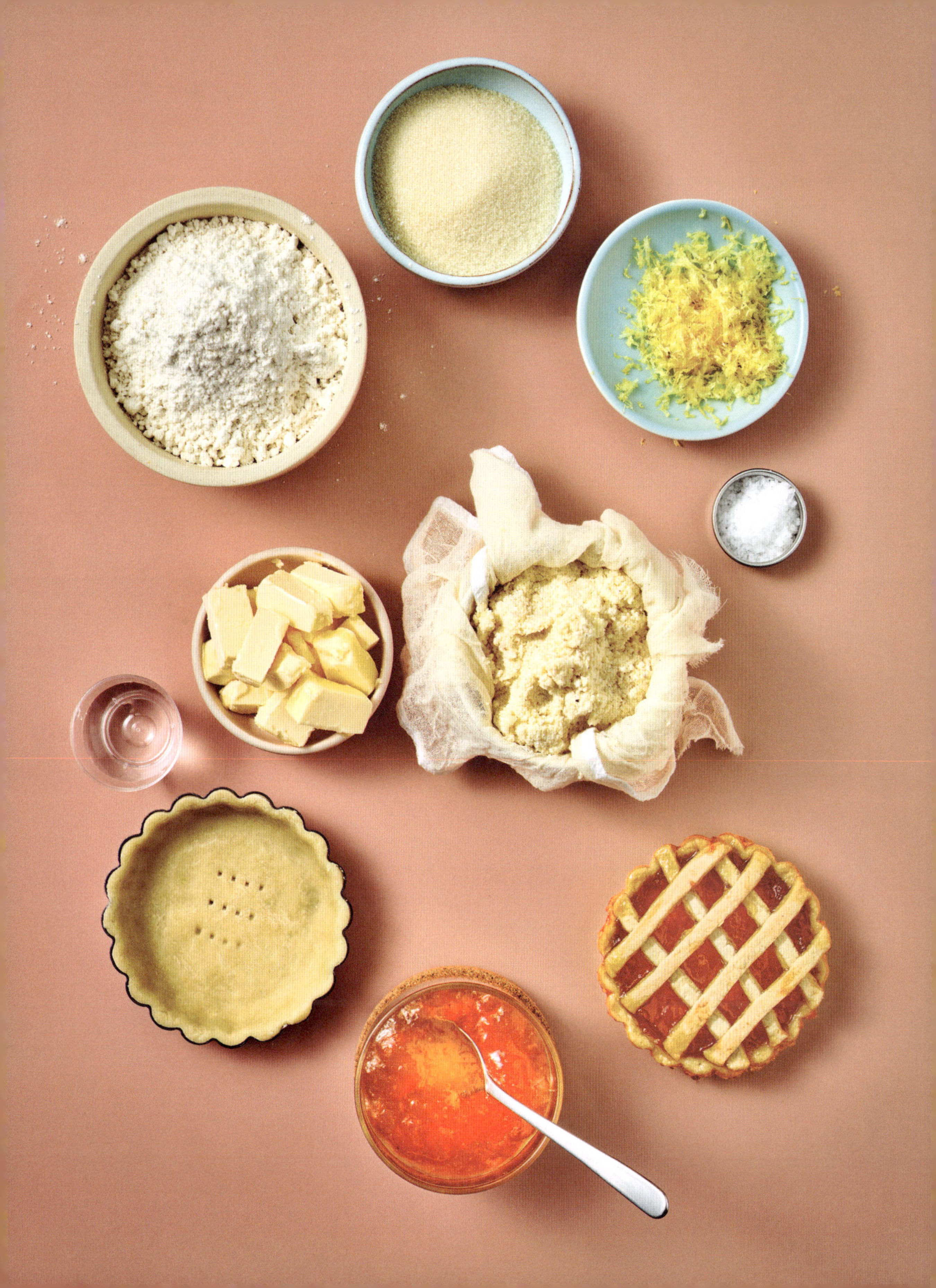

COOKING TIP:

- Keep everything cool – workspace, rolling pin and hands – while handling the dough to ensure a flaky pastry.

CREATIVE TIP:

- Experiment with fillings! Try different jams, compotes, or even savoury options like a nut paste for a versatile treat.

MINDFUL BENEFITS:

- Okara adds fiber and plant-based protein, which support sustained energy and digestive health, promoting mental clarity and focus.

Step 10: Fill each pastry shell with jam, leaving about ¼ of the shell unfilled.

Step 11: Use the remaining dough to create lattice strips or decorative shapes for the tops.

Step 12: Bake the *crostatina* in the preheated oven for 20–25 minutes or until the pastry is golden brown.

Step 13: Allow the tarts to cool in the tins for a few minutes before transferring to a wire rack to cool completely.

Storage:

Step 14: Store in an airtight container at room temperature for up to 3 days. For longer storage, refrigerate for up to 1 week or freeze for up to 3 months. To reheat, thaw and warm in an oven at 150°C/300°F/Gas 2 for 5–7 minutes.

• Recipe on the next page

CAMILLE (Carrot Muffins)

Camille muffins are a celebration of mindful, zero-waste baking, boasting a natural sweetness and moist crumb.

This humble treat reflects both the resourcefulness of the past and the creativity of modern kitchens, where reducing food waste is as important as celebrating flavour. The history of carrot-based desserts dates back to the Middle Ages when sugar was a luxury item, and carrots, with their natural sweetness, became a clever substitute.

In Italy, this tradition evolved into the beloved *Torta Camilla*, named for its individual portions and cherished for its simple, wholesome ingredients. Meanwhile, in Great Britain and the USA, carrots became essential during sugar shortages in World War II, giving rise to variations like carrot cake, often enriched with frosting, nuts or spices. This recipe takes the principles of the *Torta Camilla* even further by incorporating juicing pulp, honouring a zero-waste ethos while elevating the humble carrot to new heights.

INGREDIENTS

- 2 tbsp ground flaxseed
- 6 tbsp water
- 180g (6oz/1½ cups) plain or all-purpose flour (or gluten-free flour)
- 48g (1¾ oz/½ cup) almond flour
- 1 tsp baking powder
- ½ tsp bicarbonate of soda or baking soda
- ½ tsp ground cinnamon
- ¼ tsp ground nutmeg
- ¼ tsp salt
- 100g (3½oz/½ cup) brown sugar or coconut sugar
- 120g (4oz/½ cup) unsweetened apple sauce
- 55g (2oz/¼ cup) vegetable oil or melted coconut oil
- 1 tsp vanilla extract
- 110g (4oz/1 cup) carrot pulp (from juiced carrots)

Prepare the Flax Eggs:

Step 1: In a small bowl, combine the ground flaxseed and water.

Step 2: Stir well and let sit for 5–10 minutes until it thickens to a gel-like consistency.

Make the Muffins:

Step 3: Preheat your oven to 175°C/350°F/Gas 4. Line a muffin tin with paper liners or lightly grease it.

Step 4: In a large bowl, combine the plain flour, almond flour, baking powder, bicarbonate of soda, cinnamon, nutmeg and salt. Mix well.

Step 5: In another bowl, whisk together the brown sugar, apple sauce, vegetable oil, flax eggs and vanilla extract until smooth.

Step 6: Add the carrot pulp to the wet ingredients and mix until well combined.

Step 7: Gradually add the dry ingredients to the wet mixture, stirring until just combined. Avoid overmixing to keep the muffins tender.

Fill the Muffin Tin:
Step 8: Divide the batter evenly among the prepared muffin cups, filling each about two-thirds full.

Bake:
Step 9: Bake in the preheated oven for 20–25 minutes or until a toothpick inserted into the centre comes out clean.

Cool:
Step 10: Allow the muffins to cool in the tin for 10 minutes, then transfer to a wire rack to cool completely.

Storage:
Once cooled, store muffins in an airtight container at room temperature for up to 3 days. Refrigerate for up to 1 week or freeze for up to 3 months. To refresh frozen muffins, thaw at room temperature or warm in the oven at 150°C/300°F/Gas 2 for 5–7 minutes.

COOKING TIP:

• For a sweeter muffin, fold in raisins or chocolate chips before baking.

CREATIVE TIP:

• Add a pinch of ginger or cardamom for a flavourful twist, or sprinkle nuts and seeds on top for extra texture.

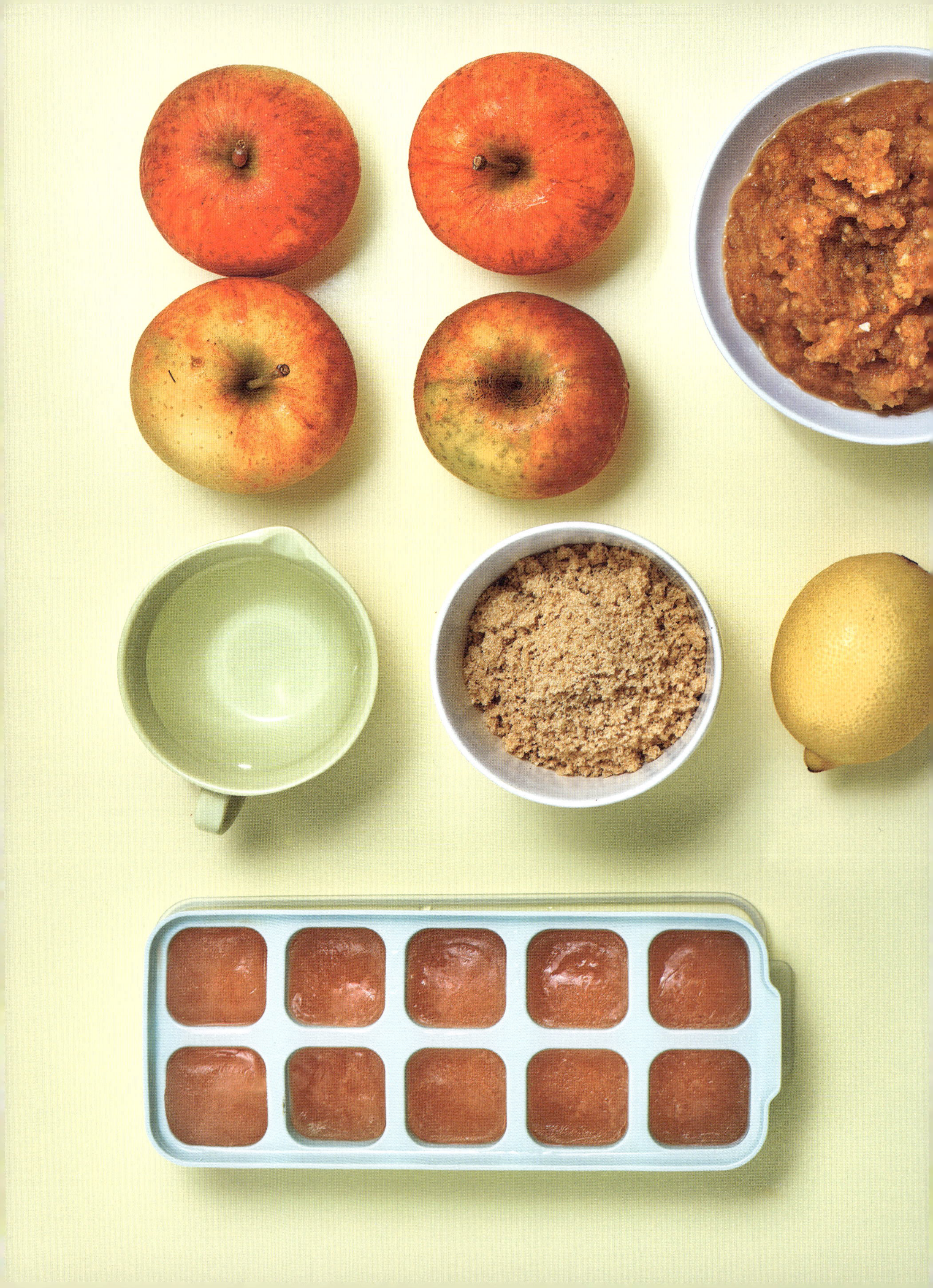

• Recipes on the next page

HOMEMADE APPLE PECTIN

Pectin is a natural thickening agent – a clever way to turn leftover apple pulp into something valuable for your kitchen.

Perfect for jams, jellies and preserves, this natural alternative provides structure and consistency without relying on store-bought additives. Here you are giving a second life to apple pulp that might otherwise be discarded.

The process is enriched by the addition of lemon juice, which not only enhances the flavour but also aids in the pectin extraction, making this a sustainable and effective addition to your map.

INGREDIENTS

- Leftover apple pulp (from around 6–7 large, not-too-ripe apples)
- 960–1,200 ml/32½–40½fl oz/4–5 cups water (adjust depending on the pulp)
- 1–2 lemons

COOKING TIP:

- Less ripe and traditional apple varieties tend to yield higher pectin content. Adjust the recipe based on the apples you use.

CREATIVE TIP:

- Experiment with different apple varieties or add citrus fruits like oranges for a unique flavour profile.

Prepare the Apple Pulp:
Step 1: After juicing the apples, keep the leftover pulp. It's fine if seeds and skin are included – these contribute to the pectin content.

Cook the Pulp:
Step 2: Place the apple pulp in a pot and add just enough water to cover it. Bring to a boil over a medium-high heat, then reduce to a simmer. Let it cook for 45 minutes to an hour, stirring occasionally to prevent sticking and ensure maximum pectin extraction.

Add Lemon Juice:
Step 3: In the last 10 minutes of simmering, add the juice of 1–2 lemons. This boosts the pectin extraction process.

Strain the Mixture:
Step 4: Strain the cooked mixture through a fine-mesh strainer or muslin cloth. Let the liquid drain naturally for 2–3 hours or overnight. Avoid pressing the pulp to keep the liquid clear. The collected liquid is your apple pectin.

Storage:
Step 5: Store the pectin in the fridge for up to a week or freeze/can it for long-term use.

ZERO-WASTE FRUIT JAM

Jams have always been a way to preserve and capture the essence of ripe fruits for enjoyment long after the harvest has passed.

This zero-waste fruit jam takes that tradition a step further, transforming leftover fruit pulp from juicing into a vibrant and flavourful spread. Whether slathered on toast, spooned over yogurts or desserts, or tucked into pastries, this jam is another delicious reminder that nothing in the kitchen is ever wasted.

INGREDIENTS

- 350g/12oz fruit juice pulp (any combination you like)
- 100g/3½oz/½ cup sugar
- 30g/1oz/¼ cup homemade apple pectin (see page 140)
- Juice of 1 lemon (for additional pectin and flavor)

COOKING TIP:

- Adjust the amount of sugar depending on the natural sweetness of the fruit pulp. Taste as you go to achieve the perfect balance.

CREATIVE TIP:

- Experiment with unique fruit combinations and enhance the flavour with spices like cinnamon, nutmeg or ginger.

Reduce Moisture Content:
Step 1: If the pulp is very wet, cook it gently in a pot over low heat to reduce its moisture content. This concentrates the flavors and begins the jam-making process.

Add Sugar and Pectin:
Step 2: Once the pulp has thickened slightly, add the sugar, homemade apple pectin and lemon juice. Stir to combine.

Cook the Jam:
Step 3: Continue cooking over low heat, stirring frequently to prevent burning, until the mixture thickens and reaches the setting point. This may take 30–60 minutes.

Test for Doneness:
Step 4: To check if the jam is ready, place a small amount on a chilled plate. If it wrinkles when you push it with your finger, it's done.

Cool the Jam:
Step 5: Allow the jam to cool before using it in your crostatina (see page 132) or as a spread.

Storage:
Transfer the cooled jam into sterilized jars and store in the refrigerator for up to 3 weeks or process in a water bath for longer storage.

4 THE REFRIGERATOR:
The Cold Storage Vault

"Veganism is not about being perfect. It is about doing the least harm and the most good."
Colleen Patrick-Goudreau

Welcome to the heart of your Mindful Kitchen Map, where preparation meets purpose.

The refrigerator, often seen as a static storage space, transforms here into a dynamic resource – a vault of nourishment, creativity and intentional living.

In this chapter, you'll master the craft of creating plant-based essentials that breathe life into your meals. From the lush creaminess of oat milk to the robust richness of soy and hemp, every recipe elevates simple ingredients into pantry staples.

Explore the alchemy of a bubbling cashew spread, the elegance of cooking and whipping creams, and an array of savoury sauces designed to transform even the simplest dishes.

Dive deeper into the art of vegan proteins with homemade tofu, tempeh and seitan and uncover the secrets behind my cherished vegan cheeses. This chapter also celebrates vitality with a focus on gut health and the "Doctor's Away" series – a testament to the power of living foods. From cold-pressed juices and vibrant green drinks to probiotic-rich kombucha, kefir and rejuvelac, you'll stock your fridge with energy and wellness. Explore living seed breads and sea moss recipes as nourishing investments in the future of your health.

The Refrigerator: The Cold Storage Vault is definitely not about what you keep – it's about what you create.

It's a space where your intentional choices ripple into every meal and every day, aligning your kitchen with the mindful, sustainable life you seek.

MILKS

Plant-based milks are the cornerstone of your fridge, offering versatility and nourishment in every pour.

From soy and oat to hemp, coconut and rice, these homemade alternatives are fresh, additive-free and customizable to your taste.

Each milk has its unique characteristics – soy for richness, oat for creaminess, hemp for earthiness, coconut for tropical flair, and rice for lightness – making them indispensable staples in your refrigerator.

These recipes guide you through creating these milks with precision, ensuring your creations are nutrient-rich and tailored to your dietary needs.

Beyond their culinary applications, these milks contribute to mental wellbeing. Ingredients like soy, hemp and oats provide essential nutrients that support focus, reduce anxiety and promote overall cognitive health.

Dive into the recipes and discover the art of plant-based milk-making – a journey of mindful kitchen practice.

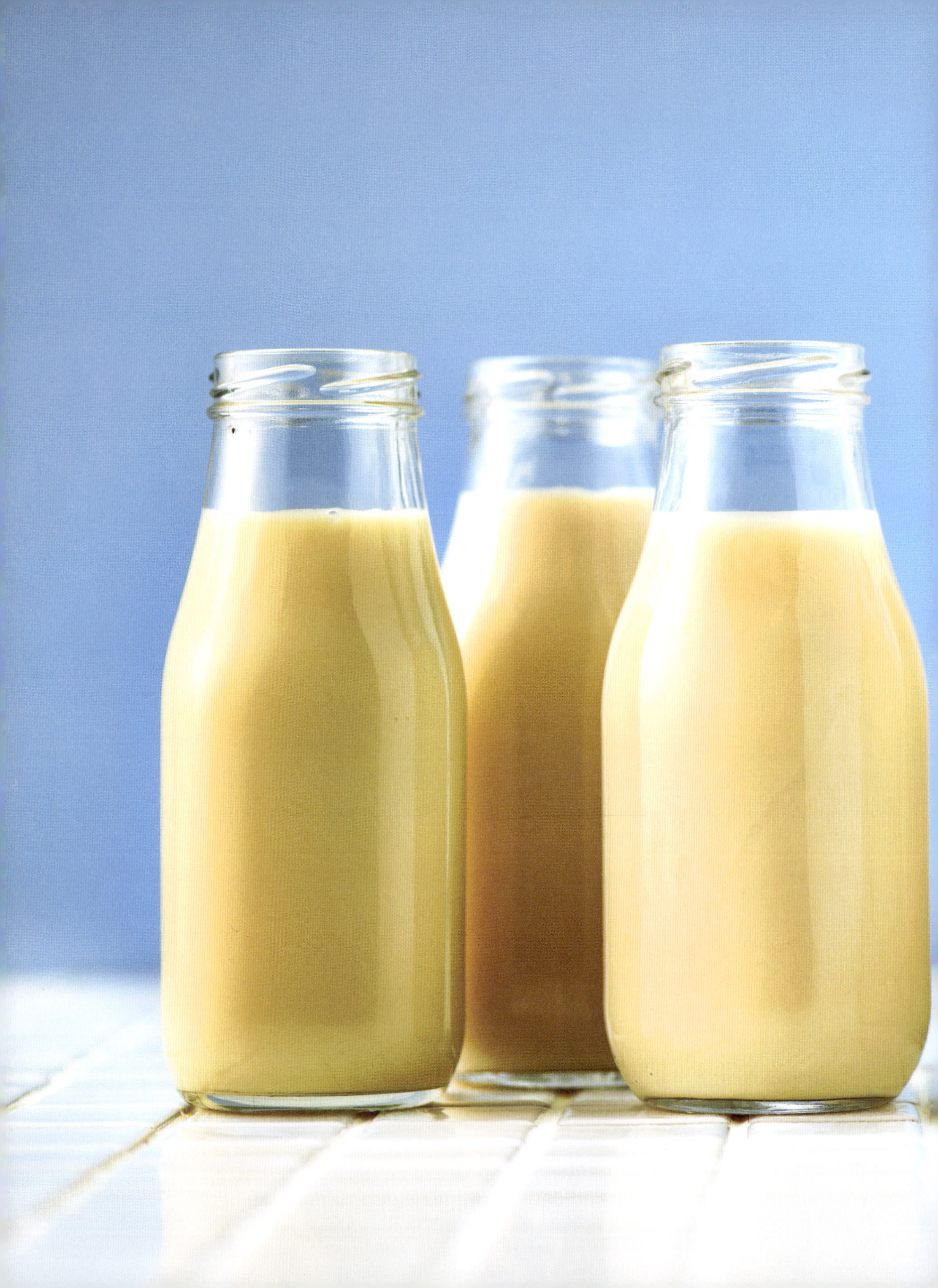

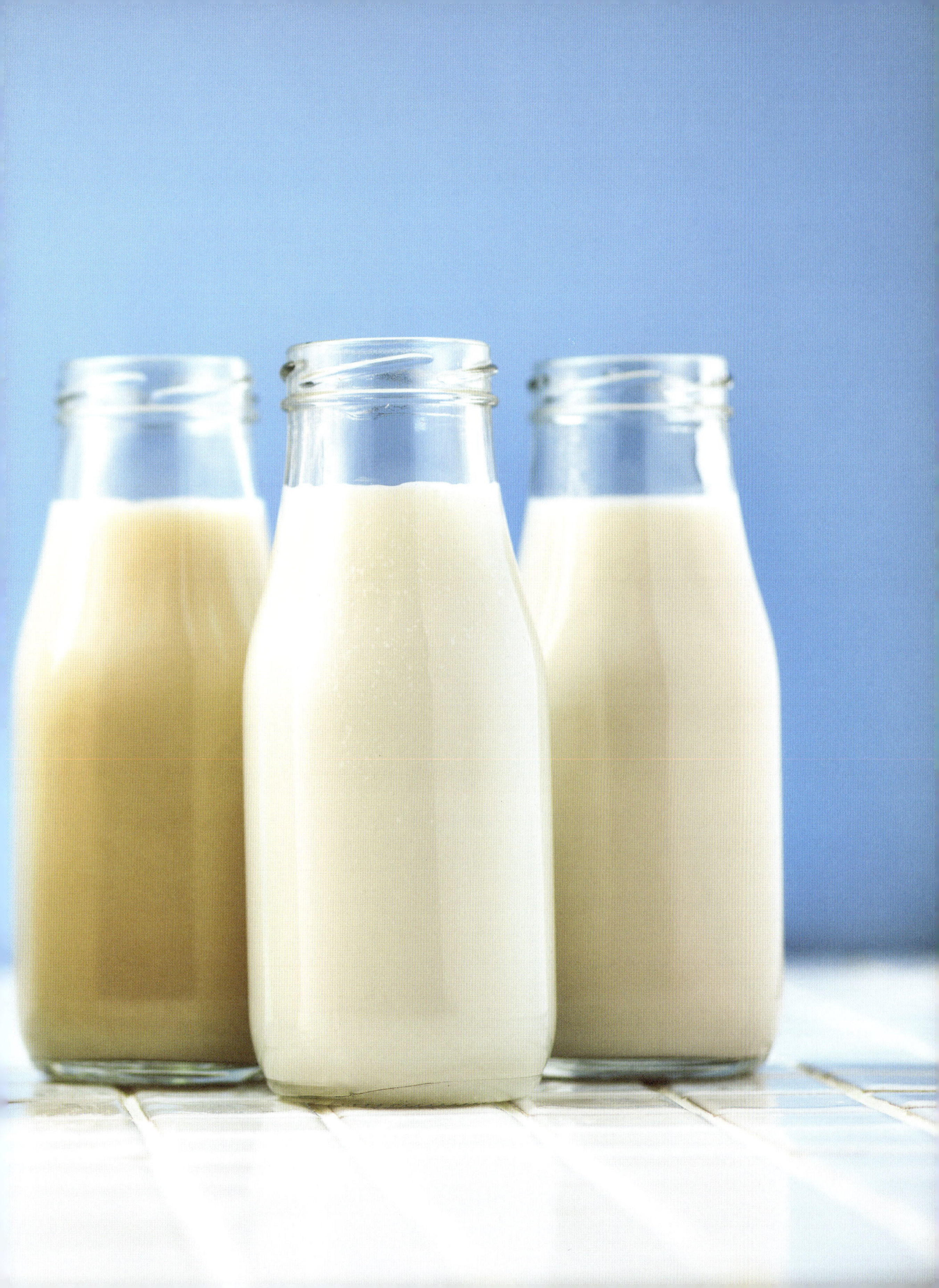

HOMEMADE SOY MILK

INGREDIENTS

- 180g/6 ⅓ oz/1 cup dried soybeans
- 1.9L/64fl oz/8 cups water (for soaking)
- 1.4L–1.9L/48–64fl oz/6–8 cups fresh water (for blending)
- 1–2 tbsp maple syrup or sugar (optional)
- 1 tsp vanilla extract (optional)
- A pinch of salt

FLAVOUR VARIATIONS:

- Add cocoa powder for chocolate soy milk.
- Blend in strawberries or other fruits for a fruity twist.

MINDFUL BENEFITS:

- Soy contains isoflavones, which are compounds that have been shown to support cognitive function and reduce the risk of age-related cognitive decline.

- High in Magnesium: Soybeans are a natural source of magnesium, a mineral that plays a crucial role in brain health by regulating neurotransmitters and reducing stress.

Soak the Soybeans:
Step 1: Place soybeans in a large bowl and cover with water. Allow them to soak overnight or for at least 8 hours. Ensure you use plenty of water, as the beans will expand.

Rinse and Remove Skins (Optional):
Step 2: After soaking, rinse the soybeans under cold water. To remove the skins for smoother milk, gently squeeze the beans between your fingers.

Blend:
Step 3: Drain the soybeans and blend them with fresh water (use less for creamier milk) on high until the mixture is smooth.

Cook:
Step 4: Pour the blended mixture into a large pot. Bring to a boil over medium-high heat, then reduce to a simmer, stirring occasionally to prevent sticking. Simmer for about 20 minutes, skimming foam or skins from the surface as needed.

Strain:
Step 5: Allow the mixture to cool slightly, then strain through a nut milk bag, muslin cloth or fine-mesh strainer into a large bowl. Press or squeeze to extract as much liquid as possible.

Flavour (Optional):
Step 6: Return the strained milk to the pot. Add maple syrup or sugar, vanilla extract and a pinch of salt. Warm gently, stirring until the sweetener dissolves. Adjust sweetness to taste.

Storage:
Step 7: Once the milk has cooled, transfer it to a bottle or jar and refrigerate. Shake well before use, as separation is natural. Consume within 3–5 days.

HOMEMADE OAT MILK

SAFETY TIPS:

- **Soaking:** This essential step hydrates soybeans, softening them for blending and reducing antinutrients like phytic acid and lectins. These compounds can interfere with nutrient absorption.

- **Boiling:** Always boil soybeans thoroughly to reduce antinutrients further. This process also ensures the soybeans are fully softened, resulting in smoother milk and better digestibility.

- **Raw Consumption:** Avoid consuming raw or improperly processed soybeans. Lectins, in particular, can cause digestive discomfort if not properly broken down.

- **Moderation:** Even homemade soy milk should be consumed as part of a balanced diet. Overconsumption of soy products may not suit everyone due to individual sensitivities or dietary restrictions.

INGREDIENTS

- 90g/3oz/1 cup rolled oats
- 960ml/32fl oz/4 cups water (for soaking and blending)
- ½ tbsp amylase
- ½ tbsp glucoamylase
- ½ tbsp maple syrup or honey (optional)
- 1 tsp vanilla extract (optional)
- A pinch of salt

USAGE:

- Enjoy chilled on its own, added to coffee or tea, or poured over cereal.

COOKING TIP:

- Adjust sweetness and flavour as needed. Add a pinch of cinnamon or blend in a few dates for variety.

Soak and Enzyme Treatment:
Step 1: Heat water to approximately 66°C/150°F and combine with the oats in a large bowl. Add amylase and glucoamylase enzymes, stirring to combine. Let sit for 30–45 minutes, stirring occasionally. The mixture should taste lightly sweet after the enzyme treatment.

Blend and Strain:
Step 2: Transfer the oat-water mixture to a blender. Blend on high for 30 seconds. Strain through a nut milk bag or fine-mesh strainer into a bowl, squeezing out as much liquid as possible.

Flavour (Optional):
Step 3: Return the strained milk to a bowl. Stir in maple syrup or honey, vanilla extract and a pinch of salt to taste.

Storage:
Step 4: Pour the oat milk into a clean bottle or jar and refrigerate. Shake well before use. Use within 5 days.

CREATIVE TIP:

- Use leftover oat pulp in baking recipes, such as muffins or cookies, or as a thickener for soups.

THE REFRIGERATOR

HOMEMADE COCONUT MILK

INGREDIENTS

- 160g/5½oz/2 cups unsweetened dried shredded coconut
- 960ml/32fl oz/4 cups hot water
- 1–2 tbsp maple syrup or agave (optional)
- 1 tsp vanilla extract (optional)
- A pinch of salt

USAGE:

- Perfect for smoothies, curries, desserts, or as a coffee creamer.

COOKING TIP:

- Adjust sweetness and flavour as desired. Try adding cinnamon or dates for unique variations.

CREATIVE TIP:

- Use leftover coconut pulp in baking (see page 126), as a natural exfoliating scrub, or mix it into granola for added fibre.

Blend:
Step 1: Combine the dried coconut and hot water in a blender. Let sit for a few minutes to soften, then blend on high for 2 minutes until smooth and creamy.

Strain:
Step 2: Pour the mixture through a nut milk bag or fine-mesh strainer into a bowl. Squeeze out as much liquid as possible. Reserve the pulp for other uses.

Flavour (Optional):
Step 3: Return strained milk to the blender and add maple syrup or agave, vanilla extract and salt. Blend briefly to combine.

Storage:
Step 4: Transfer to a clean bottle or jar and refrigerate. Shake well before use. Use within 4–5 days.

UNHULLED HEMP MILK

INGREDIENTS

- 135g/4¾oz/1 cup raw, unhulled hemp seeds
- 1 tsp raw chia seeds
- 960ml/32fl oz/4 cups water
- 1–2 tbsp maple syrup or agave (optional)
- 1 tsp vanilla extract (optional)
- A pinch of salt

USAGE:

- Perfect for smoothies, cereals, baked goods, or as a coffee creamer.

MINDFUL BENEFITS:

- Unhulled hemp seeds are rich in Omega-3 and Omega-6 fatty acids, supporting heart and brain health.

- Magnesium content can help reduce anxiety and promote relaxation.

COOKING TIP:

- Adjust sweetness and flavour. Try adding cinnamon or dates.

CREATIVE TIP:

- Use leftover hemp pulp in baking.

Rinse the Hemp Seeds:
Step 1: Rinse the unhulled hemp seeds under cold water to remove any debris or dust.

Blend:
Step 2: Combine the rinsed hemp seeds and chia seeds with water in a blender. Add the sweetener, vanilla extract (if using) and salt. Blend on high until thoroughly combined. The unhulled seeds create a milk with a thicker texture.

Strain:
Step 3: Pour the blended mixture through a nut milk bag or fine-mesh strainer into a large bowl. You may need to strain twice for a smoother consistency. Squeeze or press the bag to extract as much liquid as possible.

Taste and Adjust:
Step 4: Taste the hemp milk and adjust the sweetness or vanilla to your preference. If too thick, add more water until you reach the desired consistency.

Storage:
Step 5: Transfer the milk to a clean bottle or jar. Refrigerate and shake well before use. Consume within 5 days.

HULLED HEMP MILK

INGREDIENTS

- 160g/5½oz/1 cup shelled/hulled hemp seeds
- 960ml/32fl oz/4 cups water (plus more for soaking, optional)
- 1–2 tbsp maple syrup or agave syrup (optional)
- 1 tsp vanilla extract (optional)
- A pinch of salt

USAGE:

- Use in smoothies, cereals, baked goods, or as a coffee creamer.

COOKING TIP:

- Customize sweetness and flavour with ingredients like cinnamon or dates.

CREATIVE TIP:

- Repurpose leftover hemp pulp in baked goods or granola (see page 66), or mix with oil for a natural exfoliant.

Soaking (Optional):
Step 1: If desired, soak the hulled hemp seeds in water for 1–2 hours to improve texture. Drain and rinse before blending.

Blend:
Step 2: Add hemp seeds and water to a blender. Include optional maple syrup, vanilla extract and salt. Blend on high for about 1 minute until creamy.

Strain:
Step 3: Strain the blended mixture through a nut milk bag or fine-mesh strainer into a large bowl. Squeeze to extract as much liquid as possible.

Taste and Adjust:
Step 4: Taste the milk and adjust the sweetness or vanilla to your preference. Add more water if the milk is too thick.

Storage:
Step 5: Transfer to a clean bottle or jar and refrigerate. Shake before use. Consume within 5 days.

HOMEMADE RICE MILK

INGREDIENTS

- 185g/6½oz/1 cup cooked white rice (preferably long-grain, for its mild flavour and smooth texture)
- 960ml/32fl oz/4 cups of water (plus more for cooking the rice)
- 1–2 tbsp maple syrup or agave syrup (optional)
- 1 tsp vanilla extract (optional)
- A pinch of salt

USAGE:

- Enjoy chilled as a drink or poured over cereal.

- Use in smoothies, or as a substitute for dairy milk in baking and cooking.

MINDFUL BENEFITS:

- Rice provides complex carbohydrates for sustained energy. Stabilizing blood sugar through complex carbs can help support focus and reduce anxiety.

CREATIVE TIP:

- Repurpose the leftover rice pulp in baking, soups, or as an exfoliant in homemade skincare treatments.

Prepare the Rice:
Step 1: Start with cooked white rice. If you haven't cooked your rice yet, follow the instructions on the package. You'll need about ½ cup of uncooked rice to make 1 cup of cooked rice. Allow the rice to cool slightly before proceeding.

Blend:
Step 2: Place the cooked rice in a blender. Add the water, your chosen sweetener, vanilla extract (if using) and a pinch of salt. Blend on high speed for 1–2 minutes until smooth.

Strain:
Step 3: Pour the blended mixture through a nut milk bag or a fine-mesh strainer into a large bowl. If using a sieve, consider straining twice for a smoother consistency. Gently press or squeeze to extract as much liquid as possible.

Taste and Adjust:
Step 4: Sample your rice milk. Adjust the sweetness or vanilla flavour as needed, blending again briefly if you make changes.

Storage:
Step 5: Transfer the rice milk to a clean bottle or jar and refrigerate. Shake well before each use, as natural separation may occur. Consume within 5 days.

HOMEMADE VEGAN COOKING CREAM

Vegan cooking cream is a versatile and rich dairy-free alternative perfect for enhancing soups, sauces, and baked dishes. Use this vegan cooking cream in recipes that call for heavy/double cream.

INGREDIENTS

- 200ml/7fl oz/scant 1 cup plant-based milk
- 200ml/7fl oz/scant 1 cup cold-pressed sunflower oil
- 4 tbsp cornflour/cornstarch
- Additional 200ml/7fl oz/scant 1 cup plant-based milk for the slurry

MINDFUL BENEFITS:

- Sunflower oil is rich in vitamin E and healthy fats, supporting heart health and brain function.

COOKING TIP:

- For a thicker cream, add an extra tablespoon of cornflour. For a thinner consistency, reduce the amount.

CREATIVE TIP:

- Add your favourite herbs or spices to the cream while cooking for added flavour.

Make an Emulsion:
Step 1: In a blender or food processor, combine the plant-based milk and cold-pressed sunflower oil. Blend on high speed until the mixture is emulsified and smooth.

Prepare a Slurry:
Step 2: In a small bowl, mix the cornflour/cornstarch with the additional plant-based milk to create a smooth slurry. Ensure there are no lumps.

Combine and Cook:
Step 3: Transfer the emulsified mixture to a small saucepan. Gradually add the cornflour slurry while whisking constantly to prevent lumps from forming.

Step 4: Heat the mixture over medium-low heat, whisking continuously until it thickens to the consistency of cream. This should take about 3-5 minutes. Once thickened, remove the saucepan from the heat and let the cream cool.

Storage:
Step 5: Pour the cool cream into a container or jar and refrigerate. Use within 5–7 days.

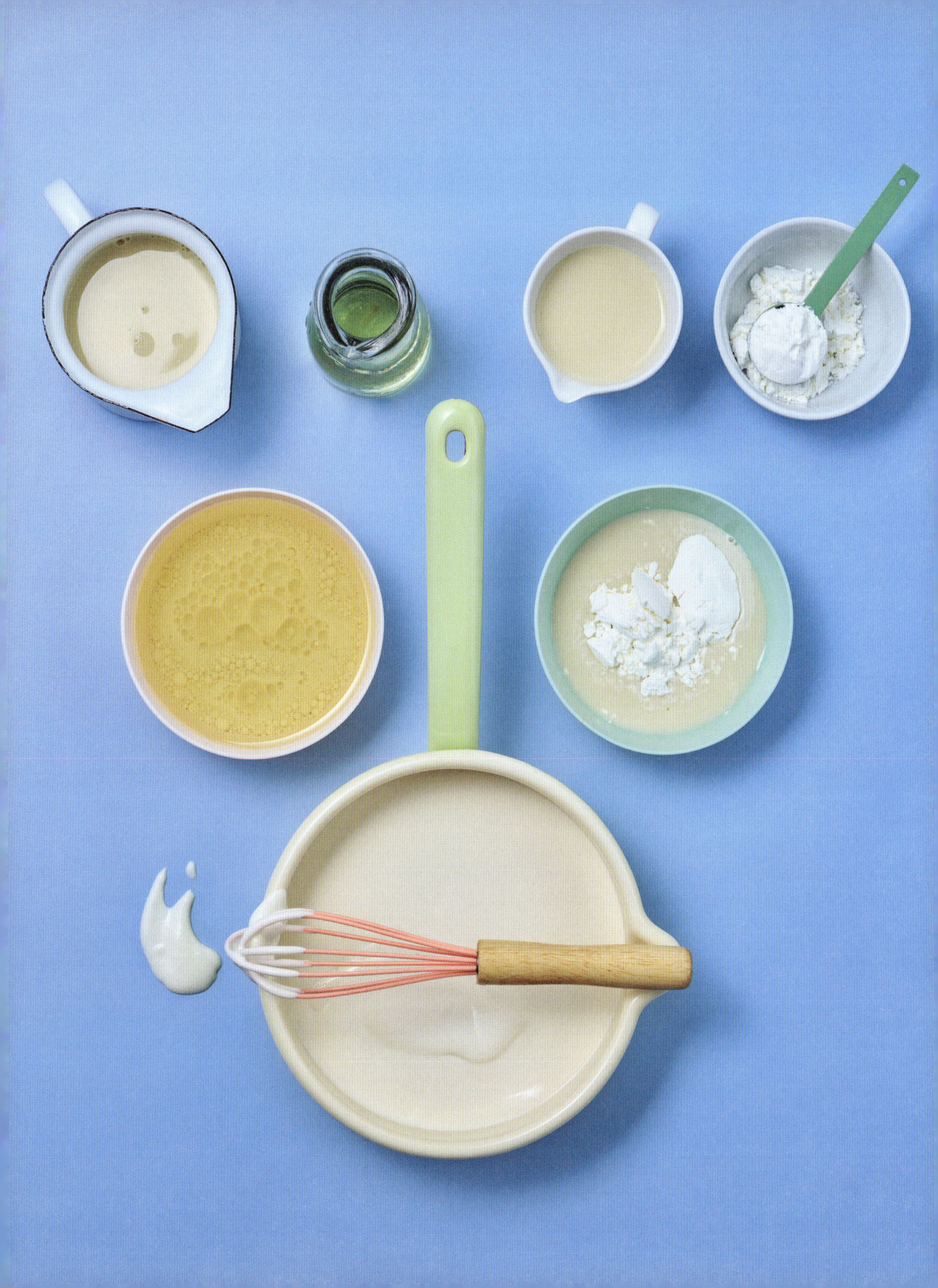

VEGAN WHIPPING CREAM (Non-Coconut)

Fluffy, light and irresistibly creamy, this vegan whipping cream is the perfect dairy-free alternative for topping desserts, fruit and more. It doesn't rely on coconut milk, making it a great option for a neutral flavour.

INGREDIENTS

- 120ml/4fl oz/½ cup aquafaba (liquid from a can of chickpeas)
- 2–3 tbsp powdered sugar
- 1 tsp vanilla extract (optional)
- ¼ tsp cream of tartar (optional, for stability)

Whip:

Step 1: Pour aquafaba into a mixing bowl. Add cream of tartar, if using, for stability.

Step 2: Using a hand or stand mixer, whip the aquafaba on high speed until soft peaks form (3–5 minutes).

Step 3: Gradually add powdered sugar and vanilla extract while continuing to whip until stiff peaks form (an additional 5–7 minutes).

Serve and Store:

Step 4: Use immediately as a dessert topping or refrigerate for up to 3 days. Re-whip if needed.

MINDFUL BENEFITS:

- **Aquafaba is a low-calorie, fat-free** ingredient that mimics the properties of egg whites, offering a plant-based alternative without added fats.

COOKING TIP:

- Use chilled aquafaba and equipment.

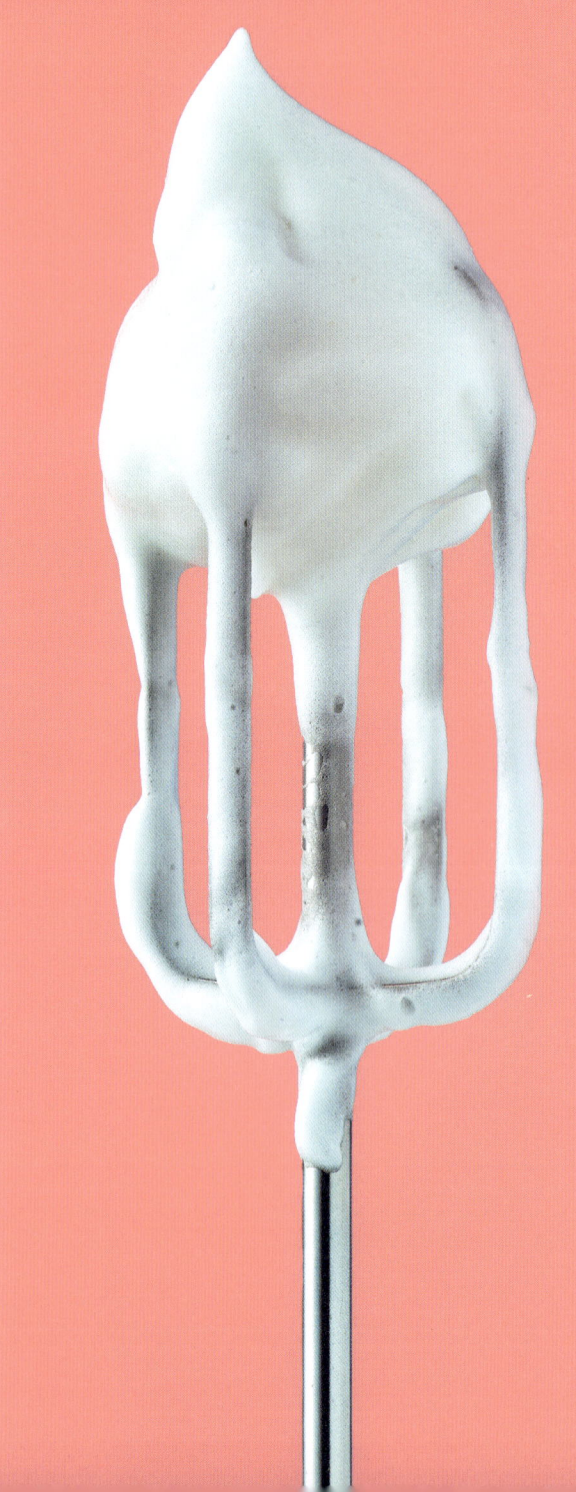

VEGAN WHIPPING CREAM
(Coconut)

This rich, creamy whipped topping is perfect for desserts, coffee, fruits and more, delivering a tropical touch.

INGREDIENTS

- 400ml/14fl oz/1 ⅔ cups coconut cream
- 2–3 tbsp powdered sugar
- 1 tsp vanilla extract (optional)

Chill:
Step 1: Refrigerate the coconut cream overnight to solidify it.

Whip:
Step 2: Scoop the solid cream into a mixing bowl, leaving the liquid behind. Add powdered sugar and vanilla extract (if using).

Step 3: Whip on high speed until soft peaks form (3–5 minutes).

Serve and Store:
Step 4: Use immediately or refrigerate for up to 3 days. Re-whip if necessary.

MINDFUL BENEFITS:

- The aroma of coconut and vanilla can promote relaxation and mental clarity, offering a calming sensory experience.

COOKING TIP:

- Ensure coconut cream is well chilled for the best whipping results.

CREATIVE TIP:

- Experiment with cocoa powder or other flavorings for variety.

VEGAN BUTTER

Making your own vegan butter is about reclaiming control over the ingredients you use and the impact you make.

This smooth, creamy butter is easy to prepare and perfect for spreading on toast, baking or cooking.

It's a versatile alternative to store-bought options, free from unnecessary additives and made with simple, wholesome ingredients.

This straightforward method gives you a delicious, sustainable reason to step away from supermarket shelves, reduce your environmental footprint and save money.

INGREDIENTS

- 200ml/7fl oz/scant 1 cup odourless coconut oil
- 150ml/5fl oz/ ⅔ cup unsweetened plant milk
- 1 tbsp miso
- 2 tbsp lecithin
- Juice of 1 lemon
- Pinch of salt

COOKING TIP:

- Adjust the salt and lemon juice to suit your taste preferences. You can also add herbs or spices to create flavoured vegan butter.

CREATIVE TIP:

- Use silicone moulds to shape your vegan butter into fun designs, adding a decorative touch to your dining table.

Melt and Mix:
Step 1: In a small saucepan, gently melt the coconut oil over low heat until it becomes liquid.

Step 2: In a blender or food processor, combine the melted coconut oil, unsweetened plant milk, miso, lecithin, lemon juice and a pinch of salt. Blend until the mixture is smooth and well-emulsified.

Blend and Chill:
Step 3: Continue blending for a few minutes to ensure all ingredients are fully incorporated and the mixture is creamy.

Step 4: Pour the mixture into a container or mould. Use a spatula to scrape out all the butter mixture from the blender.

Set:
Step 5: Place the container in the refrigerator and allow the vegan butter to set for a few hours or until it becomes firm. Once set, your vegan butter is ready to use.

Storage:
Step 6: Store it in the refrigerator and use within 1–2 weeks.

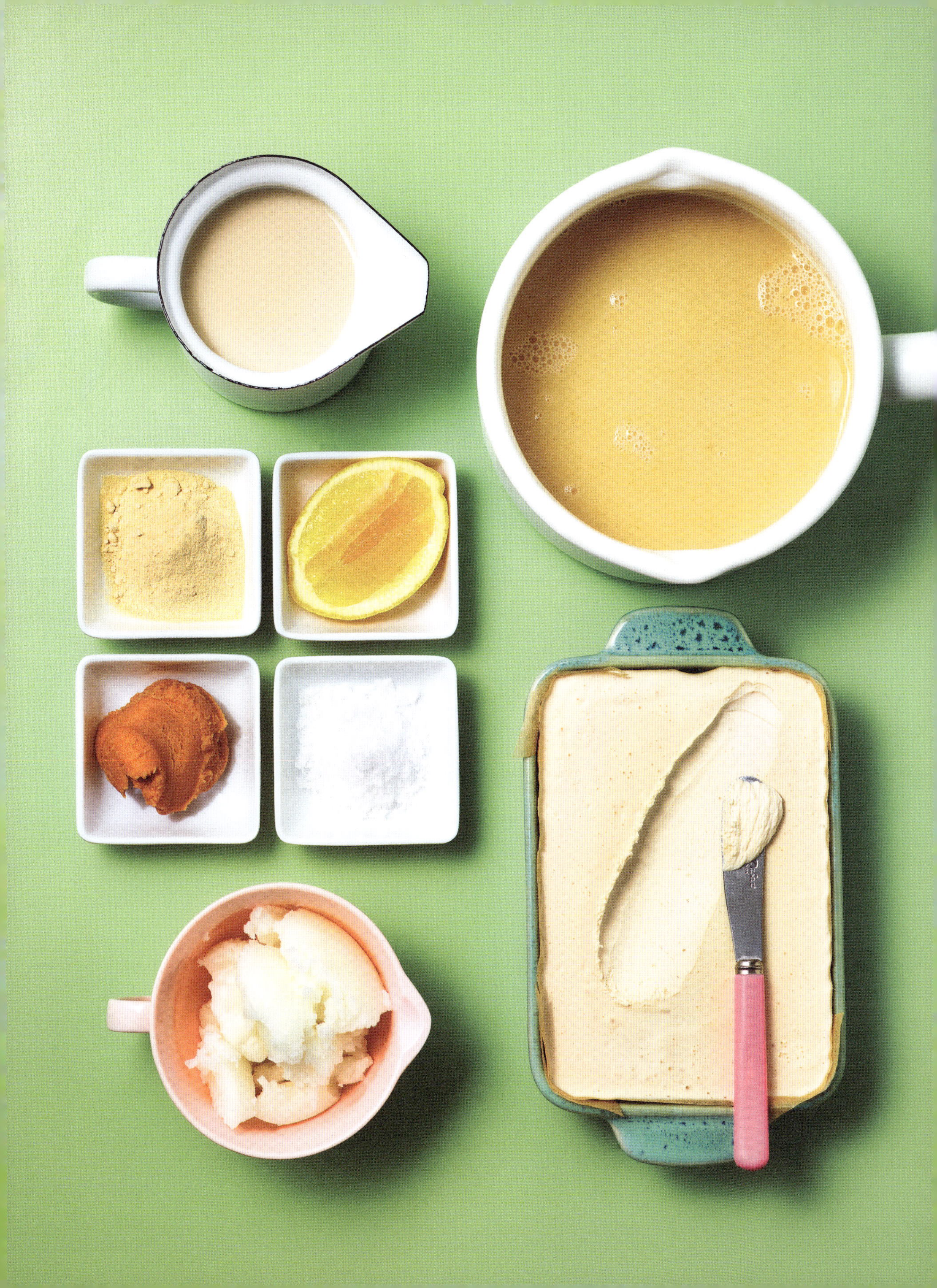

VEGAN PARMESAN

"Good food shouldn't harm – it needs to elevate."

Crafting your own vegan parmesan is a statement. A choice to simplify, to create something better than store-bought, and to redefine how we approach flavour.

This recipe is about control – over what you eat, how it's made and the impact you have.

It's straightforward, quick and packed with umami-rich complexity. With just a few ingredients and a bit of time, you'll have a versatile, flavourful topping that complements everything from pasta to salads or any dish that calls for a cheesy sprinkle.

INGREDIENTS

- 250ml/8½fl oz/1 cup unsweetened soy milk
- 90g/3oz/scant ½ cup odourless coconut oil
- 2 tbsp rice vinegar
- 1 tbsp French mustard
- 4 tbsp miso (yellow miso recommended, but any type works)
- 2 tsp salt
- 160g/5½oz/1 cup potato starch
- 4 tbsp nutritional yeast

COOKING TIP:

- Ensure the mixture is blended thoroughly to avoid lumps and achieve the smoothest possible texture in your final product.

Blend Together:
Step 1: In a blender, combine all the ingredients. Blend until the mixture is smooth and has a mayonnaise-like texture.

Cook the Mix:
Step 2: Pour the mixture into a plastic or glass rectangular container. Steam for 50 minutes using your preferred steaming method, such as a steamer basket, steaming pot or steaming oven.

Cool and Set:
Step 3: Refrigerate the steamed mixture for about 2 hours until it sets completely.

Storage:
- Store in the fridge for up to 10 days.
- Freezing: Wrap portions tightly in plastic wrap or store in an airtight container. Freeze for up to 3 months.

MINDFUL BENEFITS:

- Unsweetened soy milk and odorless coconut oil make this a heart-friendly alternative to parmesan, as it is cholesterol-free.

- Perfect for those who are lactose intolerant or sensitive to dairy.

- Nutritional yeast is packed with vitamins and minerals, supporting overall health and filling potential dietary gaps for those on plant-based diets.

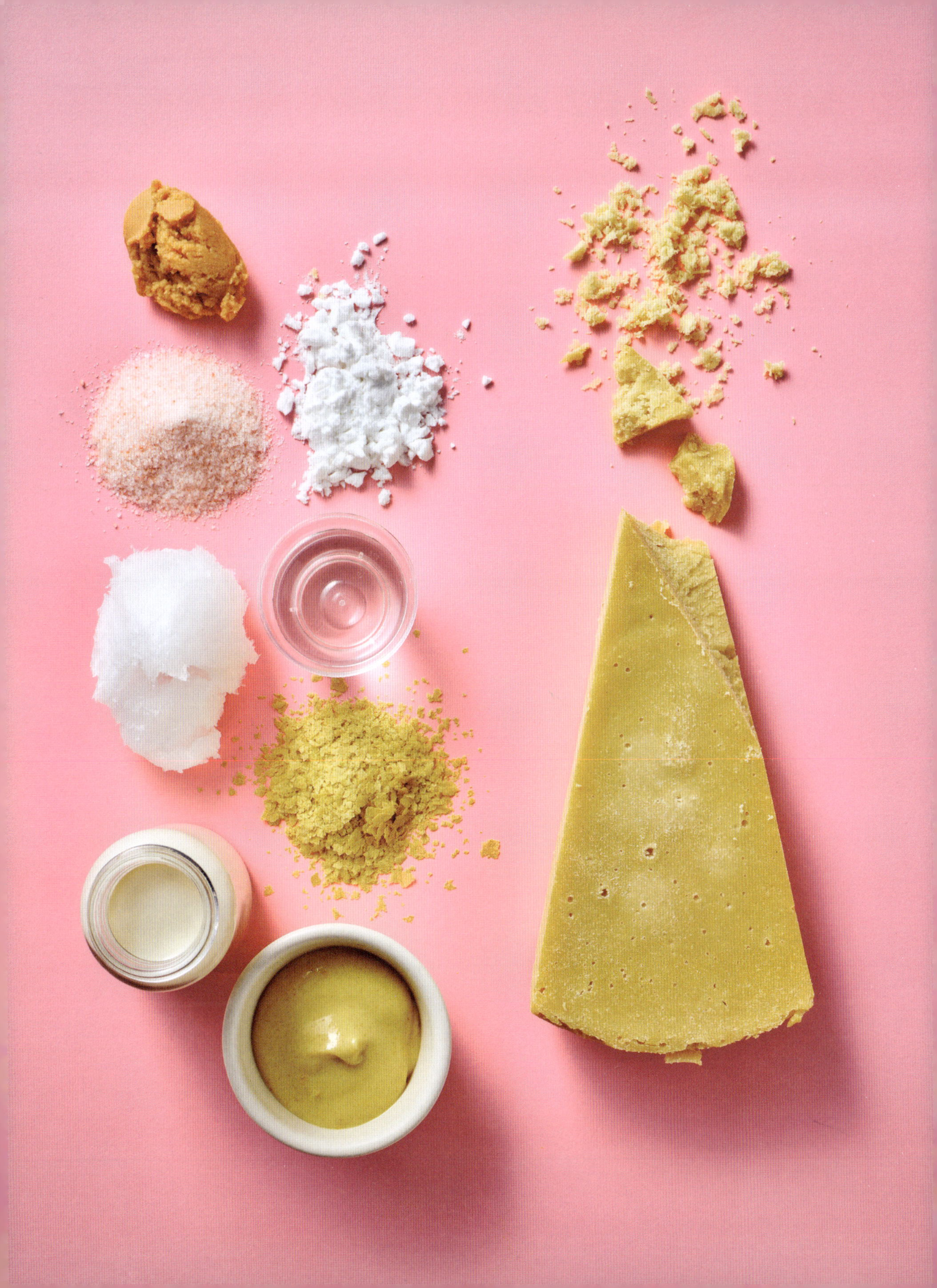

MELTY MOZZARELLA

This melty mozzarella is the ultimate plant-based cheese for dishes that call for gooey, stretchy goodness. Designed specifically for melting, it shines on pizza, in lasagna or as the perfect ingredient for mozzarella sticks. Unlike traditional mozzarella, this vegan version isn't intended for fresh use but delivers unparalleled creaminess when melted.

Now, let's take a closer look at one of the ingredients we'll use: kappa carrageenan – and clear up the confusion.

There's a controversy that stems from studies on poligeenan, a degraded form of carrageenan not used in food.

Food-grade carrageenan is entirely different – it's safe for consumption and approved by the FDA, EFSA, and other global authorities (as much as I trust them anyway).

In my opinion there's no credible evidence linking food-grade carrageenan to digestive issues. In fact, it's been used safely for centuries and even boasts potential health benefits due to its source, the seaweed *Kappaphycus alvarezii*.

So let's put the myth to rest and embrace this remarkable recipe.

INGREDIENTS

- 80g/2¾oz cashews, boiled
- 50g/1¾oz odourless coconut oil
- 35g/1¾oz potato starch
- 10g/¼oz white miso paste
- 12½g/½oz kappa carrageenan
- 15ml/½fl oz lemon juice
- 10ml/¼fl oz apple cider vinegar (see page 122)
- 10g/¼oz salt
- 375ml/12½fl oz boiling water

MINDFUL BENEFITS:

• Cashews provide healthy fats and protein, supporting sustained energy and brain function.

Boil the Cashews:
Step 1: Boil the cashews for 10 minutes to soften them, ensuring a smooth blend.

Blend the Ingredients:
Step 2: In a high-speed blender, combine the boiled cashews, coconut oil, potato starch, miso paste, kappa carrageenan, lemon juice, apple cider vinegar, salt and boiling water. Blend until smooth. The kappa carrageenan acts as a gelling agent, giving the mozzarella its stretchy, meltable texture.

Set the Cheese:
Step 3: Transfer the mixture to a tray or mould and refrigerate until fully set, about 2 hours. Chilling activates the kappa carrageenan, creating a firm, sliceable texture perfect for melting.

Storage:
• Store in the fridge for up to 7 days.
• To freeze, wrap tightly in plastic wrap or place in an airtight container for up to 2 months. Thaw before using.

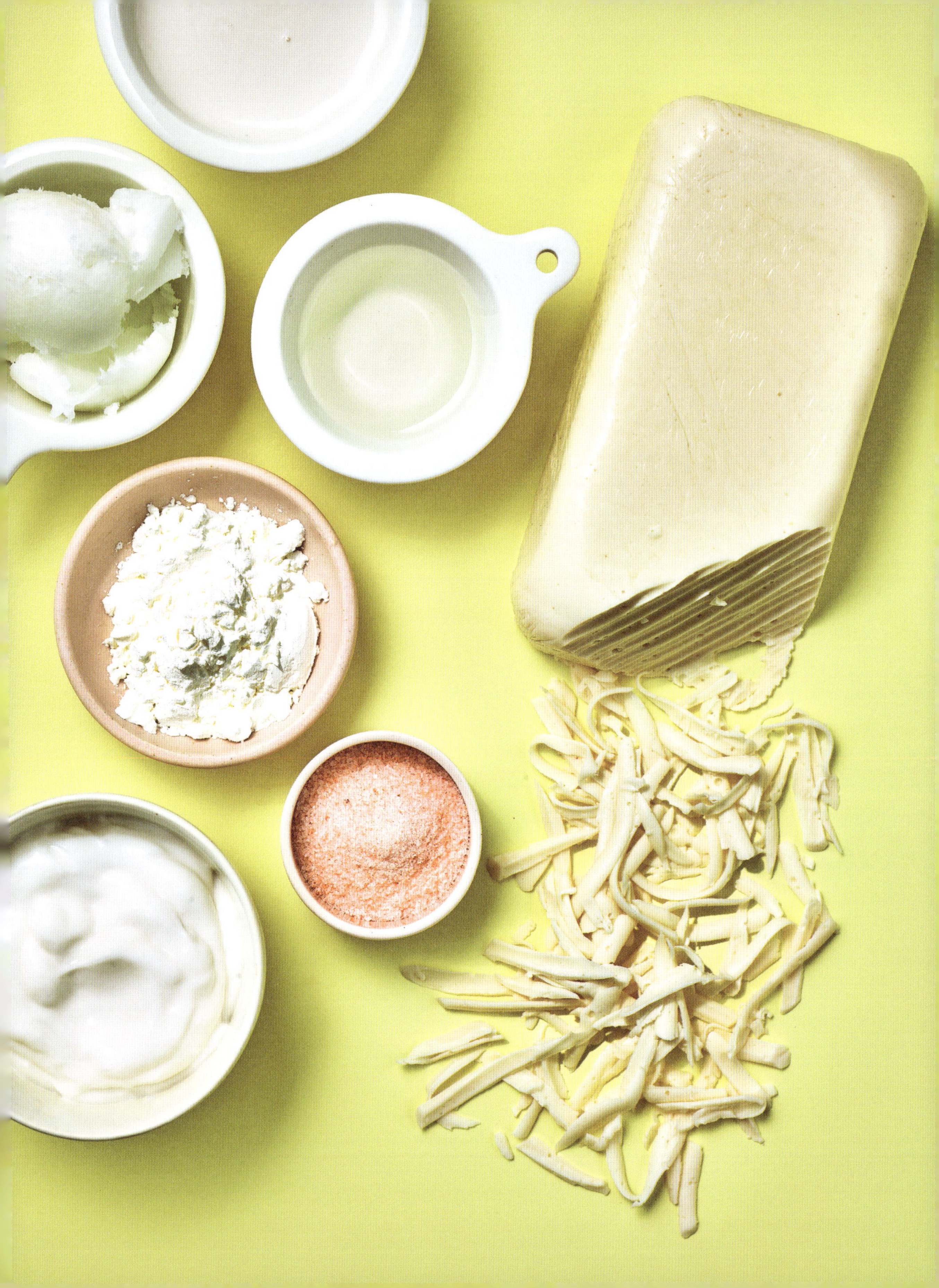

VEGAN CREAM CHEESE

Smooth, tangy and customizable, this vegan cream cheese is ideal for spreading on bagels, enriching sandwiches, or serving as a creamy dip. Crafted from curdled soy milk, it's free of additives and full of flavour, with endless options for personalization.

INGREDIENTS

- 500ml/17fl oz/2 cups unsweetened soy milk
- 2 tbsp apple cider vinegar (see page 122) (or white vinegar)
- ⅓ tsp salt (optional)
- A pinch of nutritional yeast, chives, garlic powder, dill or other flavourings (optional)

COOKING TIP:

- For a tangier flavour, add a little extra vinegar.

CREATIVE TIP:

- Try blending in roasted red peppers, sundried tomatoes or caramelized onions for unique flavour variations.

Curdle the Milk:
Step 1: Heat the unsweetened soy milk in a small saucepan over medium heat until it reaches a gentle simmer. Do not let it boil.

Step 2: Remove from heat and stir in the apple cider vinegar. Let the mixture sit for 10 minutes. The milk will separate into curds and whey.

Blend:
Step 3: While the mixture is still hot, transfer the curds to a blender or food processor. Blend until smooth and creamy.

Flavour (Optional):
Step 4: Transfer the blended cream cheese to a bowl. Mix in salt, nutritional yeast, chives, garlic powder, dill or other herbs and seasonings to taste.

Storage:
Step 5: Store the cream cheese in an airtight container in the refrigerator. Use within 3–5 days.

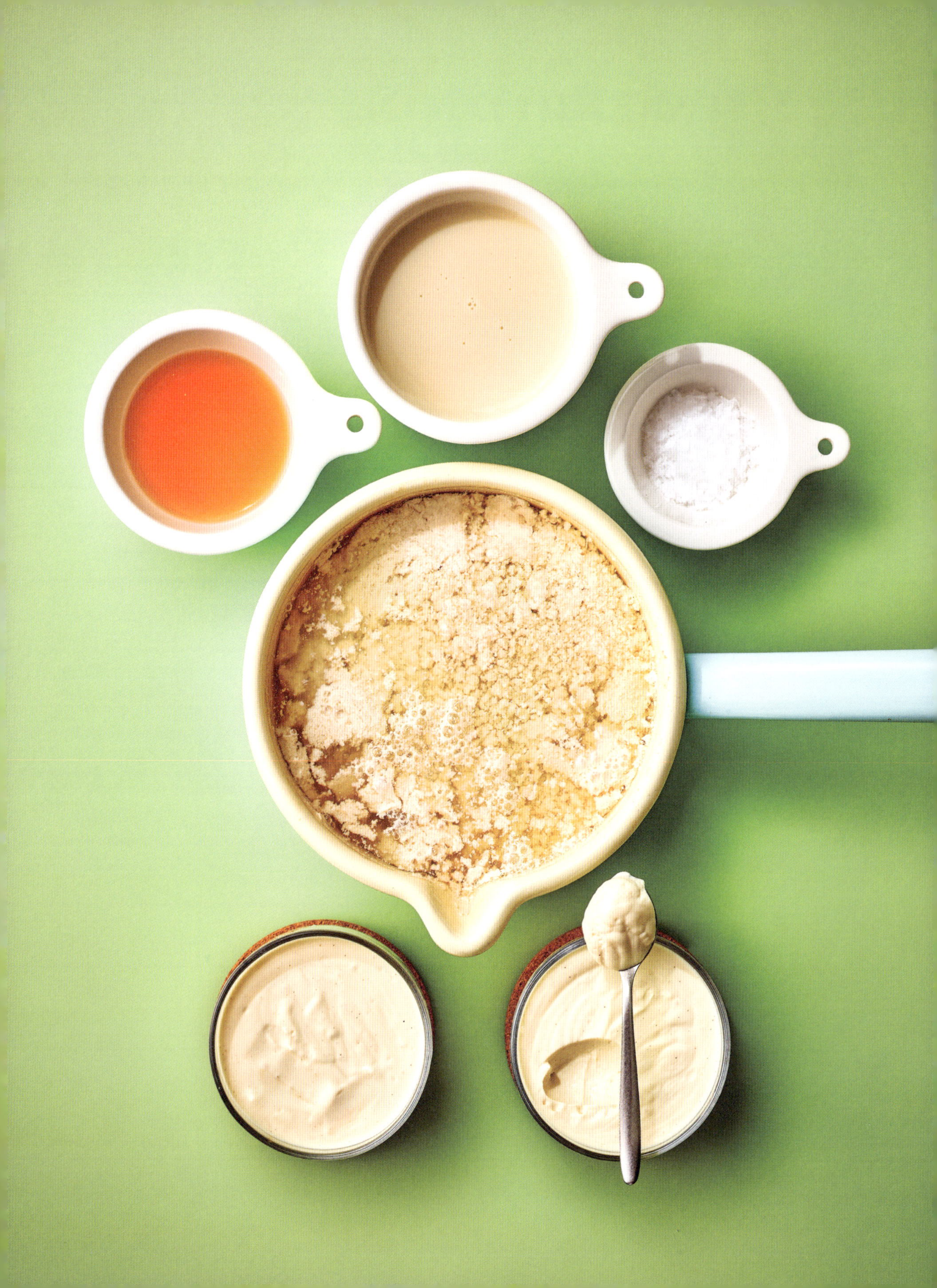

HOMEMADE VEGAN RICOTTA

With only two ingredients, this homemade vegan ricotta is simplicity at its finest. Perfect for lasagna, stuffed pasta shells, or as a creamy toast topping, this recipe offers versatility and indulgence in every bite.

INGREDIENTS

- 2L/70fl oz/8½ cups homemade almond milk (or any plant-based milk of your choice, see page 144)
- 50ml/1½fl oz/scant ¼ cup fresh lemon juice

MINDFUL BENEFITS:

- Homemade almond milk is packed with magnesium, a nutrient known to support brain health, improve sleep and reduce anxiety.

COOKING TIP:

- Always simmer the almond milk gently, bringing it only to scalding point – boiling can alter the texture of the final product.

- If not using homemade ones, use plant-based milk high in protein, such as soy or cashew, for best results. Store-bought versions often lack body and nutritional value, which can compromise the coagulation of the milk during preparation.

Curdle the Milk:

Step 1: Heat the almond milk in a large pot over medium heat until it reaches a gentle simmer. Avoid boiling, as this can affect the texture.

Step 2: Remove the pot from heat and stir in the fresh lemon juice. Allow the mixture to sit for about 10 minutes. During this time, the milk will curdle, forming curds and whey.

Strain the Mixture:

Step 3: Line a large bowl with muslin cloth or a nut milk bag. Pour the curdled mixture into the cloth, letting the whey drain into the bowl.

Step 4: Gather the edges of the cloth and gently squeeze out excess liquid. Let the ricotta drain for at least 30 minutes or until it reaches your desired consistency.

Store the Ricotta:

Step 5: Transfer the ricotta to an airtight container and refrigerate. Use within 3–5 days for optimal freshness.

CREATIVE TIP:

- Enhance your ricotta with fresh herbs, garlic or nutritional yeast for added depth of flavour. Perfect for both savoury dishes and creative pairings!

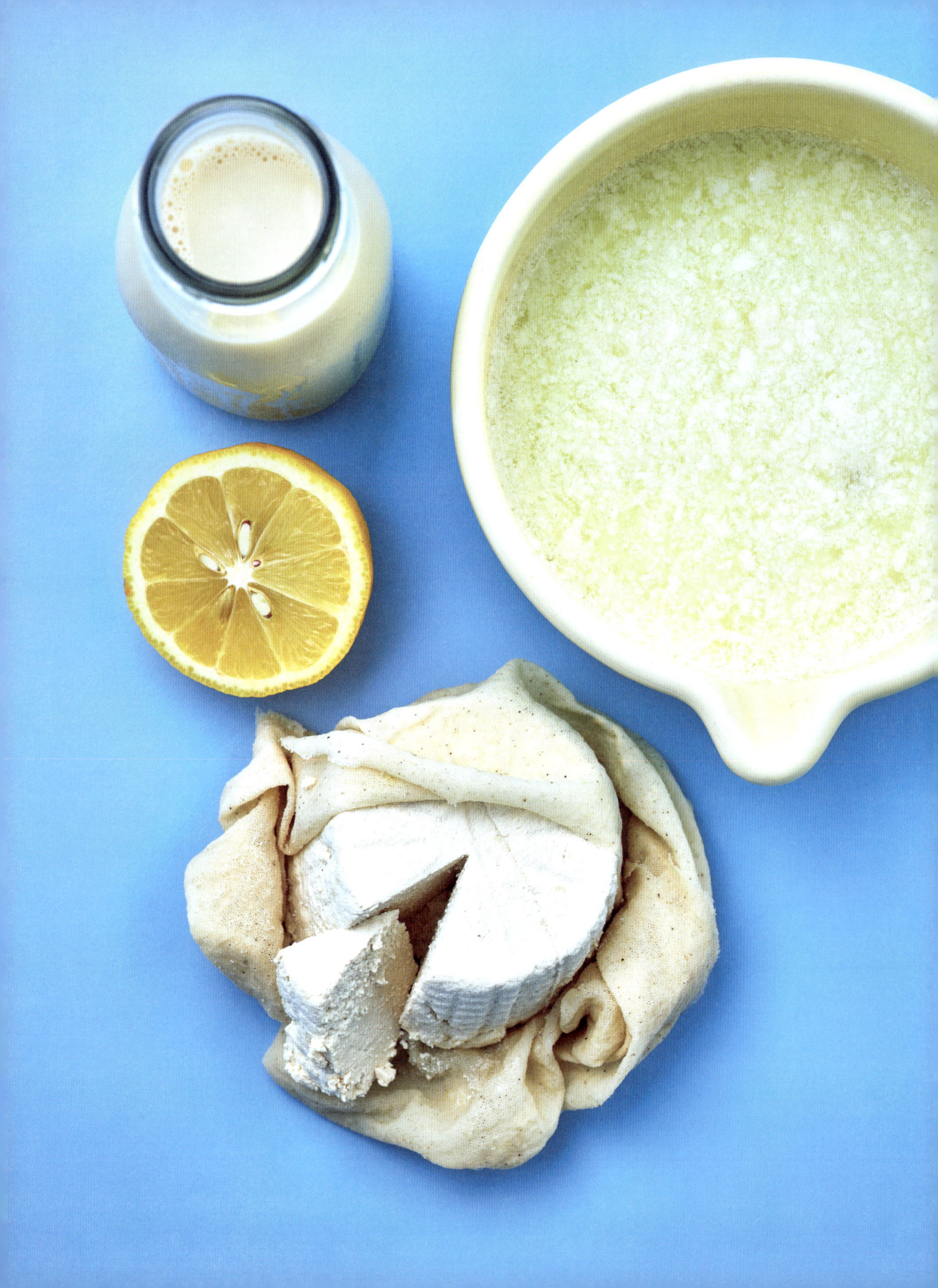

TOFU

Tofu, a cornerstone of East Asian cuisine, has a storied history that reflects both ingenuity and cultural tradition.

Originating in China over 2,000 years ago, tofu became known as the "cheese of the East" by the 15th century, showcasing its importance as a staple protein source in regions where dairy was less prevalent. The process of making tofu mirrors the cheesemaking techniques perfected in Europe, with soybeans replacing dairy milk.

The art of tofu-making follows a timeless craft. Soybeans are transformed into milk, curdled with coagulants like nigari (magnesium chloride) and then pressed into blocks. This versatile ingredient was first mentioned in Chinese texts during the Han Dynasty and later spread to Japan and Korea, becoming a culinary canvas for bold flavours and innovative dishes.

Despite its simplicity, tofu has been the subject of modern misconceptions. One persistent myth concerns its phytoestrogen content. These plant-based compounds are not identical to human oestrogen and can, in fact, offer health benefits such as supporting heart health and reducing certain cancer risks.

By embracing tofu, we honour a culinary tradition that is as nourishing as it is adaptable. Tofu is a culinary chameleon, ready to soak up flavours and textures. Its affordability and high protein content make it a cornerstone of plant-based diets.

INGREDIENTS

Makes: 600–800g/21oz–28oz tofu

- 2L/70fl oz/8½ cups soy milk (see page 146)
- 1 tbsp nigari (can easily be found online)
- 300ml/10fl oz/1¼ cups warm water

CREATIVE TIP:

- Before you press your tofu, think about flavour infusions. This is the ideal time to introduce seasonings or marinades, allowing your tofu to absorb the flavours.

Prepare the Coagulant:
Step 1: In a bowl, dissolve the nigari in the water to make your coagulant solution.

Coagulate the Soy Milk:
Step 2: Heat the soy milk in a pot until it's just about to boil (around 75–80°C/170–175°F) and then remove it from heat.

Step 3: Gently stir the soy milk and, while stirring, slowly add the nigari coagulant solution. This will cause the soy milk to curdle.

Let it Set:
Step 4: Stop stirring and allow the mixture to sit undisturbed for 15–20 minutes. During this time, curds will form and separate from the liquid, which is now known as whey.

Recipe continued on the next page ...

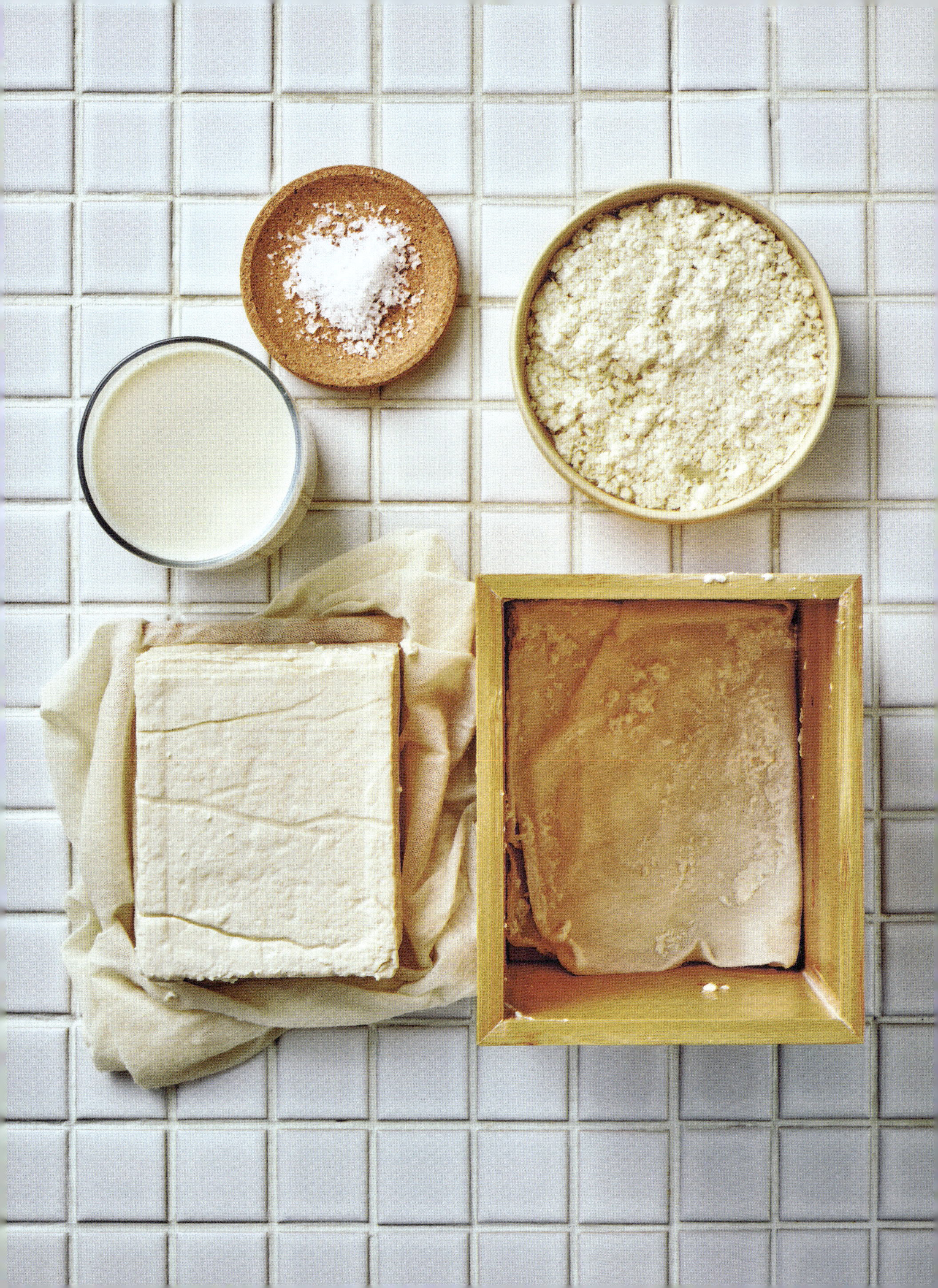

Mould the Tofu:

Step 5: Line a tofu mould or a small perforated tray with a muslin cloth/cheesecloth. Any size or shape of tray works fine for this since the tofu takes the shape of its container.

Step 6: Ladle the curds into the mould and fold the muslin cloth over the top.

Step 7: Place a weight on top to press the curds for 15–60 minutes, depending on how firm you want your tofu. The longer you press it, the firmer it will be.

Unmould:

Step 8: Once pressed, unfold the muslin cloth and gently remove your block of tofu.

Storage:

Step 9: Submerge the tofu in water in a sealed container. Change the water daily, and it will keep for about 2 weeks in the refrigerator.

USING OKARA:

• **Don't discard the okara. Freeze it or refrigerate it. This fibre-rich by-product can be added to baked goods (see page 132), veggie burgers or stir-fries for added nutrition. Spread it out on a baking sheet and dry it in a low-temperature oven or dehydrator to make okara flour.**

TEMPEH

Tempeh, tofu's fermented cousin, is a testament to the transformative power of nature and the resourcefulness of traditional food cultures.

Originating in Indonesia as far back as the 12th century, tempeh is made by fermenting soybeans into a dense, protein-packed cake bound together by the mycelium of the Rhizopus fungus. Unlike tofu, tempeh undergoes a fermentation process that not only preserves the soybeans but also enhances their nutritional profile.

This process imparts a nutty, umami-rich flavour and a firm texture, setting it apart as a culinary delight. The fermentation also breaks down the beans' complex compounds, making tempeh easier to digest and boosting its vitamin and probiotic content.

Tempeh's history is deeply tied to Javanese culinary traditions, where it was used in soups, stews and fried dishes. As globalization spread, so did tempeh, finding its place in plant-based kitchens around the world.

With tempeh, the fermentation process is where the magic happens.

It's a living, evolving creation that brings depth to dishes. Whether sliced, marinated or grilled, tempeh carries its history in every bite, offering a unique texture and a rich flavour profile that tofu cannot replicate. By making tempeh, you're participating in a centuries-old tradition of culinary ingenuity.

INGREDIENTS

Makes: 750g–1kg/ 26oz–35oz tempeh

- 500g/17½oz dry soybeans
- 2 tbsp vinegar
- 1 tsp tempeh starter (Rhizopus oligosporus spores; available online)

Soak the Soybeans:

Step 1: Rinse the soybeans and soak them in plenty of water for 18–24 hours. Use a large bowl, as the beans will double in size.

Hull and Split the Beans:

Step 2: Drain the soaked beans and rub them between your hands to remove as many hulls as possible. Not all hulls will come off, but aim for a significant amount.

Step 3: Split the beans in half by gently squeezing them. This process is made easier by soaking.

Cook the Soybeans:

Step 4: Place the hulled and split beans in a large pot and cover them with water.

Step 5: Bring to a boil, then reduce to a simmer. Cook until the beans are tender but still firm, about 30–45 minutes.

Recipe continued on the next page ...

MINDFUL BENEFITS:

- **Fermentation enhances digestibility:** Tempeh's probiotics support gut health, which is increasingly recognized for its connection to mental wellbeing. A healthy gut microbiome can positively influence mood, reduce symptoms of anxiety and depression, and enhance overall cognitive function.

- **Rich in vitamins and minerals:** Tempeh contains magnesium, which plays a key role in regulating neurotransmitters and promoting relaxation. Adequate magnesium levels can reduce anxiety and improve sleep quality, both of which are essential for mental clarity and focus.

- **Promotes the gut-brain connection:** Fermentation increases bioavailability of nutrients like B vitamins, crucial for brain health. A strong gut-brain connection, supported by probiotics, helps regulate stress responses and improve emotional balance.

Step 6: Drain the beans and allow them to cool to a warm temperature.

Add the Vinegar and Tempeh Starter:
Step 7: While the beans are warm, add the vinegar and mix thoroughly.

Step 8: Sprinkle the tempeh starter evenly over the beans and stir well to ensure all beans are coated with the spores.

Pack the Beans:
Step 9: Take a large plastic bag and perforate it with holes about 5cm/2 inches apart to allow for air circulation.

Step 10: Pack the prepared beans into the bag, pressing them down to remove any air pockets, and seal the bag securely.

Ferment the Tempeh:
Step 11: Place the packed beans in a warm area to ferment. The ideal temperature is 28–30°C/84–86°F.

Step 12: Allow the beans to ferment for 24–48 hours. The tempeh is ready when a white mycelium binds the beans into a firm cake.

Cook or Store:
The tempeh can be used immediately, refrigerated for up to a week or frozen for longer storage. It's perfect for frying, grilling or adding to soups and salads.

COOKING TIP:

- Temperature control is crucial for fermentation. Too warm and the tempeh can spoil; too cold and the spores won't grow. Monitor closely to ensure optimal conditions.
- If fermentation conditions are inconsistent, consider using a yogurt maker or placing the tempeh in an oven with the light on to maintain a steady temperature.

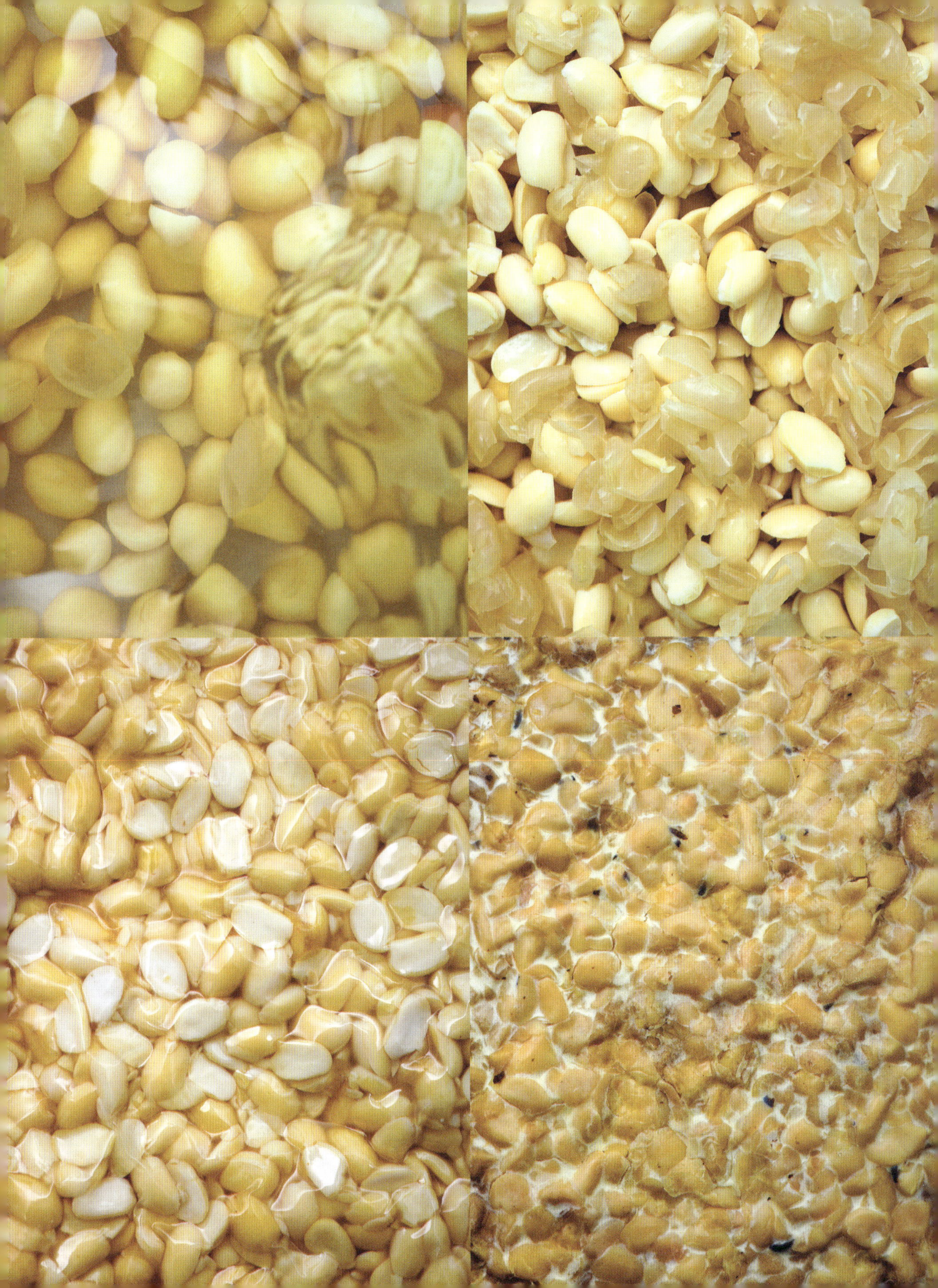

PLANT-BASED MEAT ALTERNATIVES

Transitioning to a plant-based diet isn't about giving up the familiar; it's about reframing the foods you love in ways that align with your values and goals.

For many, the texture and flavour of traditional meat dishes evoke nostalgia, comfort and connection. Plant-based meat alternatives provide a bridge – rooted in familiarity, yet paving the way for something transformative.

These recipes aren't meant to be daily staples but rather tools for a smoother journey. They mimic the essence of classic dishes – not to replicate, but to guide.

Unlike tofu or tempeh, which may feel like a completely new territory for some, these alternatives draw from flavours and textures we've grown up with.

They anchor your diet in familiarity while expanding your culinary horizon.

On a deeper level, these alternatives contribute to mental wellbeing – at least that's what happened to me.

Change can feel overwhelming, and a complete dietary shift might seem daunting.

Plant-based meat alternatives ease this transition, giving you tangible wins along the way. They offer a sense of accomplishment – proof that you're capable of adapting while staying true to yourself.

Every successful dish you make reinforces your resolve, bolsters your confidence and deepens your commitment to this new way of eating

The mental satisfaction of creating a familiar-yet-reinvented dish can be grounding and empowering.

It reminds you that change doesn't mean losing who you are – it means evolving.

With these recipes, the journey to plant-based living becomes less about what you're giving up and more about what you're gaining: new skills, vibrant health and a growing sense of alignment between your habits and your values.

SEITAN CHICKEN ESCALOPES

Seitan, often called "wheat meat", is a versatile, high-protein alternative to chicken that delivers a satisfying texture and flavour.

Perfect for breaded escalopes, this recipe uses vital wheat gluten to create a plant-based dish that's crispy on the outside and tender on the inside. Serve these escalopes with sauces, in sandwiches or on salads.

INGREDIENTS

For the dough:
- 600g/21oz/4¾ cups vital wheat gluten
- 550ml/18½fl oz/2 ⅓ cups water
- Flavorings of your choice (e.g., soy sauce, garlic powder, onion powder, herbs)

For the stock:
- 3 tbsp vegetable bouillon (see page 118)
- 60g/2oz/2 cups dried oyster mushrooms
- 1 sheet kombu algae

For the breading:
- Plain/all-purpose flour
- Gram flour/chickpea flour
- Water
- Panko breadcrumbs (optional)

CREATIVE TIP:

- Experiment with different seasonings to customize flavours to your taste.

Prepare the Seitan Dough:
Step 1: In a mixing bowl, combine the vital wheat gluten with your chosen flavorings. Gradually add water, mixing until a dough forms. Knead the dough for 2–3 minutes until smooth.

Shape the Dough:
Step 2: Divide the dough into escalopes or your desired shapes, ensuring they're of even thickness.

Prepare the Stock:
Step 3: In a large pot, combine the vegetable bouillon, oyster mushrooms, kombu and enough water to cover the seitan. Bring to a simmer.

Cook the Seitan:
Step 4: Add the escalopes to the simmering stock. Cover and cook for 45–50 minutes, ensuring the seitan is fully submerged.

Cool and Slice:
Step 5: Remove the seitan from the stock and let cool. Slice into desired thickness for escalopes.

Prepare for Breading:
Step 6: Set up a breading station with 3 bowls: one for plain flour, one for gram flour mixed with water, and one for breadcrumbs (optional).

Bread the Escalopes:
Step 7: Coat each escalope in flour, then the gram flour mixture, and finally breadcrumbs (if using).

Cook the Escalopes:
Step 8: Pan-fry in a skillet with oil until golden and crispy, or bake at 200°C/400°F/Gas 6 until crispy.

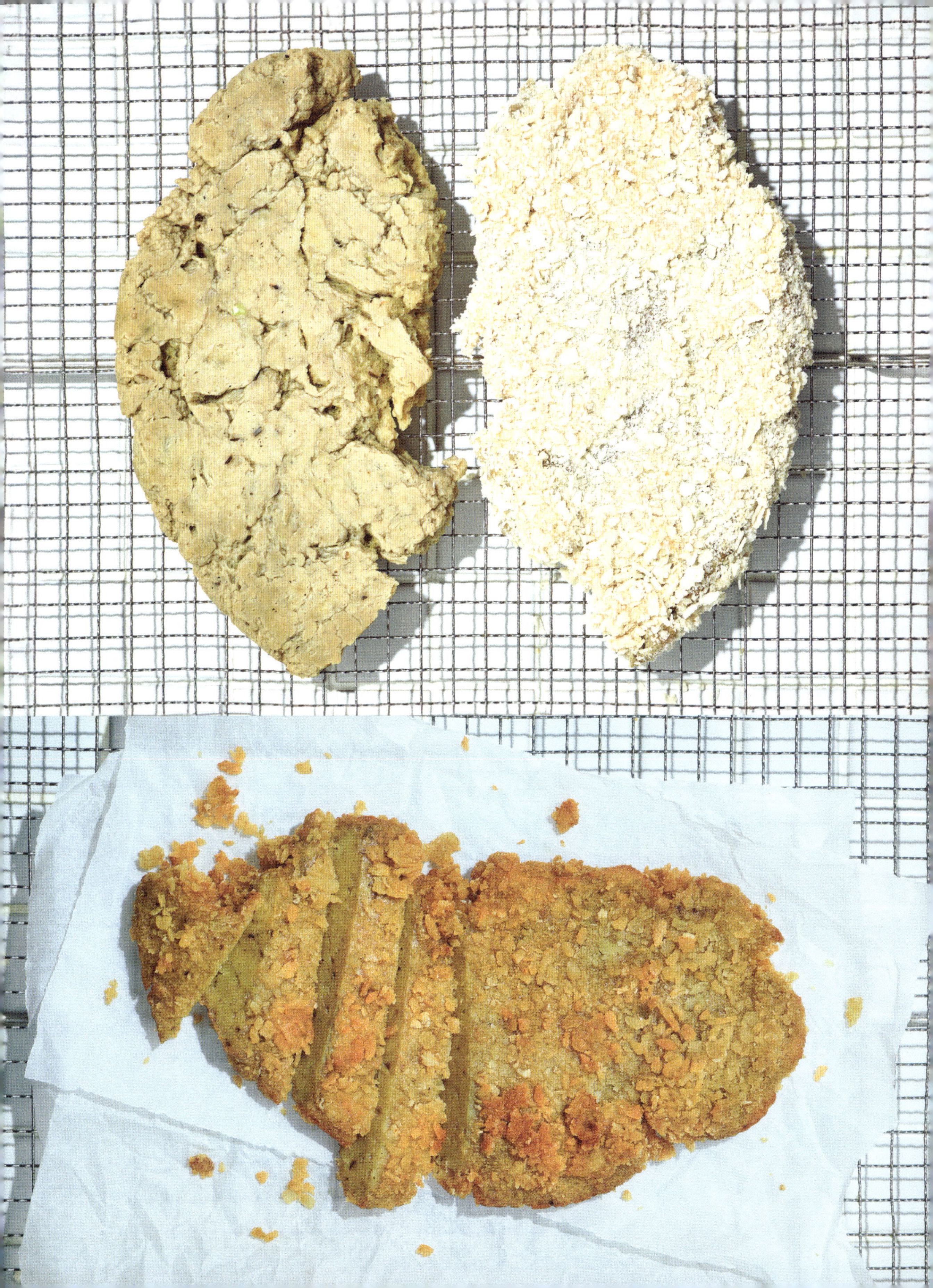

VEGAN SALAME

Salame, with its rich, spiced flavour and satisfying texture, has long been a centerpiece of charcuterie boards and comfort dishes.

This vegan version delivers all the flavour without compromise, whether you're making a sandwich, topping a pizza or creating a charcuterie board.

INGREDIENTS

- 250g/8¾oz/2 cups vital wheat gluten
- 1 tbsp toasted, crushed fennel seeds
- 2 tbsp toasted, crushed black pepper
- 2 tsp celery salt
- 2 tsp smoked paprika
- 1 tsp homemade vegetable bouillon (or substitute garlic and onion powder)
- ¼ tsp beetroot/beet powder
- 1 tsp fine sea salt
- 3 tbsp tomato purée
- 100ml/3 ⅓ fl oz light soy sauce
- 60ml/2fl oz/¼ cup odourless coconut oil
- 100ml/3½fl oz/scant ½ cup water

Prepare the Dry Ingredients:
Step 1: In a mixing bowl, combine the vital wheat gluten, fennel seeds, black pepper, celery salt, smoked paprika, vegetable bouillon, beetroot powder and sea salt.

Prepare the Wet Ingredients:
Step 2: In another bowl, whisk together tomato purée, soy sauce, coconut oil and water until well combined.

Combine and Mix:
Step 3: Pour the wet ingredients into the dry. Mix thoroughly until a dough forms. Knead the dough for 2–3 minutes until smooth.

Shape the Salame:
Step 4: Shape the dough into a compact log or sausage. Wrap it tightly in clingfilm, parchment paper or foil.

Steam the Salame:
Step 5: Place the wrapped salame in a steamer and cook for 45–50 minutes.

Cool and Slice:
Step 6: Let the salame cool completely before unwrapping and slicing.

Storage:
Step 7: Store in an airtight container in the fridge for up to 1 week or freeze for up to 3 months.

When ready to use, thaw it in the refrigerator overnight and slice as needed.

Proper storage ensures the salame retains its flavour and texture, making it ready for sandwiches, pizzas or charcuterie boards whenever you need it!

CREATIVE TIP:

• Adjust spices for a unique twist – try adding chilli powder for heat or smoked paprika for extra depth.

• Recipes on the next page

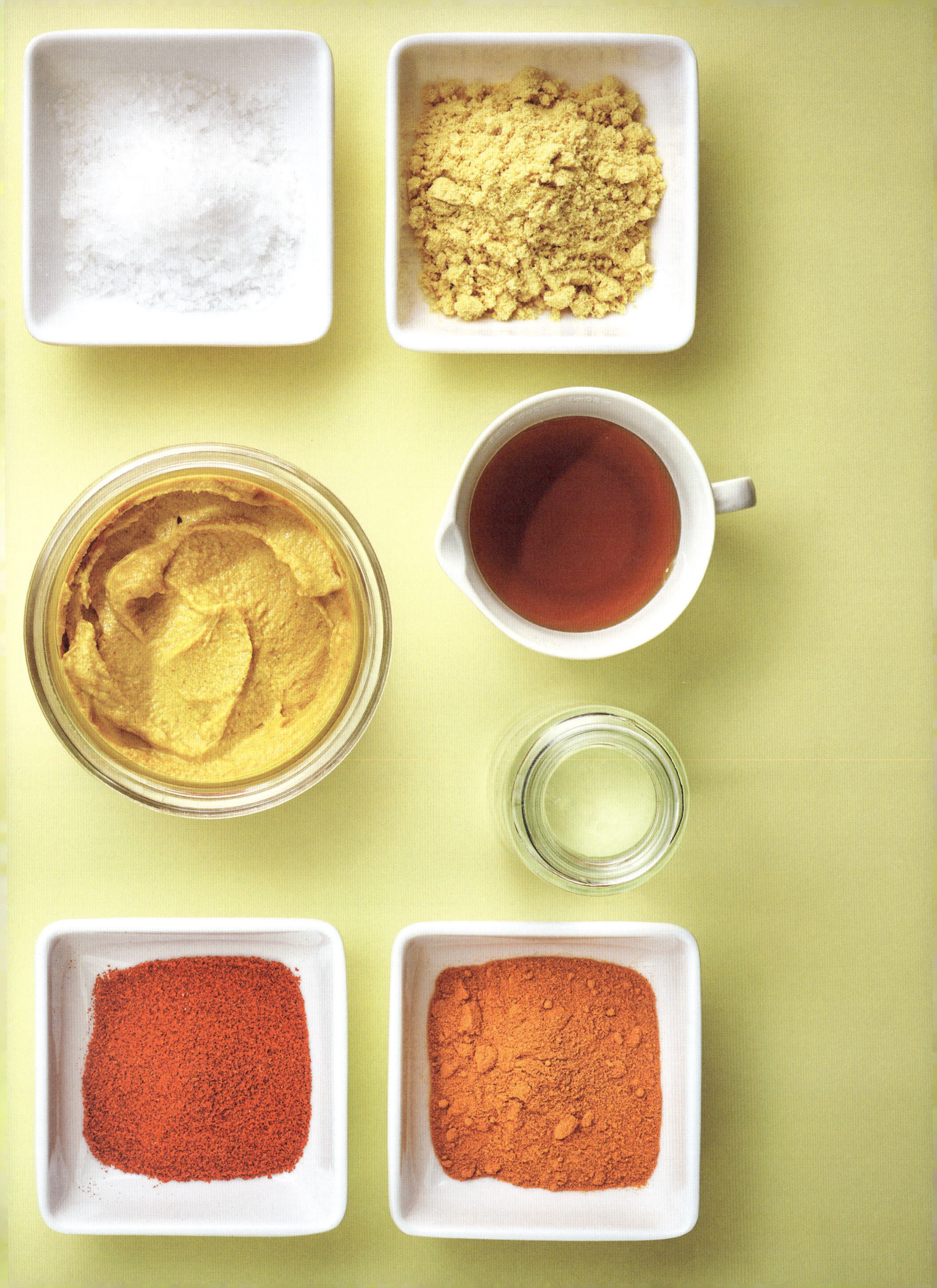

WHOLE GRAIN MUSTARD WITH MAPLE SYRUP

Mustard has been a culinary staple for millennia, its origins tracing back to ancient civilizations. The Greeks and Romans revered mustard seeds not only for their bold, spicy flavour but also for their medicinal properties.

By the Middle Ages, mustard had evolved into a household condiment across Europe, often combined with wine, vinegar or honey to create unique regional flavours.

Today, mustard remains a cornerstone of global cuisine, loved for its ability to enhance flavours.

Crafting your own mustard at home allows you to honour this timeless tradition while tailoring the recipe to suit your taste. This whole-grain mustard, enriched with the natural sweetness of maple syrup, offers a rustic texture and a vibrant, tangy flavour that elevates any dish.

INGREDIENTS

- 220g/7oz/1 cup mustard seeds (yellow, brown or a mix)
- 120ml/4fl oz/½ cup verjus (or white wine vinegar if unavailable)
- 120ml/4fl oz/½ cup apple cider vinegar (see page 122)
- 1–2 tbsp maple syrup
- Salt to taste (optional)

Soak the Mustard Seeds:
Step 1: Combine the mustard seeds, verjus and apple cider vinegar in a bowl. Stir well to ensure the seeds are fully submerged.

Overnight Soak:
Step 2: Cover the bowl and let the mixture soak at room temperature for at least 12 hours. This allows the seeds to absorb the liquid and swell, creating the base for your mustard.

Blend:
Step 3: After soaking, add the mixture to a blender along with the maple syrup. Blend to your desired consistency — coarse for a rustic texture or smoother for a creamier result.

Storage:
Step 4: Transfer the blended mustard into a sterilized jar. Seal tightly and refrigerate. The mustard will develop a deeper flavour as it matures and can be stored for several weeks.

SMOOTH YELLOW MUSTARD

While the Romans were among the first to grind mustard seeds into a paste, the bright yellow mustard we know today owes its origin to the late 19th century.

The addition of turmeric not only enhanced its flavour but also gave it the signature golden colour that became synonymous with classic American mustard.

Whether spread on sandwiches, whisked into dressings, or used as a marinade for vegetables and proteins, this recipe is a versatile kitchen essential.

INGREDIENTS

- 50g/1¾oz/½ cup mustard powder
- 120ml/4fl oz/½ cup water
- 1 tsp turmeric
- 1 tsp salt
- ½ tsp paprika
- 1 tsp honey or maple syrup

COOKING TIP:

- Adjust the water temperature when mixing to control the flavour. Cold water produces a milder mustard, while warm water creates a spicier kick.

CREATIVE TIP:

- Experiment with additional flavours by using different vinegars, adding fresh herbs, or incorporating spices like chilli powder or dill for unique twists.

Mix the Ingredients:
Step 1: In a bowl, combine the mustard powder, water, turmeric, salt, paprika, and honey or maple syrup. Stir thoroughly until the mixture is smooth and well-blended.

Cook:
Step 2: Pour the mixture into a pot and cook over medium heat, stirring constantly to prevent sticking or burning.

Step 3: Allow the mustard to simmer, reducing by about one-third, which should take 10–15 minutes. The mixture will thicken as it cooks.

Cool and Store:
Step 4: Remove from heat and let the mustard cool completely. Transfer it into a sterilized jar, seal and refrigerate. Over time, the mustard will deepen in flavour and can be stored for several weeks.

SESAME: THE SEED OF TRADITION, NUTRITION AND MENTAL WELLBEING

Sesame seeds are a quiet powerhouse.

Small and unassuming, they've been fueling human history for thousands of years, threading their way through ancient rituals, culinary traditions and even medicine. Their origins stretch back over 3,000 years to Mesopotamia, where they were prized as much for their energy-boosting properties as for their earthy, nutty flavour.

Across cultures and centuries, they've remained a staple – sustaining the rituals of Ayurveda in India, sweetening delicate halva in the Middle East, and enriching soups and oils in Asia.

But sesame is about transformation as much as it is about tradition.

Packed with calcium, magnesium, zinc and healthy fats, sesame seeds are a brain-boosting, body-fueling ingredient that bridges ancient wisdom with modern wellbeing.

From stabilizing mood and reducing stress to providing a consistent source of energy, sesame seeds are a natural ally for anyone looking to optimize their mental and physical performance.

For those navigating a plant-based lifestyle, they play an even more crucial role.

Transitioning away from familiar animal-based staples, ingredients like this bridge the gap.

They recreate creamy textures, add depth to flavours and bring the satisfying richness we crave. Whether it's tahini folded into a dressing, or a toasted sesame glaze over vegetables, sesame seeds connect you to the familiar while opening up a world of new possibilities.

The act of working with sesame seeds – roasting to a golden brown, blending or whisking them into a homemade sauce – is grounding. Each step requires focus, engaging your senses and quieting the noise of daily life.

In a world where distractions pull us in every direction, it's easy to lose sight of the simple, foundational things that keep us grounded.

Sesame seeds are a reminder that greatness often comes in small, unassuming forms …

TAHINI

My love for sesame seeds is now obvious. Tahini made it into this Kitchen Map because I consider it more than just a creamy paste; it is a culinary icon steeped in history, celebrated in kitchens from the ancient Levant to the bustling streets of modern Mediterranean markets.

The word tahini comes from the Arabic verb tahana, meaning "to grind", reflecting its artisanal roots. Across history, tahini has symbolized sustenance and luxury, appearing in sacred texts and beloved recipes alike.

In Mediterranean and Middle Eastern cuisines, tahini has been a constant presence, enriching dips like hummus, sauces and dressings with its nutty flavour.

It has crossed cultural boundaries, influencing dishes in North African, Greek and Turkish traditions. Today, it is a global favourite, prized for its balance of richness and nutritional benefits.

A source of healthful fats, protein and essential minerals like magnesium, calcium and zinc, it boasts a delicate balance of creamy texture and earthy undertones, making it an irreplaceable ingredient in both savoury and sweet creations – from robust baba ghanoush to delicate halva.

Making tahini at home connects you to this rich culinary heritage, allowing you to craft a versatile, nutrient-packed base for countless dishes.

Whether drizzled over roasted vegetables, used as a spread in sandwiches, drizzled over grain bowls or folded into a dessert, tahini is another bridge to timeless flavours and traditions.

INGREDIENTS

- 140g/5oz/1 cup sesame seeds
- 3 tbsp olive oil or sesame oil
- 2 tbsp lemon juice
- Salt to taste

Toast the Sesame Seeds:

Step 1: Heat a dry skillet over medium heat and add the sesame seeds. Toast them gently, stirring frequently, until they turn golden brown and release a nutty aroma. This should take about 5–7 minutes. Be careful not to burn them, as burned seeds can make the tahini bitter.

Cool and Blend:

Step 2: Let the toasted sesame seeds cool for a few minutes. Transfer the seeds to a food processor or blender.

Step 3: Add the olive or sesame oil, lemon juice and a pinch of salt. Blend the mixture until it becomes smooth and creamy. This process may take a few minutes, requiring occasional pauses to scrape down the sides of the bowl.

Recipe continued on the next page ...

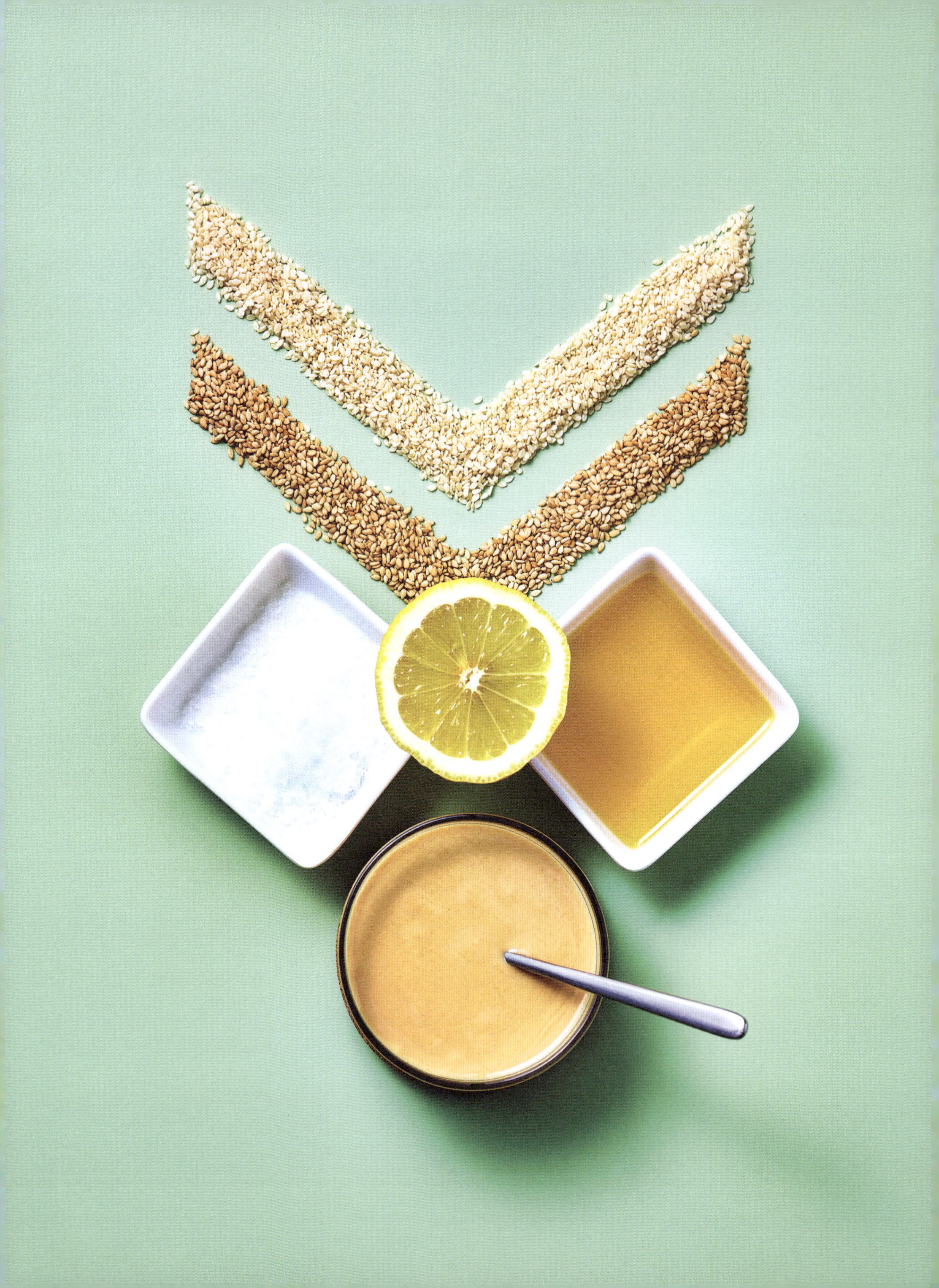

COOKING TIP:

- For a deeper flavour, use unhulled sesame seeds. They have a slightly stronger, earthier taste, which can elevate the tahini in robust dishes.

CREATIVE TIP:

- Add a clove of garlic, a pinch of cumin or a dash of chilli powder to create a spiced tahini sauce. For a sweet twist, mix in agave or maple syrup and use it as a topping for pancakes or baked goods.

Adjust Consistency:

Step 4: If the tahini is too thick, gradually add more oil, blending after each addition, until you achieve your desired consistency.

Storage:

Step 5: Transfer the tahini to an airtight container and store it in the refrigerator. It will keep for up to a month, retaining its rich flavour and creamy texture.

GUT HEALTH | DOCTOR'S AWAY

"The past is not dead. It is not even past."
William Faulkner

The gut is more than just a digestive organ – it's the keystone of our physical, mental and emotional health.

It's the conductor in the symphony of our internal systems. When the gut thrives, the brain operates with clarity, emotions stabilize, and the body finds its rhythm.

Today, we understand that diet doesn't just fuel the body – it influences gene expression, turning pathways on or off in ways that shape everything from digestion to mental clarity.

I find this connection especially profound for neurodivergent humans.

Foods rich in prebiotics, probiotics and anti-inflammatory properties help stabilize neurotransmitter production, reduce impulsivity, and create clarity in the chaos.

Here we explore raw and living foods as the antidote to modern dietary pitfalls.

These enzyme-rich, nutrient-dense foods retain the life force of their ingredients, supporting gut microbiota diversity and enhancing digestion.

Fermented foods like kombucha, kefir and rejuvelac take this a step further, delivering probiotics that nourish the gut lining, strengthen the intestinal barrier, and stimulate the production of serotonin and dopamine – neurotransmitters that anchor focus and emotional stability.

Sea moss, with its 92 essential minerals, is another standout. It soothes the gut lining, supports thyroid function, and delivers the building blocks for cellular repair.

More than biology; it's empowerment. Incorporating raw and living foods is another act of agency I would love you to take on – a declaration that you're shaping your health and future.

Preparing these foods – blending a smoothie, brewing kombucha, or soaking sea moss – grounds you in the present and turns nourishment into a practice of mindfulness.

Cooking is a practice that creates space – space to focus, reflect and connect with yourself.

Healing your gut isn't a quick fix; it's a commitment to yourself, using raw and living foods as foundation for vitality, mental clarity and emotional balance.

By embracing this journey, you're keeping the doctor away and you're stepping into a new level of energy and awareness.

Let this chapter be your starting guide to the transformative power of gut health – a key to flourishing in every aspect of your life.

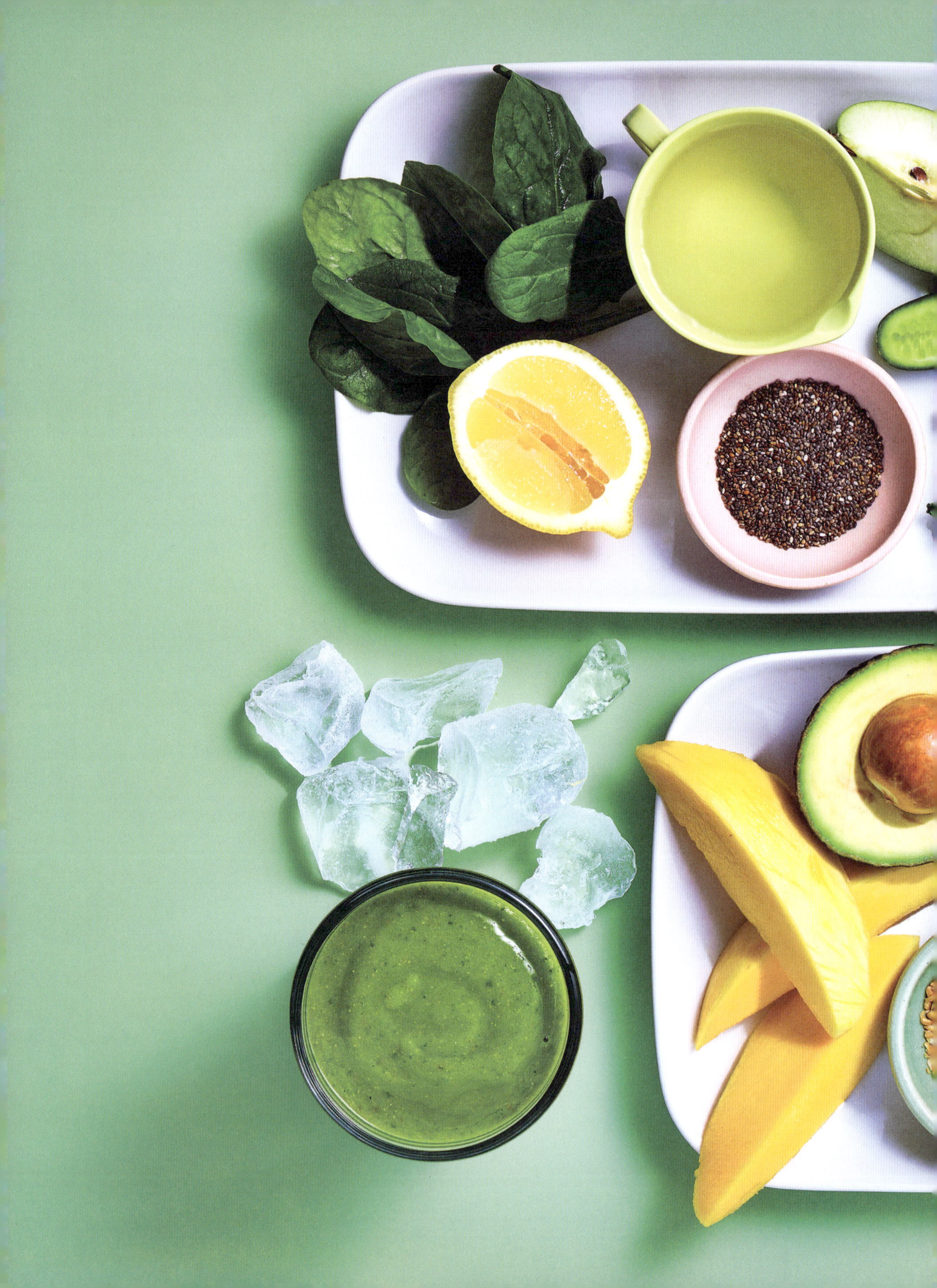

• Recipes on the next page

GREEN BLEND SMOOTHIE

Not a trend – a blend of nutrient-dense greens, hydrating fruits and vibrant flavors, this smoothie offers a daily opportunity to reset and refuel.

It is perfect as a quick breakfast, a mid-day refreshment or a post-workout boost.

INGREDIENTS

- 30g/1½oz/1 cup fresh spinach leaves
- 33g/1oz/½ cup kale, stems removed
- 1 green apple, cored and chopped
- ½ cucumber, chopped
- ½ lemon, juiced
- 1 tbsp chia seeds
- 240ml/9fl oz/1 cup coconut water
- ½ cup ice cubes

MINDFUL BENEFITS:

- Spinach and kale provide an excellent source of vitamins A, C and K, as well as iron and calcium, supporting everything from bone health to immune function. The natural hydration from coconut water aids in electrolyte balance.

- The consistent intake of magnesium and folate from greens, alongside the stable energy release from fruits, supports brain health and focus.

Prepare the Ingredients:

Step 1: Wash the spinach, kale, apple and cucumber thoroughly.

Step 2: Remove the stems from the kale and chop the apple and cucumber into smaller pieces.

Blend:

Step 3: Add the spinach, kale, apple, cucumber, lemon juice, chia seeds, coconut water and ice cubes to a blender.

Step 4: Blend on high speed until the mixture is smooth and creamy. If it's too thick, add more coconut water for your desired consistency.

Serve:

Step 5: Pour the smoothie into a glass and enjoy immediately for the freshest taste and maximum nutrient impact.

COOKING TIP:

- Add half an avocado or a banana for a creamier texture and an extra boost of healthy fats or potassium.

CREATIVE TIP:

- Swap in different greens like Swiss chard or rocket (arugula), or try fruits like pineapple or mango for a tropical twist. Fresh herbs like mint or basil can elevate the flavour profile.

TROPICAL GREEN SMOOTHIE

Transport yourself to a tropical paradise with this nutrient-packed green smoothie.

Combining the vibrant flavours of pineapple, mango and coconut with the nourishing power of spinach, kale and avocado, this smoothie offers a refreshing way to energize your day.

INGREDIENTS

- 165g/5¾oz/1 cup fresh pineapple chunks
- 165g/5¾oz/1 cup fresh mango chunks
- 33g/1oz/1 cup baby spinach leaves
- 33g/1oz/½ cup kale, stems removed
- ½ avocado
- 1 tbsp flax seeds
- 240ml/9fl oz/1 cup coconut water
- ½ cup ice cubes

MINDFUL BENEFITS:

- The greens contribute iron, magnesium and fiber.

- Natural sugars in pineapple and mango provide a gentle energy lift, enhancing focus and reducing mental fatigue. Combined with the mood-stabilizing nutrients from greens and avocado, this supports mental clarity and emotional balance.

Prepare the Ingredients:

Step 1: Wash the pineapple, mango, spinach and kale thoroughly.

Step 2: Remove the stems from the kale and chop the pineapple and mango into manageable pieces.

Blend:

Step 3: Add the pineapple, mango, spinach, kale, avocado, flax seeds, coconut water and ice cubes to the blender.

Step 4: Blend on high speed until smooth and creamy. If the smoothie is too thick, add more coconut water to achieve your preferred consistency.

Serve:

Step 5: Pour the tropical green smoothie into a glass and enjoy immediately.

COOKING TIP:

- For an added protein boost, incorporate a scoop of plant-based protein powder to create a well-rounded meal replacement.

CREATIVE TIP:

- Sprinkle shredded coconut, chia seeds, or granola on top for extra texture and nutrition.

KOMBUCHA (Mensch Cola-flavor version)

Kombucha, often hailed as the "Immortal Health Elixir", has been cherished for over 2,000 years.

This tangy, effervescent tea originated in Northeast China around 220 BC and quickly became renowned for its refreshing flavour and health-boosting properties.

Made by fermenting sweetened tea with a SCOBY (Symbiotic Culture Of Bacteria and Yeast), kombucha transforms into a probiotic-rich beverage teeming with beneficial enzymes and acids. These compounds are vital for maintaining a healthy gut, boosting digestion and supporting overall wellbeing.

The name "kombucha" is believed to have Japanese roots, stemming from a story in which a Korean physician, Kombu, used the tea ("cha" in Japanese) to heal the Japanese Emperor Ingyo in 414 AD.

From there, the tea spread across Russia, Europe and eventually to the United States of America, evolving into a global phenomenon. Modern enthusiasts prize kombucha for its rich health benefits and its ability to invigorate the gut-brain connection.

The fermentation process is what sets kombucha apart. Sweetened tea provides the base, and when combined with the SCOBY, it undergoes a magical transformation.

The yeast in the SCOBY ferments the sugar into alcohol, while bacteria convert that alcohol into acetic acid, giving kombucha its distinctive tangy flavour. The drink can be enhanced further during a secondary fermentation, where fruit juices, herbs and spices add unique flavours and carbonation.

Kombucha has different iterations across cultures. Russia's "tea kvass" uses local teas or rye bread and sweeteners, while Korea's "hongcha" is made with red tea.

These adaptations showcase kombucha's versatility and its ability to cater to regional palates.

In recent years, kombucha has re-emerged as a modern health "trend", embraced for its gut-healing benefits and DIY-friendly nature.

Brewing kombucha at home not only saves money but also allows for personalized flavour experimentation.

INGREDIENTS

Kombucha (Cola Alternative):

- 2.5l/84½fl oz/10½ cups sweetened tea (black tea preferred, brewed with 100g/3½oz/½ cup organic cane sugar)
- 2 small kombucha SCOBYs
- ⅛ tsp freshly ground nutmeg
- ¼ tsp ground cinnamon
- 1 tbsp crushed coriander seeds
- Pinch of ground clove
- Pinch of dried lavender or a fresh stalk (optional)
- Zest of 1 lemon, 1 orange and 1 lime (avoiding the white pith)
- ½ tsp citric acid (optional, for added tartness)

Step 1: Toast the spices in a dry pan over medium heat until aromatic. This releases the flavours, enhancing the final brew.

Step 2: Brew the tea using black tea leaves and dissolve the organic cane sugar while the tea is still hot. Stir until the sugar is fully dissolved, then let the tea cool to room temperature.

Step 3: Combine the toasted spices and citrus zest with the cooled tea, ensuring the mixture is well-infused.

Step 4: Transfer the spiced tea to a large 3L/100oz jar. Add the kombucha SCOBY to the jar and cover it with a breathable cloth secured with a rubber band.

Step 5: Allow the tea to ferment in a dark, room-temperature space for 7–10 days. Taste the kombucha periodically to monitor the flavour development; a longer fermentation will result in a tangier drink.

Step 6: After the first fermentation, carefully remove the SCOBY from the jar and prepare it for storage in a SCOBY hotel (see page 195) or for future use.

Step 7: Strain the fermented kombucha to remove the spices and zest, then transfer the liquid into airtight bottles for secondary fermentation. Leave some headspace in each bottle to allow for carbonation.

Step 8: Let the bottles sit at room temperature for 3–7 days to develop carbonation. "Burp" the bottles daily by opening them slightly to release excess pressure and prevent explosions.

Step 9: Once the kombucha has reached your desired level of carbonation, refrigerate the bottles to halt further fermentation.

Step 10: Enjoy your cola kombucha chilled as a refreshing, healthier alternative to commercial soda.

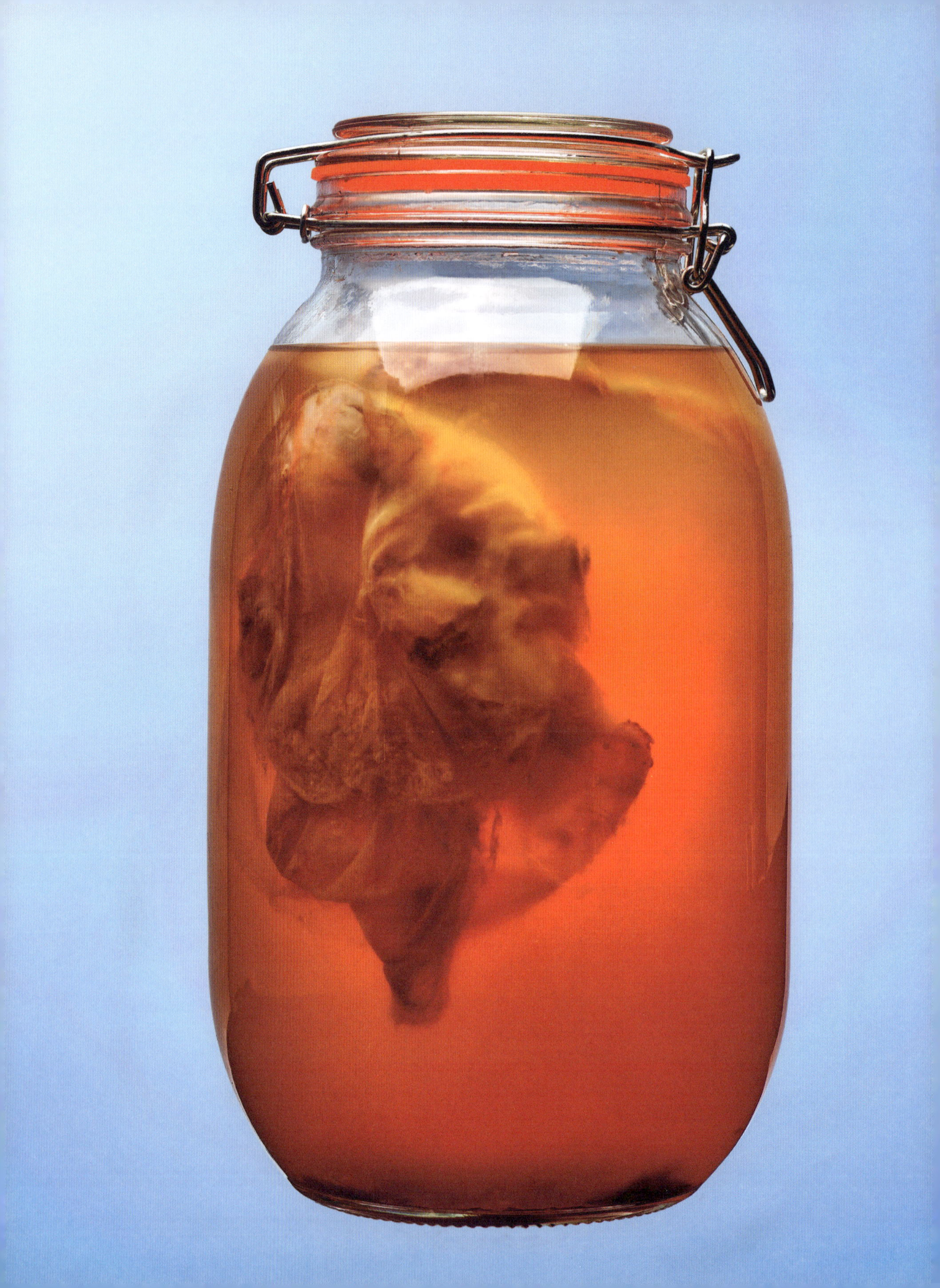

PS: WHAT IS A SCOBY HOTEL?

A SCOBY hotel is a storage solution for extra SCOBYs, ensuring you always have healthy cultures ready for future kombucha brewing. Over time, kombucha brewing generates multiple SCOBYs, and a SCOBY hotel is an efficient way to keep them alive and thriving.

Creating a SCOBY hotel is simple:

Choose a Container: Use a large, clean jar or container with a wide mouth to allow for easy access.

Add Tea: Fill the jar with a small amount of kombucha and fresh sweetened tea (the same base tea you use for brewing). This mixture feeds the SCOBYs and keeps them active.

Store the SCOBYs: Gently place your extra SCOBYs into the jar, ensuring they are fully submerged in the liquid.

Cover the Jar: Use a breathable cloth or paper towel secured with a rubber band to keep dust and pests out while allowing airflow.

Maintain the Hotel: Keep the jar at room temperature and replace or refresh the liquid every 2–4 weeks by adding more sweet tea or kombucha. This prevents mould and keeps the cultures active.

WHY YOU NEED A SCOBY HOTEL

Backup Culture: If your brewing SCOBY is damaged or becomes unhealthy, you'll have a replacement ready to go.

Experimentation: A hotel allows you to use different SCOBYs for new recipes, having different flavour notes in each.

Sustainability: Rather than discarding extra SCOBYs, you can keep them alive and repurpose them for kombucha, skincare or even compost.

In short by creating a SCOBY hotel, you're ensuring your kombucha brewing process remains sustainable and flexible while having the freedom to experiment with flavours and techniques.

HEALTH BENEFITS

• **Probiotic-Rich:** Kombucha supports a healthy gut microbiome, essential for digestion, immune function and overall wellness.

• **Detoxification:** Glucuronic acid aids liver function by binding to toxins and expelling them from the body.

• **Immune Boosting:** The antioxidants and probiotics in kombucha enhance immunity and protect against infections.

• **Energy Enhancer:** Natural caffeine and B vitamins provide a gentle energy boost without the crash of commercial sodas.

• **Joint Support:** Glucosamines in kombucha support joint health by increasing hyaluronic acid production.

CREATIVE TIPS

• Experiment with flavours by adding fruit juices, vanilla or fresh berries during the secondary fermentation.
• For a unique twist, try infusing the kombucha with herbs like basil or rosemary.

WATER KEFIR

Clean, crisp and brimming with vitality – water kefir is a time-honoured elixir that combines ancient wisdom with modern wellness.

Its roots can be traced back centuries, with fermented drinks appearing in various cultures. While dairy kefir has its origins in the Caucasus Mountains, where nomadic tribes developed the tradition of fermenting milk, water kefir (tibicos) is believed to have emerged independently in Mexico. There, naturally occurring kefir grains were found on the pads of the Opuntia cactus, used by indigenous peoples to create a sparkling, probiotic-rich beverage.

Water kefir represents the intersection of tradition and innovation.

The fermentation process transforms simple ingredients – water, sugar and kefir grains – into a lightly carbonated beverage that is both delicious and functional.

Unlike commercial sodas laden with artificial additives and empty calories, water kefir offers a wealth of benefits, supporting digestion, gut health and sustained energy.

Its versatility makes it a canvas for creativity, with endless flavour possibilities ranging from citrusy lemon-lime to tangy berry blends. Whether enjoyed on its own, as a mixer or as a base for unique mocktails, water kefir invites you to reconnect with the art of fermentation and the joy of mindful nourishment.

By fermenting water with kefir grains, you create a lightly-carbonated beverage that feels as good as it tastes.

With just a few ingredients, you can craft endless flavour combinations, each sip offering something unique.

REJUVELAC

Rejuvelac is a traditional fermented drink celebrated for its numerous health benefits and refreshing taste.

Made from sprouted grains such as wheat, rye, quinoa or barley, this slightly tangy beverage is rich in probiotics, enzymes and vitamins. It supports gut health, boosts the immune system, and provides a natural source of beneficial bacteria, which are essential for digestion and overall wellbeing.

The origins of rejuvelac are rooted in the pioneering work of Ann Wigmore, a holistic health advocate who emphasized the power of living foods in promoting vitality. Born in Lithuania, Wigmore founded the Hippocrates Health Institute in Boston, where she emphasized the role of detoxification and enzyme-rich foods in maintaining health. Her teachings remain a cornerstone of raw food philosophy, leaving a legacy in the world of wellness.

Rejuvelac became a cornerstone of her approach, offering an easy way to incorporate probiotics and enzymes into the diet. It is simple to prepare at home. By sprouting grains and fermenting them in water, you unlock a beverage teeming with live cultures that enhance digestion and promote a balanced gut microbiome.

The fermentation process also makes nutrients more bioavailable, while the enzymes aid in breaking down food and supporting nutrient absorption.

Beyond being a drink, rejuvelac is incredibly versatile. Use it as a base for smoothies, salad dressings, raw soups, or even to culture other foods like nut cheeses and vegan yogurts.

This multipurpose elixir is not only a testament to the power of fermentation but also a bridge between ancient wisdom and modern health practices.

Incorporating rejuvelac into your routine connects you to a tradition of natural wellness, offering a simple yet profound way to support your body's detoxification processes and overall vitality.

LEMON-LIME WATER KEFIR

Light, citrusy and naturally fizzy, this lemon-lime water kefir is the perfect alternative to sugary soda.

With bright, zesty flavours of fresh lemon and lime juice and a sparkling finish from the natural fermentation, it hits all the right notes!

Think of it as soda with a purpose.

INGREDIENTS

- 2.5L/84½fl oz/10½ cups filtered water for activation
- 2.5L/84½fl oz/10½ cups filtered water for brewing
- 100g/3½oz/½ cup organic cane sugar for activation
- 100g/3½oz/½ cup organic cane sugar for brewing
- 4 tbsp activated water kefir grains
- Juice of 1 lemon and 1 lime
- Pinch of citric acid for extra tartness (optional)

MINDFUL BENEFITS:

- Water kefir is loaded with probiotics that promote a healthy gut microbiome and boost the immune system.

COOKING TIP:

- Always use filtered or spring water, as chlorine and fluoride can harm the kefir grains.

Step 1: Dissolve the sugar in 2.5 liters of filtered water in a 3L/100oz jar to create an activation bath.

Step 2: Add the water kefir grains to the jar and let them soak for 24–48 hours at room temperature to activate.

Step 3: After activation, strain out the kefir grains and discard the activation water.

Step 4: In the same jar, combine lemon juice, lime juice, 2.5 liters of filtered water, the remaining sugar and the activated kefir grains. Stir to mix thoroughly.

Step 5: Cover the jar with a breathable cloth secured with a rubber band. Allow the mixture to ferment at room temperature for 24–48 hours.

Step 6: After the first fermentation, strain out the kefir grains and set them aside for your next batch.

Step 7: Transfer the flavored water kefir into airtight bottles, leaving about an inch of space at the top to allow for carbonation.

Step 8: Let the bottles sit at room temperature for another 24–48 hours for secondary fermentation. This step develops natural carbonation.

Step 9: Burp the bottles daily by opening them slightly to release pressure and prevent them from exploding.

Step 10: Once the desired level of carbonation is achieved, refrigerate the bottles to halt fermentation.

Step 11: Serve chilled and enjoy your homemade lemon-lime water kefir!

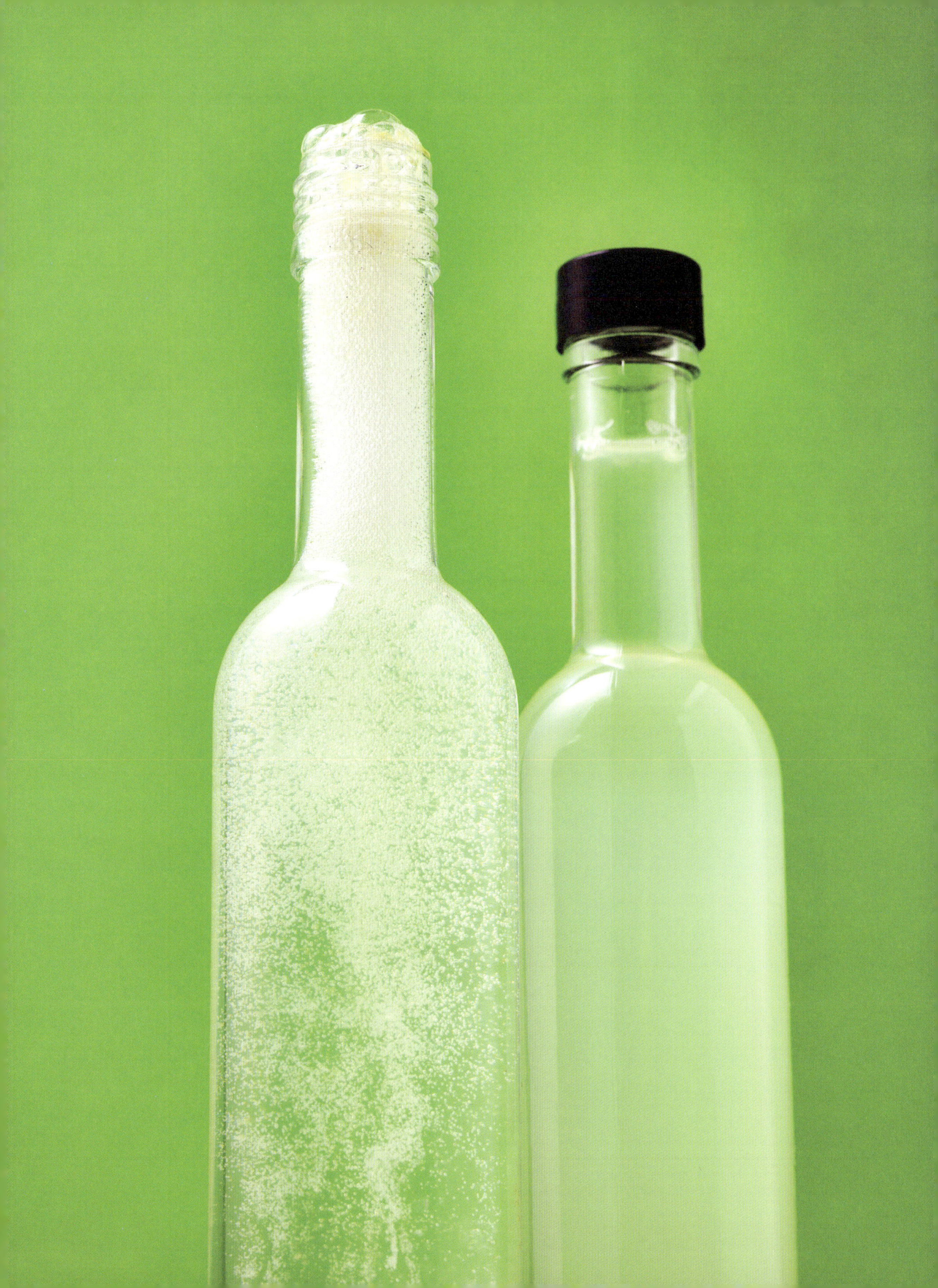

REJUVELAC RECIPE

INGREDIENTS

- 185g/6½oz/1 cup whole grains (wheat, rye, quinoa or barley)
- 960ml/32fl oz/4 cups filtered water

COOKING TIP:

- Rinse the grains thoroughly to prevent mould and ensure a clean fermentation process.

CREATIVE TIP:

- Experiment with grains and flavour additions like ginger slices or mint leaves during fermentation to craft unique variations of rejuvelac.

Step 1: Place the grains in a wide-mouth glass jar and cover them with filtered water. Let them soak for 8–12 hours.

Step 2: After soaking, drain the water and rinse the grains thoroughly. Cover the jar with a muslin cloth or sprouting lid and drain any excess water. Rinse and drain the grains 2–3 times a day for 1–3 days until they begin to sprout.

Step 3: Once sprouted, transfer the grains to a large bowl and add the filtered water, ensuring the grains are fully submerged. Allow the mixture to ferment at room temperature for 1–3 days, stirring occasionally. During this time, the water will become cloudy and a tangy, lemony aroma will develop.

Step 4: Strain the liquid into a clean jar, separating it from the grains. This liquid is your rejuvelac. Store it in the refrigerator for up to a week. You can reuse the grains to make a second batch by adding fresh water and fermenting again, though subsequent batches may be less potent.

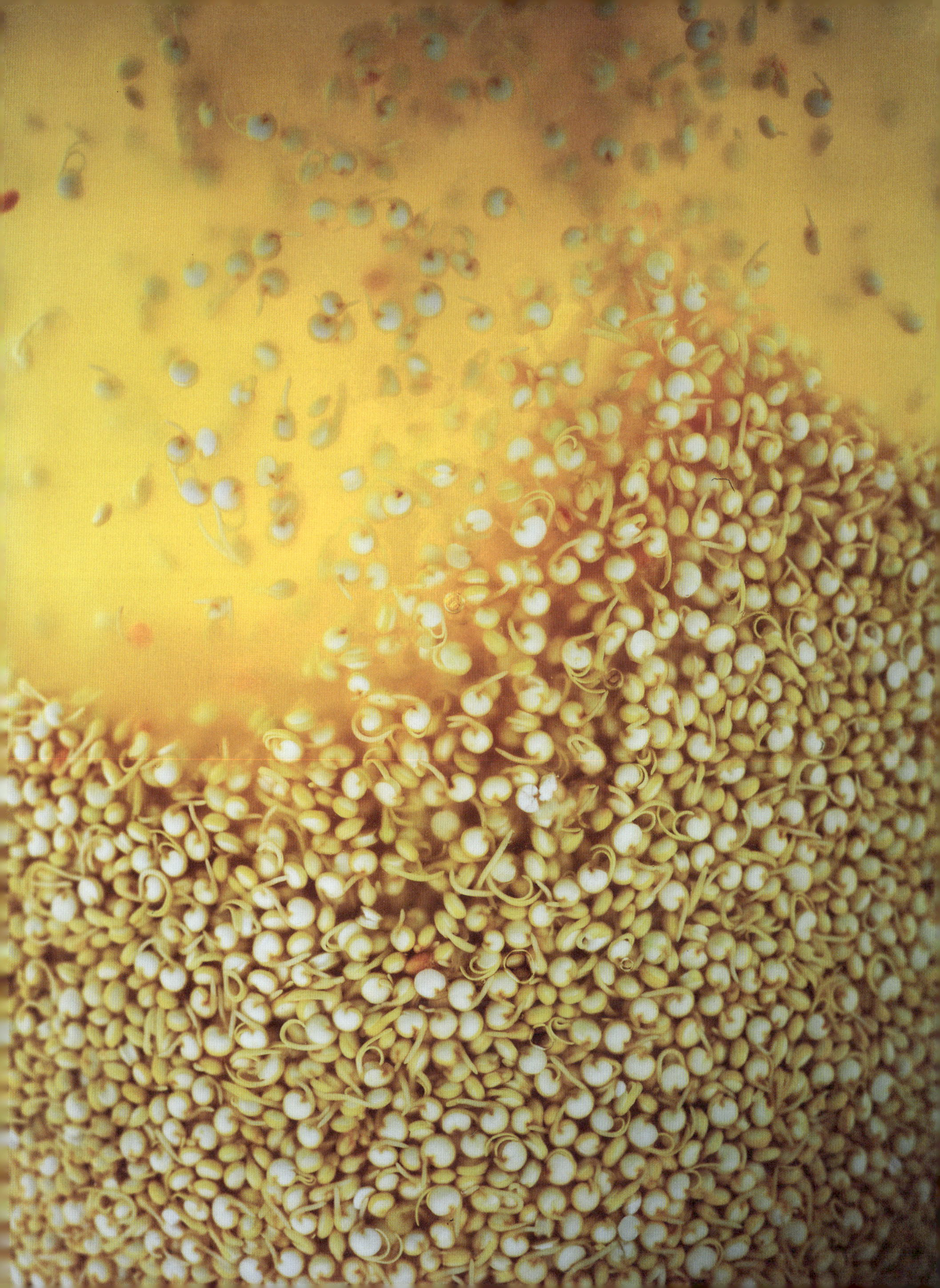

FERMENTED CASHEW SPREAD

This fermented cashew spread is a delicious and creamy alternative to traditional dairy cheese, offering a rich, tangy flavour.

Ideal as a spread on crackers or a sandwich filling. Add to pasta dishes for a creamy, tangy kick or as a base for creamy sauces.

INGREDIENTS

- 200g/7½oz/1½ cups cashews
- 180ml/6fl oz/¾ cup rejuvelac (see page 200)
- 1 tbsp soy sauce
- ½ tsp kelp powder
- ⅓ tsp Himalayan salt

MINDFUL BENEFITS:

- Cashews provide healthy fats, while the probiotics in rejuvelac support gut health and mental clarity.

CREATIVE TIP:

- Customize your cheese by adding herbs, nutritional yeast or spices for unique flavour profiles.

Blend:

Step 1: Blitz the raw cashews until powdered, then in a high-powered blender, combine with rejuvelac, soy sauce, kelp powder and salt. Blend on high until smooth and creamy, pausing to scrape down the sides as needed.

Ferment:

Step 2: Transfer the blended mixture into a clean glass or ceramic container. Cover it with a breathable cloth and let it ferment in a warm spot (24–28°C/75–80°F) for 12 hours. The mixture should develop a tangy aroma and a slightly fluffy texture, signaling that the fermentation is complete.

Storage:

Step 3: After 12 hours, the cheese will have a distinct tangy flavor. Transfer it to the refrigerator, where the flavours will continue to develop as the cheese firms up. Cooling slows down the fermentation process, preserving the cheese and allowing it to age gradually, enhancing complexity.

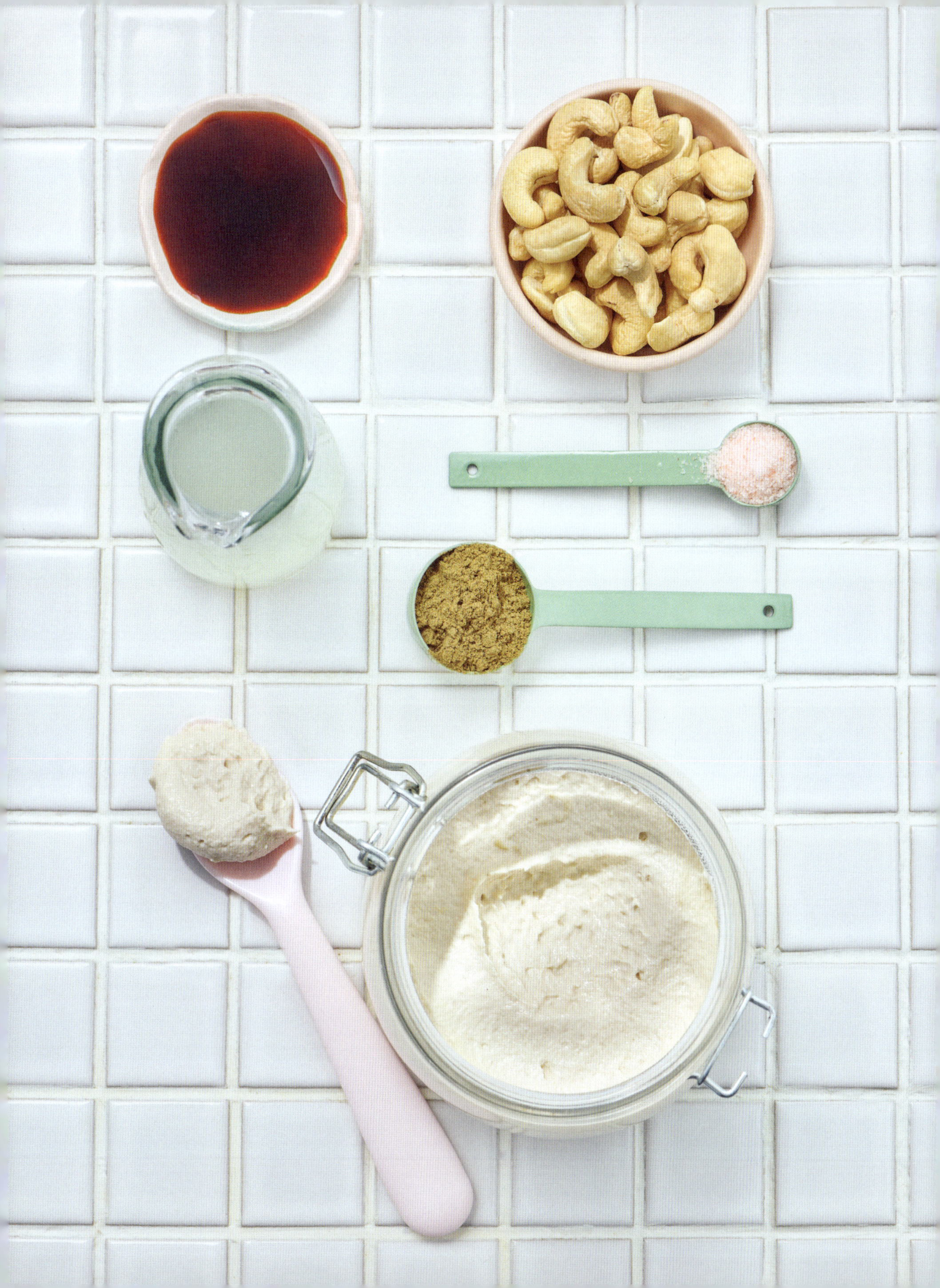

FERMENTED SEED LOAF

This fermented seed loaf is a nutrient-packed powerhouse that combines seeds, almonds and probiotics to create a dense, flavourful base for your favourite toppings.

The recipe yields a small but mighty loaf, approximately 450g to 500g (about 1lb), perfect for slicing thinly, cubing for salads or enjoying as a snack. It fits neatly into a small loaf tin, about 15cm x 7.5cm x 5cm (6" x 3" x 2") and packs enough flavour and nutrients to leave a lasting impression.

You can make this loaf your own by adding fresh herbs like parsley or vegetables such as celery and peppers to the mix, infusing it with even more character. Slice it for toppings, cube for salads, or enjoy as a snack.

INGREDIENTS

- 50g/1¾ oz/¼ cup sunflower seeds
- 50g/1¾ oz/¼ cup pumpkin seeds
- 3 tbsp sesame seeds
- 3 tbsp hemp seeds
- 100g/3½oz/¾ cup almonds
- 60ml/2fl oz/¼ cup rejuvelac (see page 200)
- 1 tbsp soy sauce
- ½ tsp kelp powder

Blend the Seeds:
Step 1: Combine the seeds and almonds in a blender or food processor. Blend until the mixture has a fine, grainy consistency.

Add Liquid Ingredients:
Step 2: Add the rejuvelac, soy sauce and kelp powder to the seed mixture. Blend again to combine, ensuring the mixture is evenly incorporated.

Ferment:
Step 3: Transfer the mixture into a loaf mold or container, pressing it down firmly to ensure it holds together. Cover with a breathable cloth and let it ferment at room temperature for a minimum of 30 hours. For a sharper, tangier flavor, leave it to ferment for up to 72 hours.

Storage:
Step 4: After fermentation, refrigerate the loaf. Slice as needed and consume within 2 weeks.

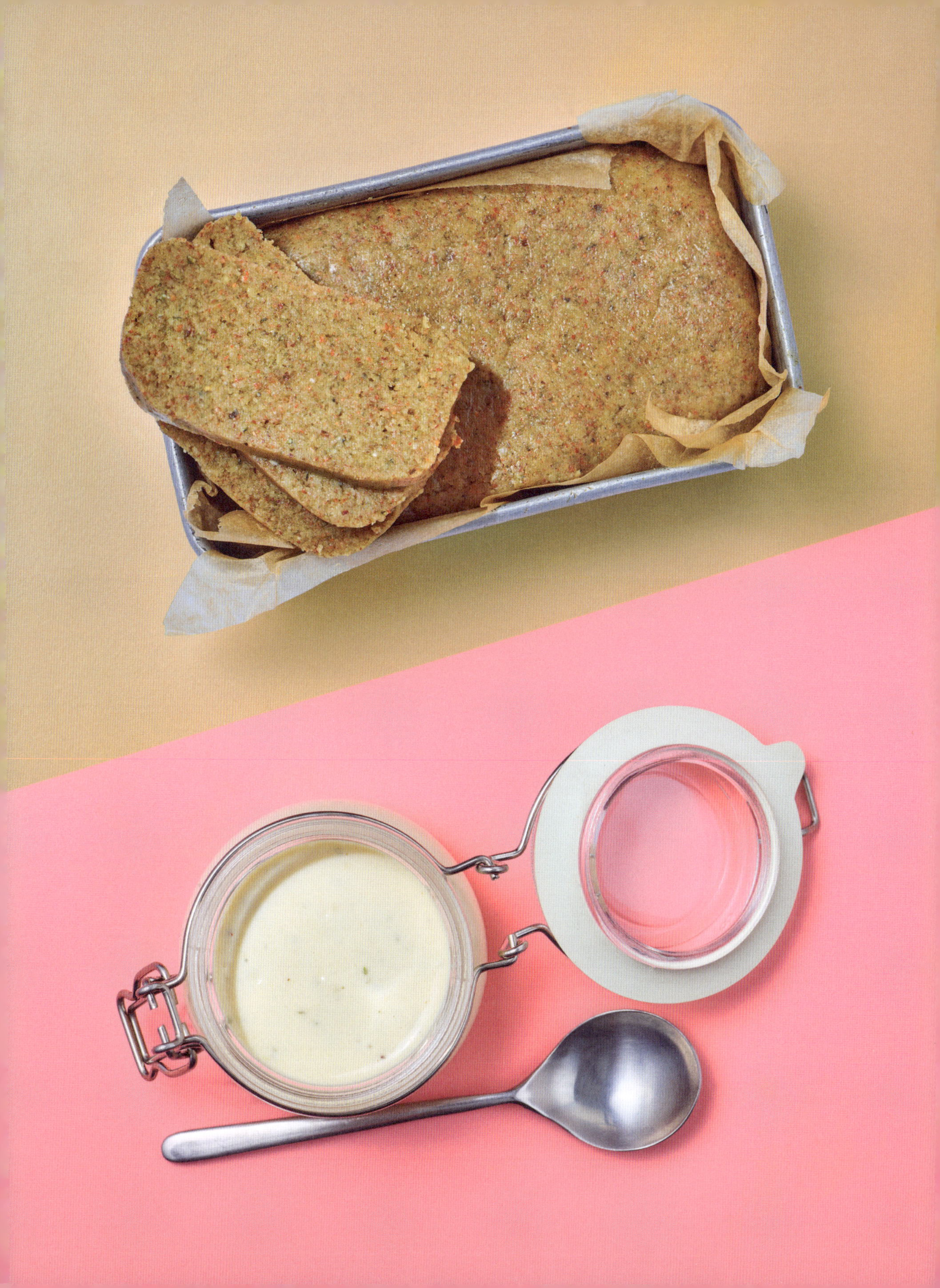

FERMENTED SEED SAUCE

Fermented seed sauce is a versatile and nutritious condiment, ideal for drizzling over salads, dipping veggies or spreading on wraps.

INGREDIENTS

- 100g/3½oz/½ cup sunflower seeds
- 50g/1¾oz/¼ cup sesame seeds
- 50g/1¾oz/⅓ cup almonds
- 100ml/3½fl oz/scant ½ cup rejuvelac (see page 200)
- 60ml extra virgin olive oil
- 8 tsp apple cider vinegar (see page 122)
- ½ tsp mustard
- ⅓ tsp Himalayan salt

Blend:
Step 1: In a blender or food processor, combine the sunflower seeds, sesame seeds, almonds, rejuvelac, olive oil, apple cider vinegar, mustard and Himalayan salt. Blend until smooth and creamy.

Fermentation:
Step 2: Transfer the mixture to a container and cover it with a breathable cloth. Let it ferment at room temperature for 12–24 hours.

Storage:
Step 3: After fermentation, transfer the sauce to an airtight container and refrigerate. Use within 1–2 weeks.

CREATIVE TIP:

- Experiment with different seeds and spices to create unique flavour profiles.

LIVE VEGAN YOGURT

Live vegan yogurt is a creamy, probiotic-rich alternative to dairy yogurt, crafted using plant-based milk and rejuvelac.

Use this live vegan yogurt as a breakfast base, snack or ingredient in smoothies and desserts.

INGREDIENTS

- 250ml/9fl oz/1 cup plant-based milk (see page 144)
- 4 tsp rejuvelac (see page 200)

COOKING TIP:

- Ensure the plant-based milk is at room temperature before combining with rejuvelac to encourage optimal fermentation.

CREATIVE TIP:

- Add fresh fruits, nuts or granola to your yogurt for a nutrient-rich and delicious treat.

Mix:
Step 1: In a mixing bowl, combine the plant-based milk and rejuvelac. Stir well to ensure everything is incorporated.

Fermentation:
Step 2: Transfer the mixture to a jar or container. Cover with a breathable cloth and let it ferment at room temperature for 12–24 hours.

Storage:
Step 3: After fermentation, transfer the yogurt to an airtight container and refrigerate. Use within 1–2 weeks.

SEAMOSS: THE OCEAN'S SUPERFOOD

Seamoss, often called Irish moss, has long been revered as nature's gift from the ocean. It is a red algae that flourishes along the rocky coasts of the Atlantic.

For centuries, it has been a quiet cornerstone of health practices in cultures from Ireland to the Caribbean. Today, in an age where the line between ancient wisdom and modern wellness is blurring, seamoss is finally emerging again as a superfood that bridges the gap between tradition and science.

With a mineral profile that reads like a nutritional symphony, seamoss contains 92 of the 102 minerals that human bodies need to thrive – iodine for the thyroid, calcium for the bones, magnesium for mental calm, and potassium for cell function.

Vitamins A, C, E and K, alongside a spectrum of B-complex nutrients, fortify its reputation as a cornerstone of vitality.

Seamoss is not just a nutritional powerhouse; it's a key to unlocking balance across physical, emotional and mental health.

For the thyroid, its rich iodine content supports a steady rhythm of energy and metabolism.

As an immune booster, it provides antioxidants and antimicrobial compounds to fortify defences against illness.

Its mucilaginous texture is soothing for the digestive system, calming inflammation and acting as a prebiotic to feed the gut microbiota – a gateway to mental clarity and mood stability.

On the skin, seamoss offers hydration, elasticity and anti-inflammatory benefits, and it is now a celebrated ingredient in natural skincare for its anti-aging properties.

Seamoss also serves as a balm for joints and bones, reducing inflammation and nourishing connective tissues.

It has even held a sacred place in folk medicine, hailed as an aphrodisiac and remedy for physical and mental fatigue in the Caribbean and as a life-saving staple during Ireland's potato famine.

In the kitchen, seamoss is a silent collaborator, adding texture and nutrition to smoothies, soups and desserts without stealing the spotlight.

Transformed into a gel, it becomes a multi-purpose base for a host of recipes, blending seamlessly into daily life.

Its sustainable harvesting further elevates its role, contributing to marine biodiversity while supporting ethical and environmentally-friendly food systems.

Beyond its physical benefits, seamoss nourishes the mind.

Rich in magnesium and potassium, it supports nervous system function and reduces anxiety, while promoting a healthy gut microbiome – a key player in the emerging understanding of the gut-brain connection. For those navigating ADHD or anxiety, seamoss offers the possibility of enhanced focus, stabilized mood and a sense of mental calm.

Seamoss is more than a superfood; it is a testament to the timeless power of nature.

It speaks to the rhythms of the ocean, the resilience of tradition, and the profound interplay between what we consume and how we feel.

SEAMOSS GEL

Add this gel to smoothies, soups, sauces and desserts for a nutritional boost.

INGREDIENTS

- 100g/3½ oz/1 cup dried seamoss
- 1 key lime
- Big bowl of purified water (ensure it is enough to keep the seamoss submerged as it expands fivefold)

COOKING TIP:

- Ensure the seamoss is well-soaked and rinsed to eliminate any residual sand or sea debris before blending.

CREATIVE TIP:

- Add a splash of vanilla or a spoonful of maple syrup to subtly enhance the flavour of the gel.

METHOD

Step 1: Rinse the dried seamoss thoroughly to remove sand and debris.

Step 2: Soak the seamoss in purified water with the juice of one key lime for 12–24 hours. The seamoss will expand and become gelatinous.

Step 3: Drain and rinse the soaked seamoss.

Step 4: Transfer the seamoss to a high-powered blender, adding just enough purified water to blend smoothly.

Step 5: Blend until the mixture achieves a smooth, gel-like consistency.

Step 6: Pour the seamoss gel into a clean, airtight container and refrigerate for up to 3 weeks.

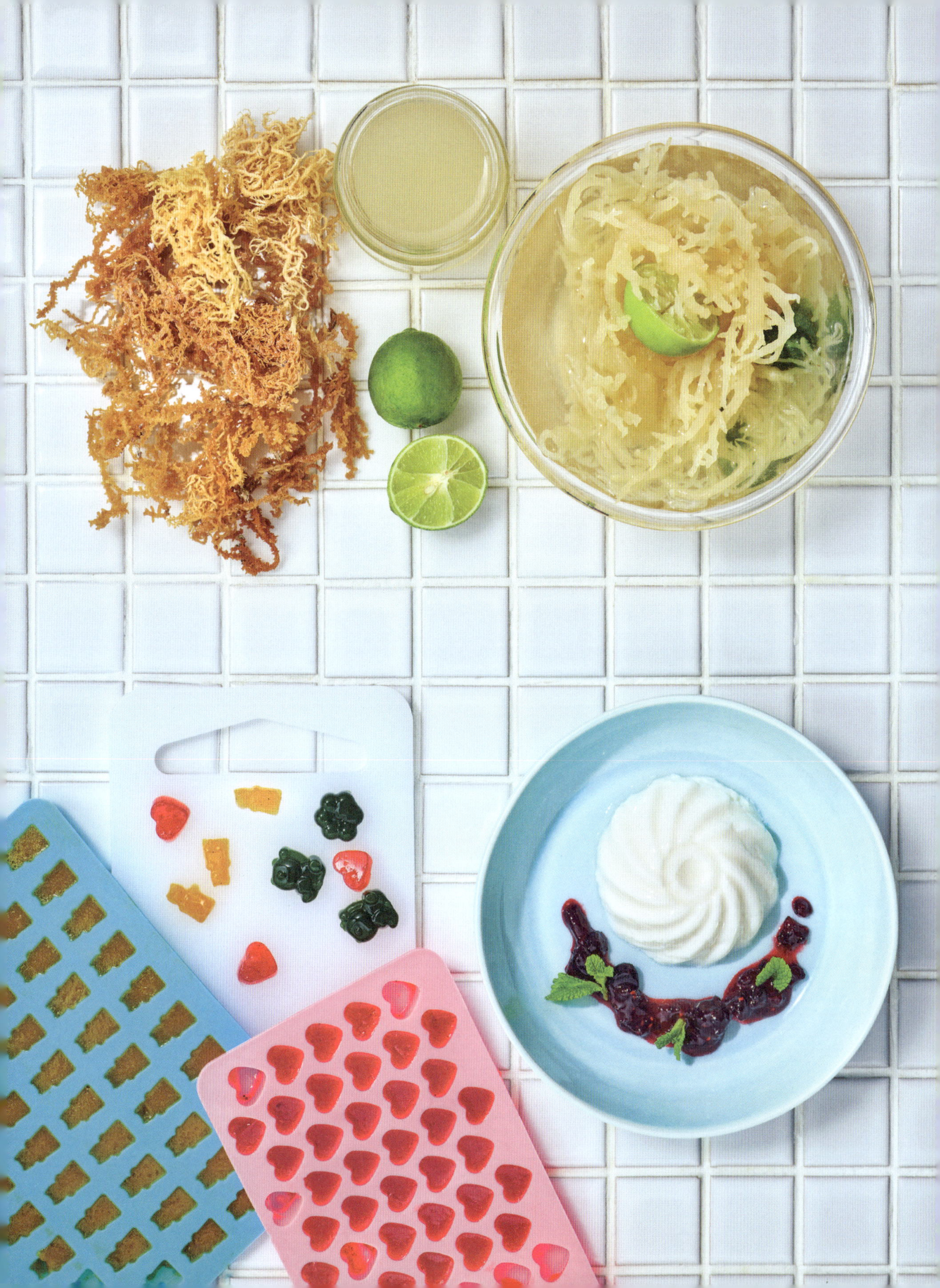

SEAMOSS PANNA COTTA

Seamoss brings a silky, nutrient-packed twist to desserts like panna cotta, delivering both indulgence and health.

Its natural gelling properties create a creamy, rich texture that pairs perfectly with coconut milk and vibrant berry sauce, making it an elegant and nutritious treat for any occasion.

INGREDIENTS

Panna Cotta:
- 320g/11oz/1 ⅓ cup seamoss gel
- 200ml/7fl oz/scant 1 cup coconut milk
- 120ml/4fl oz/½ cup plant-based milk
- 5 tbsp cornflour/cornstarch
- 2 tbsp maple syrup

Mixed Berry Sauce:
- 360g/12¾oz/2½ cups frozen mixed berries
- 120ml/4fl oz/½ cup water
- 50g/1¾ oz/¼ cup cane sugar or coconut sugar
- Pinch of cinnamon
- 1 tbsp cornflour/cornstarch

COOKING TIP:

- Stir continuously while heating to ensure a smooth texture.

CREATIVE TIP:

- Garnish with edible flowers or fresh mint leaves for a beautiful presentation.

Prepare the Panna Cotta:

Step 1: Combine the seamoss gel, coconut milk, plant-based milk, cornflour/cornstarch and maple syrup in a saucepan.

Step 2: Heat over medium heat, stirring constantly, until the mixture thickens and begins to simmer.

Step 3: Pour into molds or serving dishes and refrigerate for at least 4 hours or until set.

Prepare the Mixed Berry Sauce:

Step 4: Combine the berries, water, sugar and cinnamon in a saucepan.

Step 5: Cook over medium heat until the berries release their juices and the mixture begins to simmer.

Step 6: Dissolve the cornflour in a small amount of water and add it to the saucepan.

Step 7: Stir until the sauce thickens.

Serve:

Step 8: Remove the panna cotta from the molds or serve directly in dishes.

Step 9: Top with the berry sauce before serving.

SEAMOSS GUMMIES

Seamoss gummies are a fun, flavorful, and nutrient-packed way to enjoy the benefits of seamoss. These naturally firm gummies require no additional thickeners, relying on the magic of the ingredients and blender to achieve the perfect texture. Enjoy as a daily supplement or healthy snack.

INGREDIENTS

- 100g/3½ oz/1 cup dried seamoss
- 1 key lime
- Purified water
- 2 tbsp natural sweetener (agave syrup or maple syrup)

FLAVOUR COMBINATIONS:

Tumeric and Black Pepper:
- 1 tsp turmeric powder
- ¼ tsp black pepper

Wheatgrass and Spirulina:
- 1 tsp wheatgrass powder
- 1 tsp spirulina powder

Ginger and Hibiscus:
- 1 tsp ginger powder
- 1 tsp hibiscus powder

Step 1: Rinse the dried seamoss thoroughly to remove sand and debris.

Step 2: Soak the seamoss in purified water with the juice of one key lime for 12–24 hours.

Step 3: Drain and rinse the soaked seamoss.

Step 4: Transfer the seamoss to a high-powered blender, adding just enough purified water to blend smoothly.

Step 5: Add the natural sweetener and your chosen flavour combination (turmeric and black pepper, wheatgrass and spirulina, or ginger and hibiscus).

Step 6: Blend until smooth and gel-like.

Step 7: Pour the mixture into silicone gummy molds.

Step 8: Let the gummies set in the refrigerator for at least 2 hours.

Step 9: Remove the gummies from molds and store in an airtight container in the refrigerator for up to 2 weeks.

MINDFUL BENEFITS:

- Turmeric and black pepper boost anti-inflammatory effects.

- Wheatgrass and spirulina enhance detoxification and energy.

- Ginger and hibiscus support cardiovascular and digestive health.

CREATIVE TIP:

- Add a splash of fruit juice for natural flavour and colour enhancement.

5 THE FREEZER:
The Time Capsule

The freezer is another unsung hero of the kitchen – a time capsule preserving the peak freshness, flavour and nutritional value of food.

With the right techniques and a touch of organization, it transforms from a mere storage space into a powerful tool. Reducing food waste, saving time and ensuring access to delicious, nutritious meals becomes effortless when your freezer works for you.

Proper freezing starts with quality.

Fresh, high-grade produce and proteins freeze better, holding their texture and taste when thawed.

BEST PRACTICES FOR FREEZING

Vegetables often benefit from a quick blanch – a brief boil followed by an icy plunge – to lock in colour, crunch and nutrients.

Packaging is your next safeguard. Airtight containers, freezer bags or vacuum-sealed options shield against freezer burn and dehydration, which can strip food of its flavour and vibrancy. The goal is to eliminate air as much as possible.

Labels are your best friend – record the date and contents to streamline rotation and avoid a forgotten backlog.

Defrosting requires as much care as freezing. The refrigerator offers the safest method, allowing food to thaw gradually while minimizing the risk of bacterial growth.

In a pinch, the microwave works, but only if you cook immediately after thawing. I do not own a microwave so I do not recommend it; planning in advance is a better ally.

Some items, like soups and casseroles, can go straight from freezer to stovetop or oven, bypassing the need to defrost entirely.

Consistency is key to maintaining quality. Keep your freezer at -18°C/0°F and avoid overloading it.

Air circulation matters; it ensures even cooling throughout. An organized system – grouping similar items together and using clear containers – saves time and prevents waste.

A simple inventory list can keep track of hidden treasures and ensure nothing languishes out of sight.

Freezing doesn't kill bacteria; it pauses their growth. Proper food handling before freezing is non-negotiable. Clean hands, utensils and surfaces prevent contamination. Refreezing thawed items is best avoided; it can degrade quality and heighten food safety risks.

When done right, your freezer becomes a reliable ally. It's there for the seasonal produce you can't bear to waste, the pre-prepared meals that save the day on busy nights, or the stash of favourite ingredients that inspire spontaneous creativity.

It offers the luxury of time – preserving not just food but the possibility of future meals, ready to nourish when you need them most.

READY-TO-ENJOY MEALS

"Time is the most valuable thing a man can spend."
Theophrastus

This chapter dives into the craft of creating and storing instant meals and indulgent desserts – lifelines that are ready when you need them most.

From silky homemade tagliatelle and hearty 5-minute minestrone to perfectly crispy fries and luxuriously creamy ice creams, these recipes bridge the gap between convenience and quality, offering satisfaction without compromise.

With a touch of foresight and preparation, your freezer can become a sanctuary of possibilities.

A steaming bowl on a cold evening, a ready-to-bake pizza for a last-minute gathering, or a sweet, icy dessert to end the day – all just minutes away from being enjoyed.

For neurodivergent individuals or anyone navigating the labyrinth of a busy life, this approach creates mental space.

The small act of preparing meals in advance becomes an investment in self-care, building a buffer against stress and the temptation of unhealthy shortcuts.

By transforming your freezer into a resource, you make your kitchen – and your life – a little simpler, more efficient and infinitely more satisfying.

• Recipe on the next page

INSTANT TAGLIATELLE

Quick to cook and easy to enjoy, this pasta is the perfect no-fuss solution when you're craving something satisfying but are short on time. Just add water, heat, and dinner is served.

MAKES: 4 PORTIONS

INGREDIENTS

- 40g/1½oz/2 cups dried mushrooms
- 125ml/4fl oz/½ cup white wine
- 1 clove garlic, finely chopped
- 4 tbsp extra virgin olive oil
- 1 bunch parsley, chopped
- Salt and pepper, to taste
- 3 tbsp light cooking cream (see page 152)
- 360g/12¾oz wholewheat tagliatelle, spaghetti or linguine

Make the Sauce:

Step 1: Soak the dried mushrooms in the white wine for 10 minutes.

Step 2: In a pan over low heat, gently sauté the garlic in 2 tablespoons of olive oil.

Step 3: Squeeze the excess wine from the mushrooms, chop them, and add to the pan along with the parsley, a pinch of salt and pepper. Sauté for a few minutes.

Step 4: Deglaze the pan with the reserved mushroom-soaking wine and let it evaporate over high heat. Turn off the heat, stir in the light cream, and adjust seasoning. Spread the sauce in a thin layer onto a tray or container and freeze.

Prepare the Pasta:

Step 5: Bring a pot of salted water to a boil and cook the tagliatelle until al dente, about 3 minutes.

Step 6: Plunge the pasta into cold water to stop the cooking process, pat dry, and transfer to a bowl.

Step 7: Add 2 tablespoons of olive oil and gently toss the pasta to coat lightly, preventing sticking.

Step 8: Form nests by twirling 5–6 strands of tagliatelle around two fingers and placing them on a tray or container suitable for freezing. Repeat until all the pasta is used.

Step 9: Freeze the pasta.

Combine for Future Use:
Step 10: After 2 hours, remove the sauce and tagliatelle from the freezer. Cut the sauce into 4 cubes and distribute them with the pasta into one or more food-grade bags for individual portions.

Step 11: Seal the bags tightly and return them to the freezer.

Storage:
Step 12: Store in the freezer for up to 6 months.

Cook:
Step 13: To prepare, add the contents of a bag (tagliatelle and sauce) with 2 tablespoons of water or broth to a non-stick pan. Warm through, stirring gently, until heated and coated with sauce. Serve immediately, optionally garnished with our grated vegan parmesan cheese (see page 158)

MINDFUL BENEFITS:

- **Switching to wholewheat tagliatelle increases the fiber content, which supports digestive health and helps regulate blood sugar levels. Using your freshly-made light cooking cream reduces calories and fat without sacrificing creaminess.**

5-MINUTE MINESTRONE

Yes, you read that right. With just 20 minutes of preparation over the weekend, you can enjoy this hearty and nutritious soup in a few minutes whenever you like. Stored in your freezer, these meal pouches last up to 6 months, ensuring you always have a comforting and nourishing Italian classic on hand.

When ready to enjoy, simply empty a pouch into a pot, add water to cover the ingredients and bring to a boil. Simmer for about 5 minutes until everything is heated through. Your minestrone soup is ready to serve.

INGREDIENTS

Mix 1:
- 5 medium carrots, chopped
- 2 celery stalks, chopped

Mix 2:
- 2 sweet potatoes, diced
- 2 white potatoes, diced

Mix 3:
- 1 onion, chopped
- ½ bunch of green beans, chopped
- 1 courgette/zucchini, chopped
- 300g/10½oz/1½ cups cooked white beans (see page 104)
- 1 tsp per pouch homemade bouillon (see page 118)
- 1 tsp per pouch homemade tomato purée (see page 94)
- A pinch per pouch of fresh parsley, chopped

Prepare the Mixes:

Step 1: Blanch the chopped carrots and celery in boiling water for 4 minutes. Drain and let cool.

Step 2: Blanch the diced sweet potatoes and regular potatoes in boiling water for 6 minutes. Drain and let cool.

Step 3: Blanch the chopped onion, green beans and courgette/zucchini in boiling water for 2 minutes. Drain and let cool.

Assemble the Pouches:

Step 4: For each pouch, add 2 tablespoons of Mix 1 (carrots and celery), 2 tablespoons of Mix 2 (sweet potatoes and white potatoes) and 2 tablespoons of Mix 3 (onion, green beans and courgette).

Step 5: Add 2 tablespoons of cooked white beans, 1 teaspoon of homemade bouillon, 1 teaspoon of homemade tomato purée and a pinch of fresh parsley to each pouch.

Seal:

Step 6: Place each assembled pouch into a freezer-safe bag. Remove as much air as possible before sealing.

Storage:

Step 7: Label the bags with the date and contents. Store in the freezer for up to 6 months.

COOKING TIP:

- Blanching vegetables before freezing helps preserve their colour, texture, and nutritional value.

CREATIVE TIP:

- Customize your soup by experimenting with additional herbs and spices or adding other vegetables you enjoy.

• Recipe on the next page

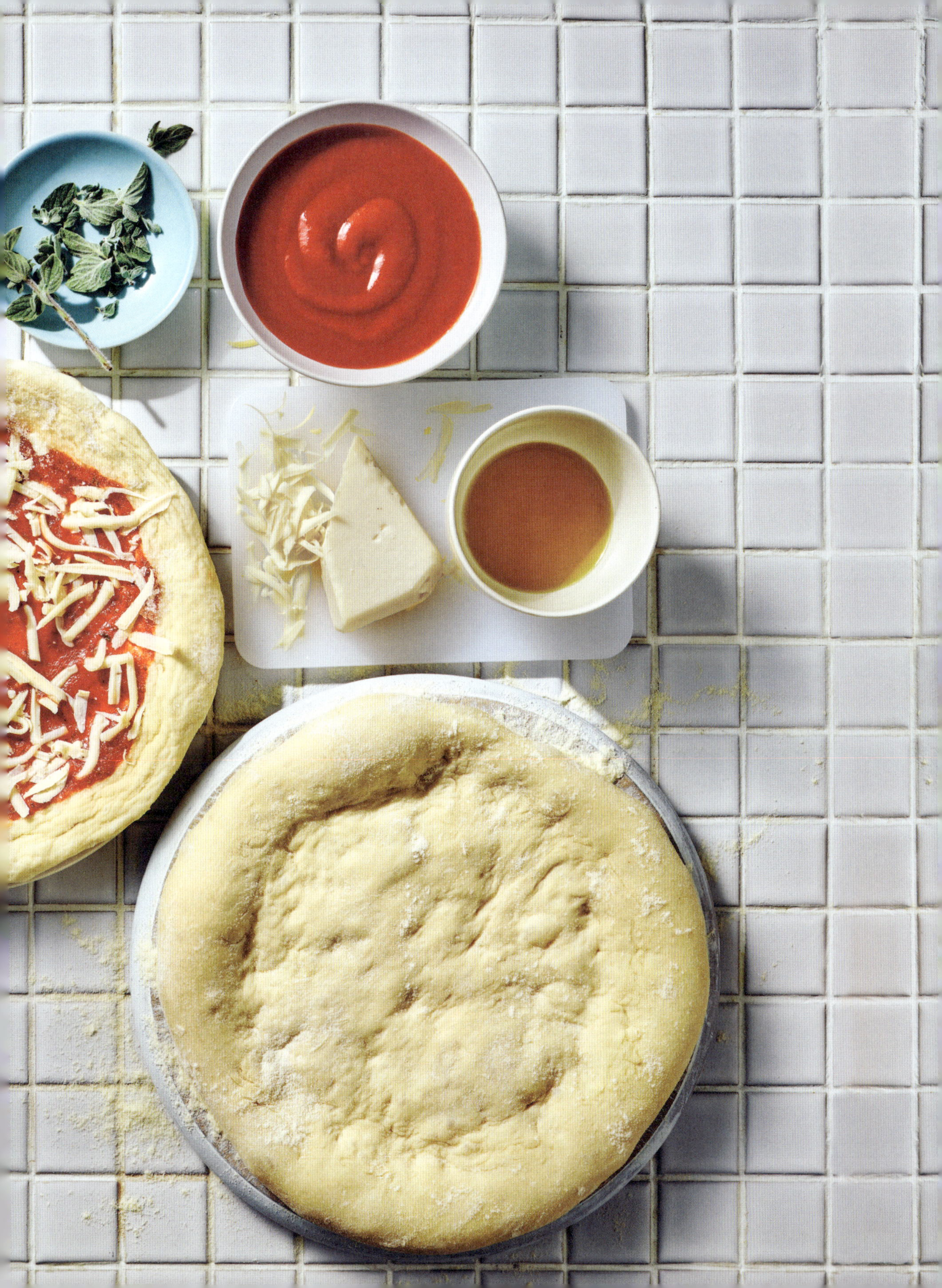

ANYTIME PIZZA

Imagine the aroma of freshly baked pizza wafting through your kitchen, any time you desire, without the wait.

This recipe transforms the dream of quick, artisanal pizza into a reality. With just 30 minutes of active preparation, you can stock your freezer with personalized pizzas that rival any pizzeria.

MAKES: 4 PORTIONS

INGREDIENTS

For the dough:
- 400g/14oz/1 ⅔ cups water, room temperature
- 1 tsp sugar
- 14g/½oz fresh yeast
- 640g/22½oz/5 ⅓ cups Manitoba flour (or a strong flour if unavailable)
- 2½ tsp fine sea salt
- 2 tbsp extra virgin olive oil, plus extra for greasing
- Semolina flour, for stretching

For the sauce:
- 400g/14oz high-quality tomato pulp
- Generous pinch of sea salt
- Fresh oregano, to taste

For toppings:
- Fresh mozzarella (see page 160)
- Any additional toppings you love

Activate the Yeast:

Step 1: Warm the water to about 43°C/110°F– the perfect temperature to wake up your yeast without giving it a thermal shock.

Step 2: Stir in the sugar until it dissolves.

Step 3: Sprinkle the fresh yeast into the water, stir gently and set aside for 5–10 minutes until frothy.

Mix the Dough:

Step 4: In a large mixing bowl, whisk together the Manitoba flour and fine sea salt.

Step 5: Add the activated yeast mixture and olive oil. Mix until a shaggy dough forms, then bring it together with your hands.

Knead the Dough:

Step 6: Sprinkle semolina flour on your surface and knead the dough for about 10 minutes until smooth. Test by stretching a small piece; if it doesn't tear, it's ready.

First Rise:

Step 7: Lightly oil a bowl, place the dough inside, and cover with a damp cloth. Let it rise in a warm, draft-free place for 1 hour or until it doubles in size.

Portion and Second Rise:

Step 8: Punch down the dough and divide it into 4 equal portions. Roll into balls, place on a tray, cover with cling film, and let rise for another hour until puffed.

Prepare the Sauce:

Step 9: Blend the tomato pulp with sea salt and fresh oregano. Adjust to taste. A pinch of sugar can balance acidity. If you like it rustic, a few pulses will do; for a silkier sauce, let the blender run a bit longer.

Assemble the Pizzas for Freezing:
Step 10: Roll out each dough ball on a lightly-floured surface. Place each base on a parchment-lined baking sheet or pizza tray.

Step 11: Top with tomato sauce, fresh mozzarella and desired toppings.

Freeze:
Step 12: Freeze pizzas uncovered on trays for 2–3 hours until solid.

Storage:
• Once frozen, wrap each pizza tightly in cling film or transfer to vacuum-sealable bags for up to 3 months.
• Ensure pizzas are fully frozen before vacuum packing to avoid damaging toppings or compressing the crust.

Cook:
• To bake, place the frozen pizza directly in a conventional oven preheated to maximum power (8–9 minutes).
• If using a pizza stone, reduce cooking time to 4–5 minutes. For an electric pizza oven, bake for 3 minutes.

COOKING TIP:

• **Pre-bake the Crust:** Pre-bake your pizza dough for 5–6 minutes before adding toppings. This prevents sogginess and ensures a crispy crust, especially for frozen pizzas.

5 MINUTE FRIES

Quick to cook and easy to enjoy, this pasta is the perfect no-fuss solution when Enjoy crispy, delicious fries in just 5 minutes!
 By preparing and freezing your own fries, applying this simple technique you can have a quick and tasty snack or side dish ready whenever you want.

INGREDIENTS

- 2kg/70½oz potatoes
- Water, as needed for blanching and refreshing
- Oil, as needed for frying or baking
- Salt and pepper, to taste

COOKING TIP:

- Cut the potato sticks evenly to ensure uniform cooking.

CREATIVE TIP:

- Experiment with seasonings such as garlic powder, paprika or rosemary for unique flavour twists.

Preparation:

Step 1: Peel and cut the potatoes into sticks.

Step 2: Blanch the potato sticks in boiling water for 3 minutes.

Step 3: Cool the blanched potatoes in cold water, then dry them thoroughly on a cloth.

Freeze and Store:

Step 4: Place the dried potato sticks in a food bag, preferably vacuum-sealed, and freeze. Use within 3 months.

Cooking:

Step 5: Fry the frozen potatoes in plenty of oil for 5 minutes. Alternatively, place the frozen potato sticks on a baking sheet, drizzle with a little oil, and bake in the oven at 200°C/392°F/Gas 6.

Serve:

Step 6: Season with salt and pepper, and enjoy.

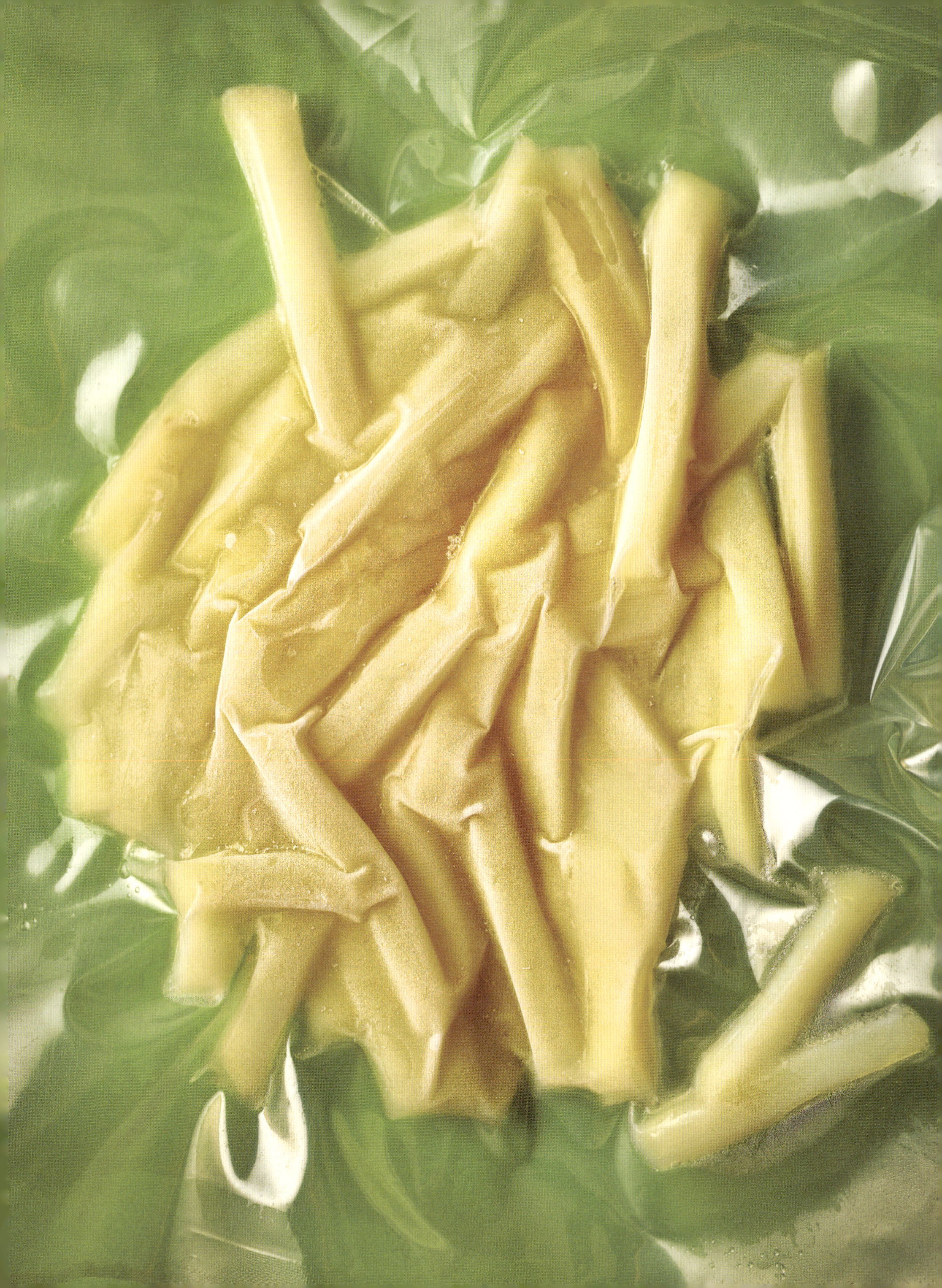

THE MANGUM

This homemade "Mangum" is a delightful twist on the classic ice cream, combining the creaminess of cashew cream with the tropical sweetness of mango purée, all encased in a crisp chocolate shell. A mini vacation on a stick!

INGREDIENTS

- 200g/7oz cashews (soaked for 4 hours or overnight to soften)
- 125g/4½oz/½ cup homemade cream (blend soaked cashews with water until thick and creamy; add a pinch of salt and a dash of vanilla extract for a gourmet touch)
- 1 tbsp maple syrup
- 2 tbsp coconut oil or butter
- 2 or 3 ripe mangos
- 200g/7oz 54% dark chocolate

MINDFUL BENEFITS:

- Cashews provide healthy fats and magnesium and mangos are packed with vitamins A and C, essential for immune and skin health, while dark chocolate contains antioxidants and promotes mental clarity.

Prepare the Cashew Cream:
Step 1: Drain the soaked cashews and blend with the homemade cream, maple syrup, and coconut oil or butter until smooth and creamy.

Make the Mango Purée:
Step 2: Peel and purée the mangos until smooth.

Assemble the Ice Cream:
Step 3: In your moulds, layer the creamy cashew mixture first, followed by the mango purée. Freeze until firm.

Prepare the Chocolate Coating:
Step 4: Melt the dark chocolate using a double boiler or in the microwave, being careful not to burn it.

Coat the Ice Creams:
Step 6: Dip or drizzle the frozen Mangums with melted chocolate, allowing them to harden. For an extra touch, sprinkle with nuts, coconut flakes or sea salt before the chocolate sets.

CREATIVE TIP:

• Experiment with other fruit purées, such as strawberries or passionfruit, for different flavour profiles – you're allowed to change the name then!

NO-CHURN ICE CREAMS

Creating your own no-churn ice creams at home is simple and very cost-effective.

These recipes are perfect for hot summer days or whenever you're craving a quick and delicious dessert.

With no need for an ice cream maker, these recipes are easy to prepare and can be customized with your favourite flavours and toppings.

Enjoy these no-churn ice creams as a refreshing dessert. They pair beautifully with fresh fruit, nuts or your favorite toppings.

If there's any leftover ice cream (unlikely!) that has crystalized, you can then blitz it again for a softer texture.

AVO AND MATCHA ICE CREAM

This creamy, refreshing ice cream combines the richness of avocado with the earthy notes of matcha for a satisfying and nutritious dessert.

INGREDIENTS

- 2 ripe avocados
- 1 can (400ml/13½fl oz) full-fat coconut milk
- 120ml/4fl oz/½ cup maple syrup or agave nectar
- 2 tbsp matcha powder
- 1 tsp vanilla extract

Blend:
Step 1: In a blender or food processor, combine the avocados, coconut milk, maple syrup, matcha powder and vanilla extract. Blend until smooth and creamy.

Freeze:
Step 2: Pour the mixture into a loaf pan or container. Cover with cling film/plastic wrap or a lid and freeze for at least 4 hours or until firm.

Serve:
Step 3: Scoop and serve. For extra flavour, sprinkle with matcha powder.

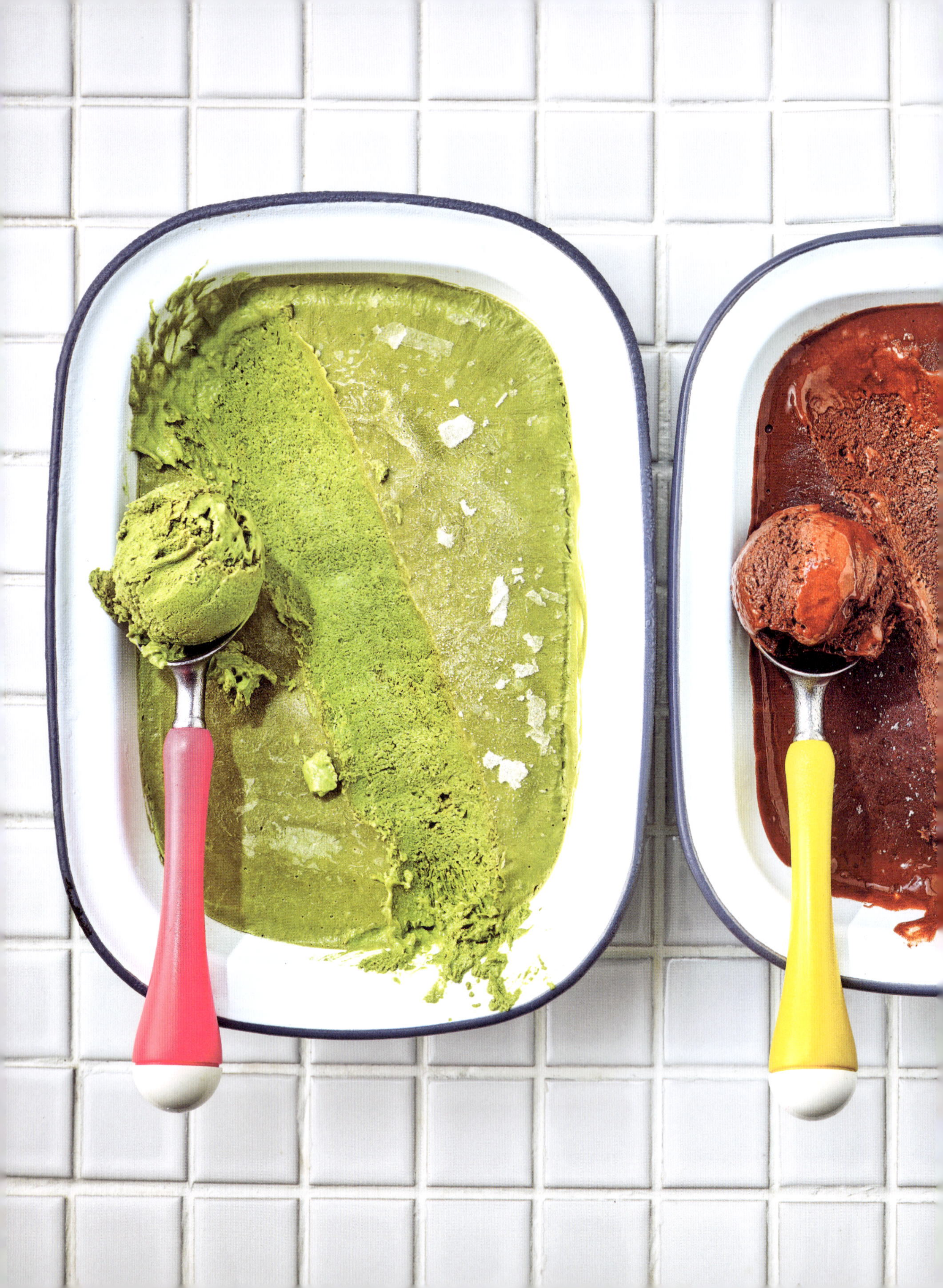

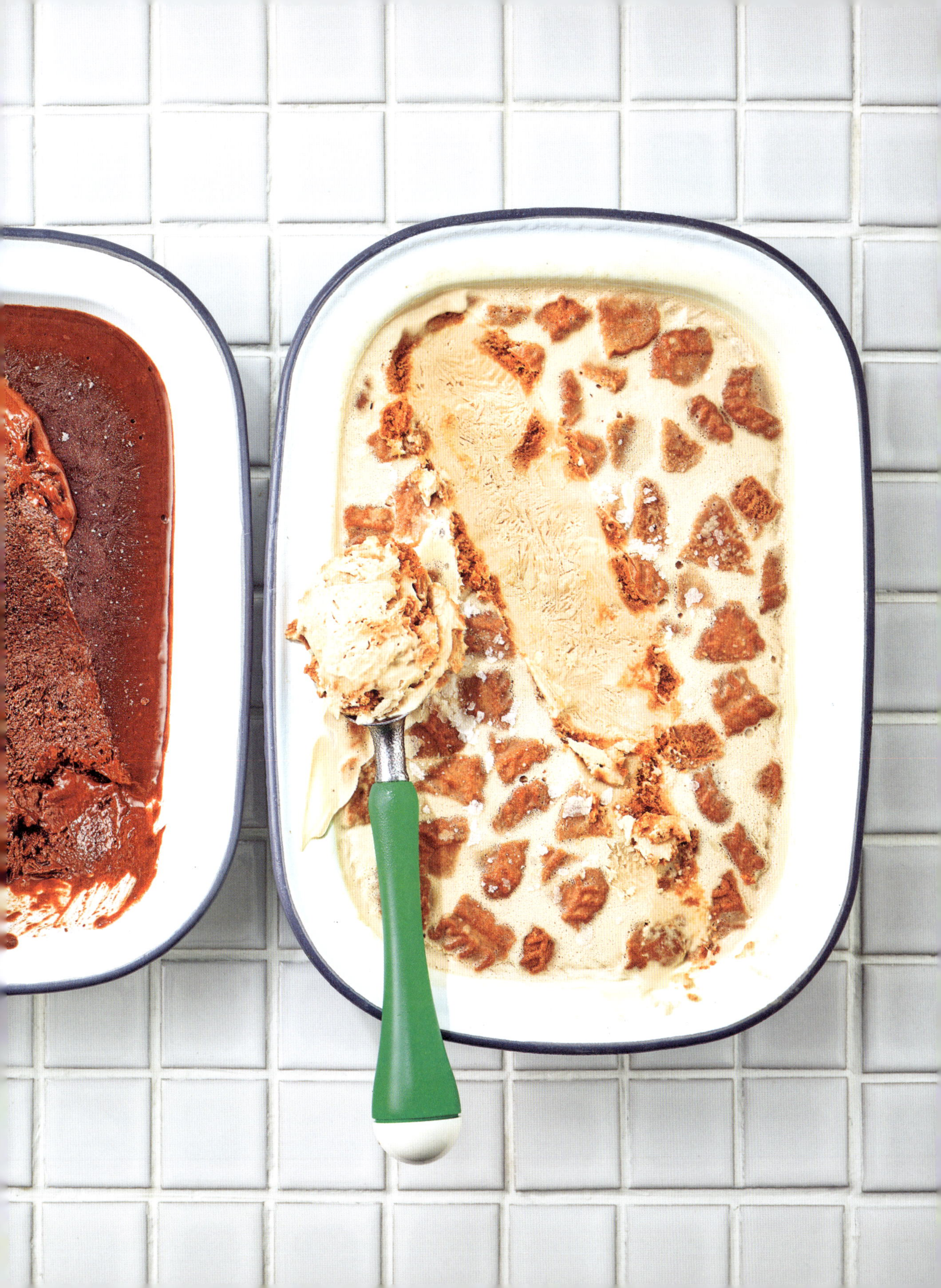

BANANA AND CACAO ICE CREAM

Rich, chocolatey and naturally sweet, this ice cream pairs beautifully with a drizzle of syrup or cacao nibs for added texture.

INGREDIENTS

- 4 ripe bananas or plantains
- 50g/1¾oz/½ cup cacao powder
- 60ml/2fl oz/¼ cup almond milk or any plant-based milk
- 88ml/3fl oz/¼ cup honey or maple syrup
- 1 tsp vanilla extract

Slice and Freeze:
Step 1: Slice the bananas or plantains and freeze for at least 2 hours or until solid.

Blend:
Step 2: Combine the frozen banana slices, cacao powder, almond milk, honey or maple syrup, and vanilla extract in a blender. Blend until smooth and creamy.

Freeze:
Step 3: Pour the mixture into a loaf pan or container. Cover and freeze for 1 hour for a firmer texture.

Serve:
Step 4: Scoop and enjoy with a drizzle of chocolate syrup or a sprinkle of cacao nibs.

COCONUT AND BISCOFF ICE CREAM

Decadent and creamy, this ice cream combines the richness of coconut milk with the sweet, spiced flavour of Biscoff for an indulgent dessert.

INGREDIENTS

- 2 cans (400ml/13½fl oz each) full-fat coconut milk
- 160g/5½oz/½ cup Biscoff spread
- 60ml/2fl oz/¼ cup maple syrup or agave nectar
- 1 tsp vanilla extract
- 55g/2oz/½ cup crushed Biscoff cookies

MINDFUL BENEFITS:

- These dairy-free ice creams are free from artificial additives and preservatives and are low in refined sugars. They provide healthy fats from avocados and coconut milk, antioxidants from matcha and cacao, and natural sweetness from the fruit.

Whisk:
Step 1: In a large bowl, whisk together the coconut milk, Biscoff spread, maple syrup and vanilla extract until well combined.

Fold in the Cookies:
Step 2: Gently fold in the crushed Biscoff cookies.

Freeze:
Step 3: Pour the mixture into a loaf pan or container. Cover and freeze for at least 2 hours or until firm.

Serve:
Step 4: Scoop and enjoy, garnished with extra crushed Biscoff cookies if desired.

CREATIVE TIP:

- Experiment with different flavours and textures, like a pinch of cinnamon, a swirl of nut butter or a handful of chocolate chips.

- Serve your ice cream in decorative bowls or cones, garnished with fresh fruit or a drizzle of syrup, for a visually appealing treat.

6 THE HOMEGROWN HAVEN:

"To plant a garden is to believe in tomorrow."
Audrey Hepburn

In an age where convenience often overshadows sustainability, the simple act of growing your own food can be a revolutionary statement of self-sufficiency and environmental consciousness.

Whether you have a sprawling garden or a cosy balcony, cultivating your own plants is a rewarding journey that reconnects you with nature and grounds you in the present moment.

You don't need acres of land to start your own garden.

With a bit of creativity, even the smallest balcony can become a thriving oasis of herbs, vegetables and flowers.

Urban gardening is not just about the food it yields; it's a testament to resilience and adaptability.

Every pot of herbs or box of tomatoes is a step toward food sovereignty, giving you control over what you eat and reducing your reliance on industrial agriculture.

The benefits are as abundant as the harvest: the freshness of sun-ripened produce, the satisfaction of reducing your carbon footprint and the cost savings that come with propagating and saving seeds.

Beyond this, gardening is a living classroom, offering invaluable lessons about plant cycles, biodiversity and ecosystems

Food sovereignty is about reclaiming the right to healthy, culturally appropriate food grown through sustainable methods. When you grow your own food, you decide what enters your soil, your plants and ultimately your body.

It's an act of autonomy, ensuring you and your loved ones have access to nutrient-dense, chemical-free produce.

In an era dominated by agribusiness, cultivating even a modest garden is a statement of independence and care for the environment.

In our fast-paced, hyperconnected world, tending to a garden provides a rare and restorative contact with nature. The physical activity of planting, watering and harvesting nourishes the body, while the sensory immersion in textures, scents and sounds calms the mind.

Gardening reduces stress, enhances mood and sharpens cognitive function, offering a vital grounding experience in an otherwise chaotic world.

Perhaps the most profound lesson of gardening lies in its imperfection.

Plants may fail, pests may come and weather may thwart plans, but these are opportunities for growth and adaptation.

Nature's resilience teaches us to embrace imperfection, to be patient and to find beauty in diversity and unpredictability. Like cooking and everything we have explored up to now, gardening is not about perfection; it's about participation, a partnership with the earth that fosters understanding, humility and gratitude.

CHIVE OIL

Chive oil can elevate any dish with its vibrant green colour and delicate flavour. It's a simple way to add an extra layer of elegance to soups, salads and sauces, while also making the most of fresh chives from your garden or local market.

INGREDIENTS

- 500ml/17fl oz/2 cups neutral oil (such as grapeseed or light olive oil)
- 1 bunch fresh chives

Prepare and Blend:

Step 1: Wash the chives thoroughly to remove any dirt or debris. Pat them dry with a clean kitchen towel.

Step 2: In a blender, combine the chives and neutral oil. Blend until the mixture is smooth and vibrantly green. Avoid over-blending to prevent overheating, which can dull the colour and flavour.

Chill and Separate:

Step 3: Immediately chill the blended mixture to preserve its bright green hue. You can achieve this by blending with a few ice cubes or placing the mixture in the refrigerator.

Step 4: Let the mixture sit undisturbed in a cool place to allow the water content to separate naturally from the oil. Decant the oil from the top or use a vacuum pack bag for precise separation.

Strain:
Step 5: Strain the oil through a fine-mesh sieve, muslin cloth or coffee filter to remove any solid particles, leaving a pure, clear oil.

Storage:
Step 6: Store the chive oil in an airtight glass container. Keep it at room temperature for up to 2 weeks or refrigerate for up to 1 month. Allow it to return to room temperature before using, as the oil may solidify when chilled.

PRO TIP:

- Achieving perfection in herb oils lies in the balance of technique and timing. Swift chilling post-blending preserves the freshness and colour, while patient separation ensures a clean, potent oil. This method can be applied to various herbs, opening a palette of flavours for your culinary experiments.

CULINARY APPLICATIONS AND COMPANION PLANTING:

- Using every part of the chive plant reflects the principles of zero-waste cooking. The flowers can be infused into vinegar, the stalks into oils, and the seeds into dishes like tahini, creating unique flavour profiles. In gardening, chives are excellent companion plants, particularly for apple trees, as they deter pests and promote healthier growth.

TO GROW YOUR OWN CHIVES:

- Select a sunny or partially shaded spot in your garden or a windowsill with good light; chives thrive in at least 4-6 hours of sunlight daily.
- Plant chive seeds in well-draining soil, keeping the surface moist until germination, which typically takes 7-14 days.
- Once the plants establish, trim them regularly by cutting from the base to encourage new, tender growth.
- Chives can be harvested continuously, but avoid cutting more than one-third of the plant at a time to keep it healthy and productive. Remember you can use the flowers too!

BASIL PESTO

Making this basil pesto will bring the vibrant flavours of Italian cuisine to your kitchen, offering a creamy, vegan-friendly version that's used as a pasta sauce, sandwich spread or dip. It pairs wonderfully with fresh bread, roasted vegetables or as a pizza topping.

INGREDIENTS

- 80g/2¾oz/½ cup pine nuts
- 4 tbsp nutritional yeast
- 1 clove garlic, peeled
- 80g/2¾oz/1 cup vegan parmesan (see page 158)
- 120g/4¼oz fresh basil leaves
- 50ml/1¾oz/¼ cup extra virgin olive oil

GARDENING TIP:

- The oils in freshly picked basil leaves are at their peak, giving you the most flavour-packed pesto.

- Basil benefits from regular harvesting. Pinch off the tips of the branches to encourage bushier growth and prevent the plant from flowering, as flowering can diminish flavour.

Toast the Pine Nuts:
Step 1: Toast the pine nuts in a dry skillet over medium heat, stirring often, until golden brown. Remove from heat to cool.

Blend the Base:
Step 2: In a food processor, combine the toasted pine nuts, nutritional yeast and garlic. Pulse until coarsely ground.

Step 3: Add the vegan parmesan and pulse again to incorporate.

Add Basil and Olive Oil:
Step 4: Add fresh basil leaves to the processor. Blend on a low speed while slowly drizzling in the olive oil until the mixture reaches your desired consistency.

Taste and Adjust:
Step 5: Taste and adjust seasoning with salt or a squeeze of lemon juice for brightness.

Storage:
- Sealed jars can be stored in a pantry for up to 12 months. Once opened, refrigerate and consume within 3–4 weeks.
- For longer storage, freeze in airtight containers for up to 6 months.

TO GROW YOUR OWN BASIL:

- Choose a sunny spot in your garden or a south-facing windowsill for your basil plants; they love warmth and light.
- Plant the seeds in well-draining soil and water them gently to keep the soil moist but not soggy.
- As the seedlings grow, thin them out to prevent overcrowding.
- Remember, basil is sensitive to cold, so if temperatures start to drop, protect your plants or move them indoors.

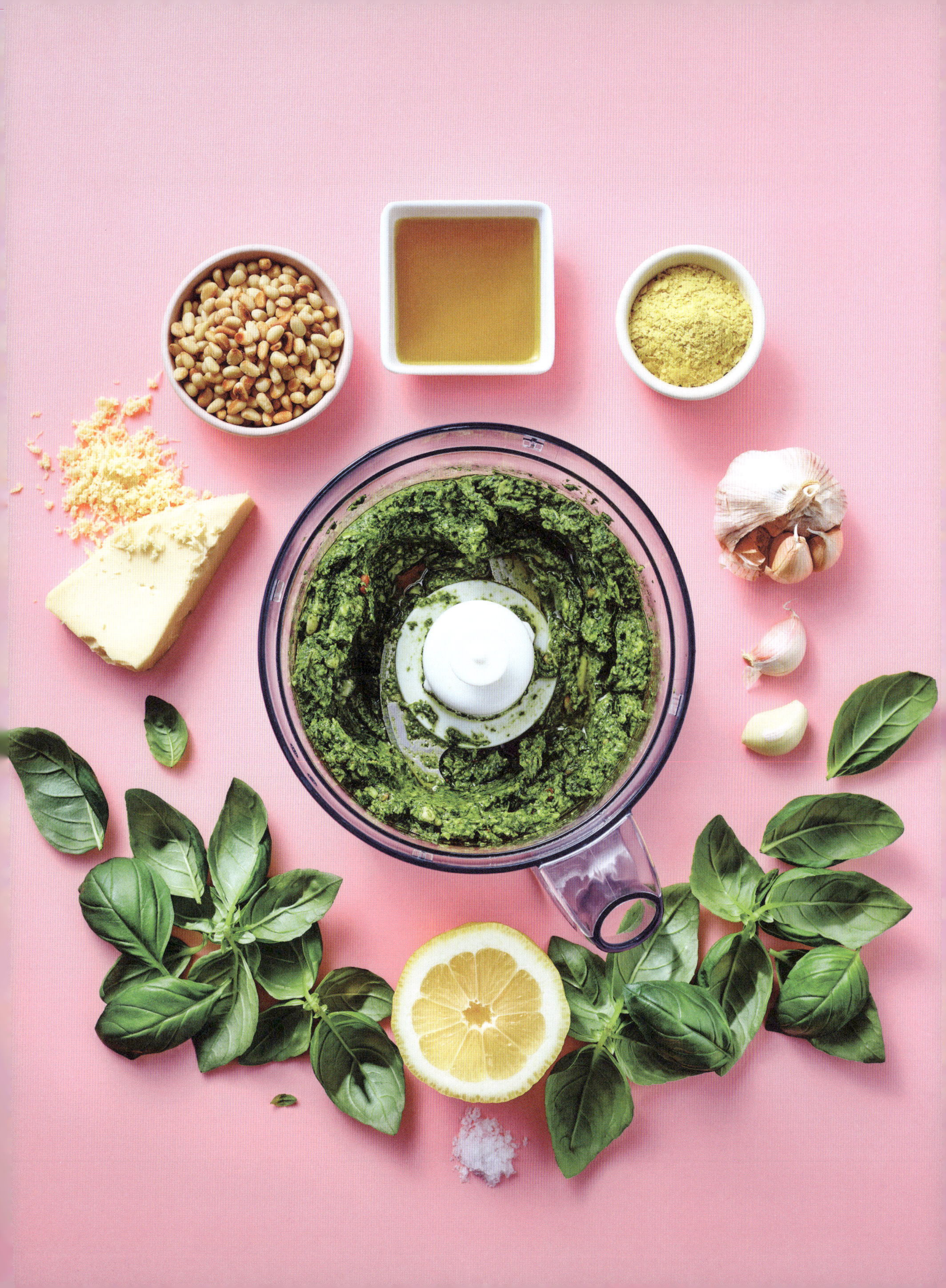

NASTURTIUM JELLY

Nasturtium jelly is a unique and vibrant spread that captures the essence of edible flowers. It's a versatile addition to breakfast, desserts or savoury dishes.

INGREDIENTS

- 40g/1½oz/1½ cups nasturtium flowers
- 700ml/24fl oz/3 cups water
- 120g/4oz/½ cup granulated sugar
- 85g/3oz/1/3 cup homemade pectin (see page 140)

CULINARY APPLICATIONS AND COMPANION PLANTING:

- Nasturtium flowers bring vibrant colour and peppery flavour to the table. Their leaves and seeds can also be used in salads, while the jelly serves as a topping for toast, a glaze for tempeh and tofu or an ingredient in desserts.

- In the garden, nasturtiums deter pests and attract pollinators, making them a valuable addition to any garden ecosystem.

Infuse the Flowers:
Step 1: Soak the nasturtium flowers in warm water overnight to extract their flavour and colour.

Prepare the Jelly:
Step 2: Strain the infusion and dissolve the sugar into the liquid.

Step 3: Add the homemade pectin and bring the mixture to a gentle boil, ensuring it doesn't overheat to maintain the pectin's effectiveness.

Jar and Cool:
Step 4: Pour the hot jelly into sterilized jars, leaving some headspace. Seal and allow to cool completely.

Storage:
- Sealed jars can be stored in a pantry for up to 12 months. Once opened, refrigerate and consume within 3–4 weeks.
- For longer storage, freeze in airtight containers for up to 6 months.

GARDENING TIPS FOR GROWING NASTURTIUMS:

- **PLANTING:** Directly sow seeds in well-drained soil. They can also be started indoors a few weeks before the last frost and transplanted outside.
- **SPACING:** Space seeds about 25–30cm/10–12 inches apart to allow for growth and airflow.
- **MAINTENANCE:** Nasturtiums require minimal maintenance. Deadhead spent flowers to encourage more blooms.
- **HARVESTING:** Harvest flowers and seeds regularly to keep the plants productive. Use the flowers in salads, and pickle the seeds for capers.

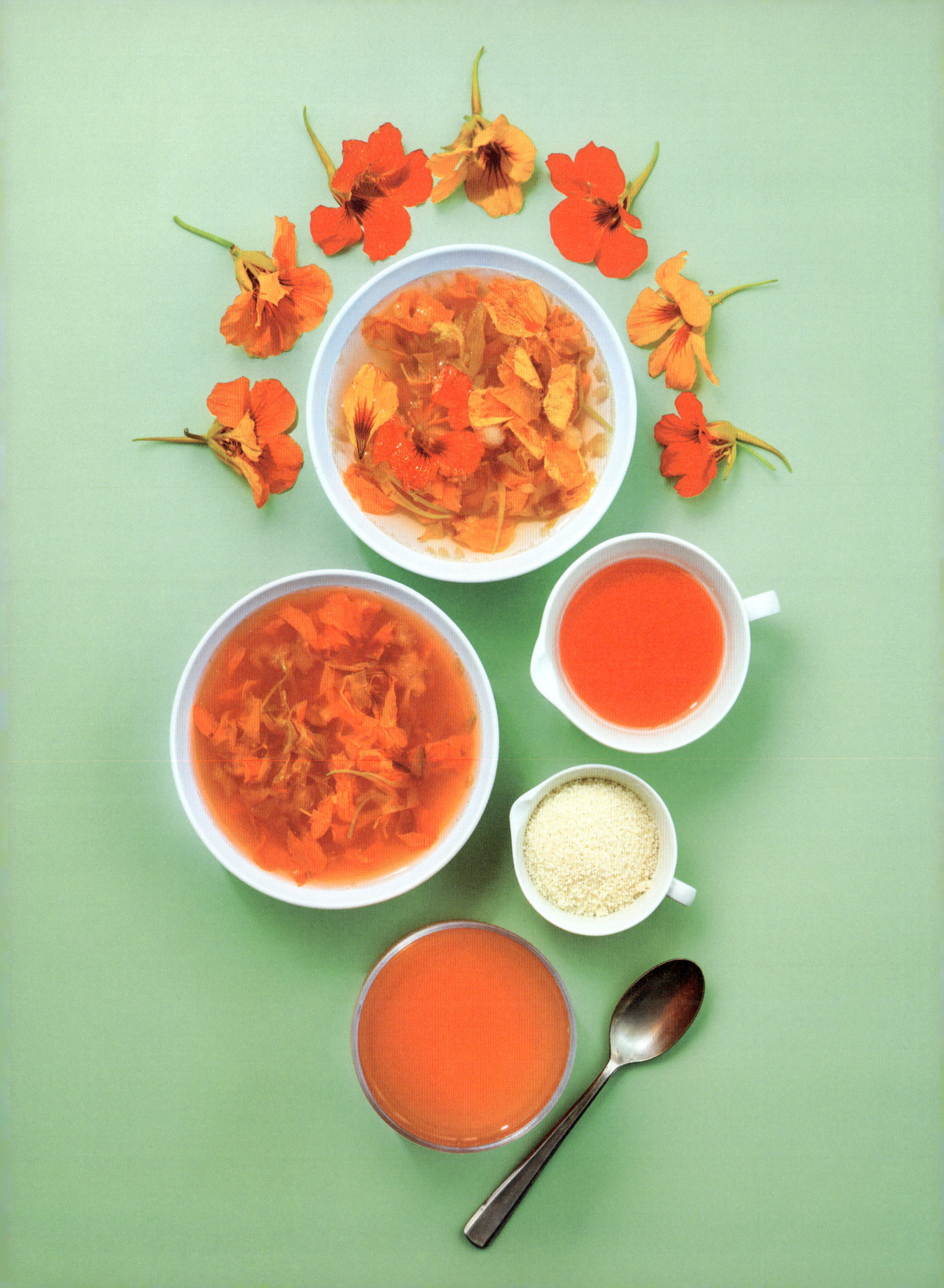

NASTURTIUM CAPERS

Nasturtium seeds are a delightful secret, offering a natural, peppery kick that elevates gourmet dishes. Pickled nasturtium capers are a versatile addition to your kitchen, perfect for garnishing salads, enriching sauces or adding a burst of flavour to spreads.

INGREDIENTS

- 200–250g/7–8¾oz fresh nasturtium seeds
- 1 tbsp salt (for brine)
- 500ml/17fl oz/2 cups water (for brine and pickling)
- Pickling solution (homemade apple cider vinegar (see page 122), water, star anise)

COOKING TIP:

- Experiment with the pickling solution – try adding dill, garlic or chilli for a customized flavour. Adjust the brining time if you prefer a milder or stronger caper.

CREATIVE TIP:

- Use nasturtium capers as an unexpected replacement for traditional capers in recipes like pasta puttanesca or tapenade.

Harvest:
Step 1: Collect green, plump nasturtium seeds directly from the plant, ensuring they are firm and fresh.

Prepare the Brine:
Step 2: Dissolve 1 tablespoon of salt into 500ml/17fl oz/2 cups of water to create a brine.

Brine the Seeds:
Step 3: Submerge the nasturtium seeds in the brine solution and let them soak overnight to reduce bitterness and prepare them for pickling.

Drain and Rinse:
Step 4: The next day, drain the seeds and rinse them thoroughly under cold water to remove any excess salt.

Pickling Process:
Step 5: Pack the rinsed seeds into a sterilized glass jar.

Step 6: Cover the seeds with your pickling solution, which may include homemade apple cider vinegar, water and a star anise pod for an aromatic touch.

Step 7: Seal the jar tightly and let it sit at room temperature for at least 3 days for the flavours to infuse. For a more robust flavour, allow the capers to pickle for 2 weeks.

Storage:
- Properly sealed, the capers can be stored in the refrigerator for up to 6 months.

CHARD AND FENNEL KIMCHI

This vegan kimchi gives a creative twist to the traditional Korean dish, utilizing Swiss chard and fennel to deliver a distinctive flavour profile.

Packed with probiotics and loaded with tangy, spicy goodness, it's an excellent way to boost your intake of greens while enjoying the benefits of fermentation.

Use this kimchi as a side dish, topping for rice or noodles or even as an ingredient in wraps and sandwiches for added zest.

INGREDIENTS

- 1 large bunch of Swiss chard, chopped
- 1 bulb fennel, thinly sliced
- 72g/2½oz/¼ cup sea salt
- 946ml/32fl oz/4 cups water
- 120ml/4fl oz/½ cup vegan fish sauce (see page 102)
- 4 tbsp Korean red pepper flakes (Gochugaru)
- 1 small carrot, julienned
- 4–5 spring onions/scallions, chopped
- 5 cloves garlic, minced
- 1 thumb-sized piece of ginger, grated
- 1 tbsp sugar

Prepare the Vegetables:
Step 1: Rinse the Swiss chard and fennel thoroughly. Chop the chard into bite-sized pieces and thinly slice the fennel.

Brine the Vegetables:
Step 2: Dissolve the sea salt in the water to create a brine. Soak the chopped chard and sliced fennel in the brine for 1–2 hours to soften the vegetables and draw out excess moisture.

Rinse and Drain:
Step 3: After soaking, drain the vegetables and rinse them thoroughly to remove excess salt. Squeeze out any remaining water and set aside.

Mix the Seasoning Paste:
Step 4: In a large bowl, combine vegan fish sauce, Korean red pepper flakes, julienned carrot, chopped spring onions/scallions, minced garlic, grated ginger and sugar. Mix well to create a thick paste.

Coat the Vegetables:
Step 5: Add the drained chard and fennel to the seasoning paste. Use gloved hands to massage the paste into the vegetables until fully coated.

Pack and Ferment:
Step 6: Pack the kimchi mixture tightly into a sterilized jar, pressing down to remove air bubbles and ensure the vegetables are submerged in their own juices. Leave some headspace for expansion.

Recipe continued on the next page ...

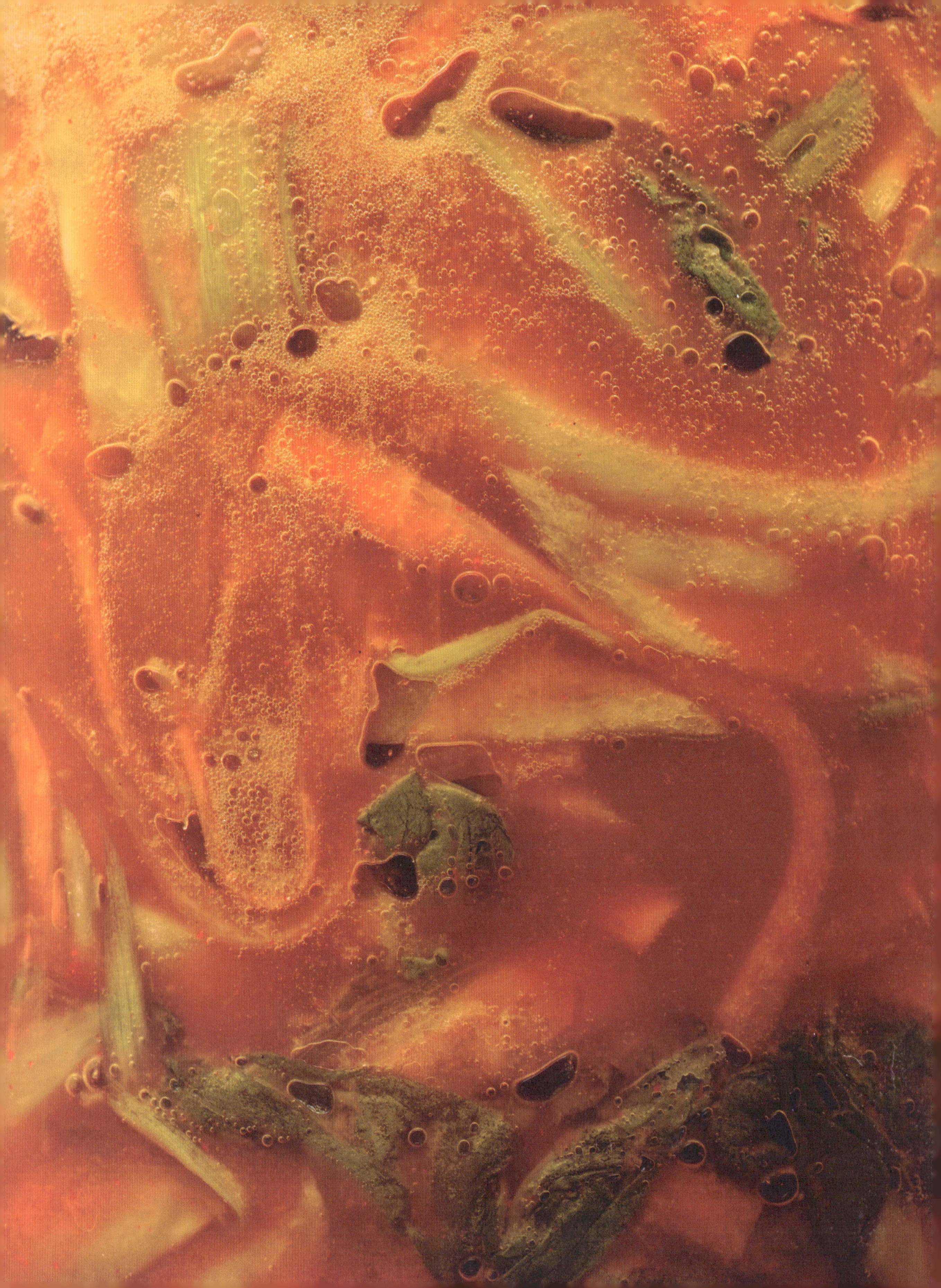

COOKING TIP:

• Adjust the spice level by modifying the amount of Korean red pepper flakes to suit your taste.

CREATIVE TIP:

• Add vegetables like daikon radish, cucumber or napa cabbage for additional textures and flavours.

Step 7: Cover loosely and ferment at room temperature for 2–5 days. Check daily to press down the vegetables and release any gas build-up.

Storage:
Step 8: Once fermented to your liking, seal the jar tightly and store in the refrigerator. Enjoy over several weeks as the flavour develops.

GARDENING TIPS FOR SWISS CHARD AND FENNEL:

CHARD:
• **PLANTING:** Sow seeds directly in well-drained soil. Chard can tolerate some shade but thrives in full sun.
• **SPACING:** Space seeds about 30–45cm/12–18 inches apart to allow room for growth.
• **MAINTENANCE:** Water regularly and harvest outer leaves to encourage continuous growth.
• **HARVESTING:** Harvest leaves when they are young and tender, but before they become too large and tough.

FENNEL:
• **PLANTING:** Directly sow seeds in well-drained soil in a sunny spot. Fennel prefers cool weather, so plant in early spring or late summer.
• **SPACING:** Space seeds about 30–45cm/12–18 inches apart.
• **MAINTENANCE:** Keep soil moist and weed-free. Fennel does not transplant well, so sow seeds where they are to grow.
• **HARVESTING:** Harvest fennel bulbs when they are about the size of a tennis ball. Use the fronds as an herb in salads and dishes.

CRISPY CHILLI OIL

This crispy chilli oil combines spicy, smoky and savoury notes to elevate any dish. Whether drizzled over noodles, stirred into soups or paired with dumplings and spring rolls, this homemade version ensures a fresh, preservative-free condiment for all your meals.

INGREDIENTS

- 250ml/9fl oz/1 cup vegetable oil (or another neutral oil)
- 22g/¾oz/½ cup dried red chillies, crushed
- 2 cloves garlic, minced
- 1 small shallot, finely chopped
- 1 tsp salt
- 1 tsp sugar
- 1 tbsp soy sauce
- 1 tbsp rice vinegar
- 1 tsp Sichuan peppercorns (optional)
- 1 tbsp sesame seeds (optional)

MINDFUL BENEFITS:

- Chillies are high in vitamins A and C, supporting immunity and reducing inflammation. Capsaicin, the active compound in chillies, also enhance mood by releasing endorphins.

Prepare the Ingredients:
Step 1: Crush the dried red chillies into small flakes. Mince the garlic and finely chop the shallot.

Fry the Aromatics:
Step 2: Heat the vegetable oil in a saucepan to 180°C/350°F. Add the minced garlic, shallot and Sichuan peppercorns, if using. Fry until golden and crispy, then remove from heat.

Combine the Flavors:
Step 3: In a heatproof bowl, mix the crushed chillies, salt, sugar, soy sauce and rice vinegar. Carefully pour the hot oil over the chilli mixture and then add the fried aromatics.

Cool and Store:
Step 4: Let the mixture cool to room temperature before stirring in sesame seeds (optional). Transfer to a sterilized jar and store in the refrigerator for up to 1 month.

COOKING TIP:

- Monitor the oil temperature closely to avoid burning the aromatics, which can result in bitterness.

CREATIVE TIP:

- Add additional aromatics such as cinnamon, star anise or dried mushrooms for a personalized flavour profile.

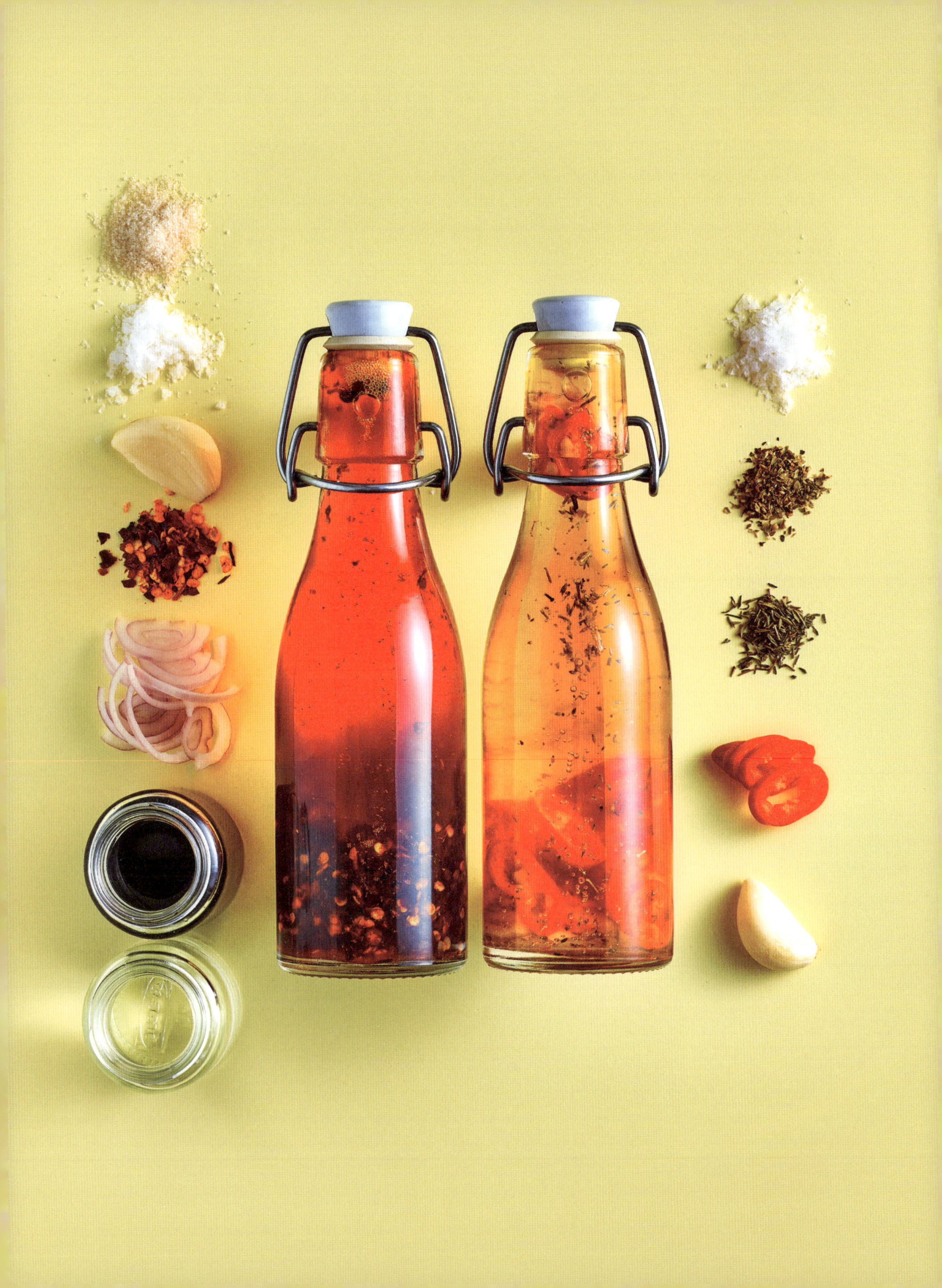

GARLIC CHILLI-INFUSED OIL

Garlic Chilli Infused Oil combines the bold flavours of garlic and chilli in a versatile condiment that enhances any dish.

This oil is perfect for sautéing vegetables, marinating proteins, drizzling over pasta, salads and pizzas, or adding a spicy kick to any of your favourite recipes.

INGREDIENTS

- 250ml/9fl oz/1 cup olive oil (or other neutral oil)
- 5 cloves garlic, sliced
- 2–3 fresh red chillies, sliced
- 1 tsp salt
- 1 tsp dried oregano (optional)
- 1 tsp dried thyme (optional)

Prepare the Ingredients:
Step 1: Slice the garlic cloves and fresh red chillies.

Infuse:
Step 2: In a small saucepan, heat the olive oil over medium-low heat.

Step 3: Add the sliced garlic and chillies to the warm oil. Gently heat for about 10–15 minutes, ensuring the garlic does not burn while the flavours infuse. Remove from the heat.

Add Seasoning:
Step 4: Stir in the salt and optional dried herbs. Allow the oil to cool to room temperature, letting the flavours deepen.

Strain:
Step 5: Strain the oil into a sterilized jar to remove the garlic and chilli slices, or leave them in for a bolder taste and rustic appearance.

Storage:
Store in the refrigerator for up to 1 month.

GARDENING TIPS

FOR GROWING CHILLIES
Choosing the Right Variety: Select a chilli variety suited to your growing conditions. Mild chillies like Anaheim or spicy varieties like Habanero or Thai chillies thrive in warm climates, while smaller varieties can grow well in containers indoors.

- STARTING INDOORS: Plant chilli seeds 6–8 weeks before the last frost date. Keep the soil moist and warm (21–29°C/70–85°F).
- TRANSPLANTING: Once seedlings have true leaves and temperatures are consistently above 15°C/60°F, harden them off and plant outdoors in full sun.
- SOIL: Use well-draining, fertile soil with a pH of 6.0–7.0.
- WATERING: Keep the soil moist but not soggy. Mulch to retain moisture and suppress weeds.
- FERTILIZING: Feed monthly with a balanced fertilizer to support growth and fruit production.
- HARVESTING: Harvest chillies when they reach their mature color. Use scissors to avoid damaging the plant.

GROWING GARLIC:
- PLANTING TIME: Plant garlic cloves in autumn, 6 weeks before the ground freezes.
- SOIL PREPARATION: Enrich the soil with compost or manure. Ensure it drains well and has a pH of 6.0–7.0.
- PLANTING CLOVES: Place cloves root-side down, 5cm/2 inches deep and 10–15cm/4–6 inches apart. Cover with mulch.
- WATERING: Keep the soil moist in the growing season but reduce watering as bulbs mature.
- HARVESTING: When the leaves yellow, lift the bulbs carefully, cure them in a dry area, and store in a cool, dark place.

7 NOT THE END:
The Recipe for a Holistic Kitchen

Take a moment.

Before you move forward, close this book and step back into your world. Let's pause to reflect on the progress of your journey with me.

I told you it wasn't like any map; its purpose wasn't to dictate your every step but to guide your journey.

A framework, not a formula. A tool for you to navigate the beautiful, messy complexity of food, cooking, and life itself.

Throughout these pages, I like to think you've explored ideas, chapters and recipes that led you to something more.

From stocking a pantry to curating a library of possibility.

From growing a windowsill garden to forging a deeper connection with the earth.

From a chaotic fuelling station to a sanctuary of creativity and nourishment.

Most importantly you've found a way of cooking and living that prioritizes mindfulness, creativity and connection.

Think about where you started. Maybe it stemmed from curiosity. Maybe it was overwhelm.

Maybe you were searching for clarity in a kitchen that felt too much – or not enough. Wherever you began, you're here now. And that matters.

You've chosen to lean into something bigger. To explore what it means to create, care and connect – not just with the food on your plate but with yourself and the world around you.

Every choice you've made – from sourcing ingredients to preparing meals with intention – has been a step toward a more mindful, sustainable and ethical way of living.

This journey wasn't about following a perfect path but finding your own rhythm.

It's about progress – not the kind measured by checklists or timelines, but the kind found in small rituals: a moment of clarity in the kitchen, a meal that feels like care, a habit that becomes second nature.

And here's the truth: you're not done.

You'll never be done.

Because the kitchen, like life, is never static. It evolves. Seasons change, needs shift, and so will you.

The lessons in this book? They're not rules to follow but tools – meant to grow with you, just like the map itself.

So take this moment. Look at where you've been, what you've created and how you've grown. Not as an endpoint, but as a foundation. A beginning.

Your journey isn't just about food – it's about what food makes possible.

Clarity. Presence. Connection.

And above all, a life that feels aligned with your values, your dreams and your heart.

The map has guided you here. Now, it's yours to use – however, wherever and whenever you need it.

You've got this. Let's keep going.

CREATING A LASTING CONNECTION

Now it's clear – the kitchen isn't just a room.

It's where intention meets action, a space that reflects who you are and who you're becoming.

This is the connection that you forged. A bond between the ingredients on your counter and the values in your heart. Between your daily rhythms and the deeper meaning behind them.

Between the food you create and the life you want to live.

This connection isn't fleeting. It doesn't disappears when the book is closed or the dishes are done. It endures because it's built on something real: your choices, your creativity and your care.

Every time you step into your kitchen, you nurture that connection. Mindfulness becomes habit. Cooking becomes an act of alignment – your actions mirroring your values. And this connection extends beyond you.

The ripple effect of your actions reaches far beyond your walls.

A mindful kitchen inspires mindful living, and that energy touches everything it encounters.

Sharing a meal becomes an act of joy and care. Choosing local produce supports livelihoods and strengthens communities. Reducing waste contributes to a more balanced world.

That's what you are doing. You are contributing. To your own wellbeing. To your community. To a world that needs more connection, more care, and more creativity.

This is how good becomes a medium for something greater.

So let this be the start of something bigger. Let your kitchen be a canvas for your values, a reflection of the life you're creating. And as you move forward, remember: every meal is an opportunity to connect with yourself, with others and with the world.

This connection doesn't end here. It begins now.

LIVING WITH INTENTION BEYOND THE KITCHEN
Mindfulness in Everyday Life

It all begins with the simple act of paying attention and setting intentions. While attention anchors you in the present, intention provides direction.

Attention is noticing the vibrant aroma of spices as you toast them in a hot pan. Intention is cooking that meal to nourish both body and soul.

This distinction is powerful, especially for neurodivergent minds, where focus can feel fleeting, and chaos can derail progress.

Intention offers clarity – a guide to what truly matters amidst the noise.

The care you show while preparing a meal extends to how you nurture relationships.

The presence you cultivate in cooking translates into how you engage with your work or hobbies.

The creativity sparked in the kitchen fuels how you approach challenges and pursue passions.

The kitchen's rhythm – one of patience, experimentation and discovery – mirrors how we can navigate life beyond its walls.

Living with intention isn't about doing more; it's about doing what matters, aligning your actions with your values, and creating a life that feels authentic.

Let these principles ground you as you move forward, turning everyday moments into opportunities for meaningful, sustainable joy.

EMPOWERMENT THROUGH FOOD SOVEREIGNTY

When I speak of empowerment, I speak of freedom – freedom rooted in food sovereignty.

If you've followed my content, read my blogs, or subscribed to my newsletter, you know this is a theme I hold dear. Food sovereignty is the ultimate expression of agency – reclaiming control over what nourishes us, body and soul.

At its core, it's about challenging industrial food systems and returning power to individuals and communities. It's not just about sustenance – it's about creativity, tradition and autonomy.

For me, food sovereignty is deeply personal. It began with reclaiming recipes – rejecting processed, standardized foods and crafting my own. Each meal became a statement of independence, a conscious choice to prioritize health, sustainability, and authenticity over convenience.

By taking control of what we eat, we free ourselves from reliance on mass-produced products. Making your own bread, cheese, or condiments is more than a skill – it's an act of resistance, a declaration of self-sufficiency.

At its heart, food sovereignty is about reclaiming what has been commodified. It's about finding joy in creation, embracing tradition, and taking responsibility for the impact of our choices.

Every meal prepared with care, every recipe reclaimed, is a step toward a more just and sustainable food system. It's a journey that empowers us to live in alignment with our values, celebrate our cultural identities, and create a future where food is a source of joy, connection, and love.

This isn't about perfection – it's about progress. Small, meaningful steps that align your actions with your aspirations.

The choices we make every day matter. They shape not only our own lives but the world around us.

By embracing this philosophy, you become part of a larger movement – one that uplifts communities, protects the planet, and celebrates the beauty of intentional living.

The map is in your hands now. Use it to chart a course toward a future where food is more than a commodity. Let this be the beginning of a journey that continues to inspire, nourish, and empower you every step of the way, one recipe at a time – mindfully.

MOVING FORWARD: Gratitude and Growth

This journey was never meant to be walked alone. Neither for you nor for me. Writing this book has been a journey – a winding road filled with discovery, growth and deep reflection. It wasn't created in isolation. It was shaped by every voice, every story, and every shared moment of connection.

To Irene: The north in every map I've drawn, the light in me I couldn't always see.

To Mum: My first and forever mentor, the voice in my ear, the strength behind every uncertain step. Your belief in me has carried me further than I ever imagined.

To Dad: For passing down the way to walk through life with integrity, purpose and courage.

To Ali, Oya, Esu, Ala, Ray, Cloud, Stripe and Bilbo: The chaos, the joy, the pull back to universal love. You are the distractions I need, the family I choose, the gift I've always wanted.

To my little sister Clarissa: For inspiring me to live my impact on this earth with kindness and desire, and to remind you to follow your dreams with intention, courage, and an open heart.

To Tore: for your boundless trust, a steady presence in every step of this journey.

To Roberto: Thank you for being the friend who shows up – not just when it's easy, but when it matters most.

To Ella, my editor: Thank you for pushing me to see the heart of this work, to help me shape it without losing its soul.

To Crystal and Jason, my agents: Thank you for believing in this before it existed.

To my mentors: Your words live in my head, your lessons etched in every step I take. This book carries your fingerprints.

And to all those I may have forgotten to name but who have been here all along: You are seen, you are appreciated, and you are part of this journey in every way.

To my followers: You are the heartbeat of this journey. Every comment, every share, every moment you've taken to engage has reminded me why this matters. This is ours as much as it is mine.

To the farmers who nurture the soil, the chefs who transform it, the artisans who preserve traditions, and the communities and families who gather to share meals – this book is, in part, a celebration of your work. You remind us that food is never just food. It's resilience, connection, and the stories we carry forward.

To the earth: Our ultimate provider, teacher and partner. Thank you for your abundance, your resilience, and your quiet wisdom. May we honour you with every seed we plant, every meal we share and every mindful choice we make.

And to you, the reader: Thank you for showing up. For opening these pages with curiosity, for embracing new ideas, and for navigating this journey with me. Your willingness to engage, experiment and make this map your own is what gives it meaning.

This is not the end. It's the beginning of something much bigger – a life where food is more than a commodity, where the kitchen is more than a space, and where every meal becomes an act of care, creativity and connection.

INDEX

Note: page numbers in **bold** refer to illustrations.

A

accessibility 9
activation
    butters 72–4, **75**
    yeast 224
age-related cognitive decline 146
agency 16
air-drying 48
almond 73, 204, 206
    activated almond butter 74, **75**
    almond and seed flour **35**, 41
almond milk 164, 234
amylase 147
anti-inflammatory foods 38, 41, 59, 61, 186, 208, 248
antioxidants 53, 59, 74, 101, 103, 124, 195, 208, 228
anxiety 6–7, 29, 41, 77, 92, 124, 143, 149, 164, 170, 209
apple 190
    homemade apple pectin **138–9**, 140
apple cider vinegar 100–1, 180, 206
    recipe **120–1**, 122–3
aquafaba 154
Attention Deficit Hyperactivity Disorder (ADHD) 7, 10, 12, 14–16, 29, 209
    diagnosis 14, 16
    and the gut 15
    and the heart 18–19
    medication 14
avocado 191
    avo and matcha ice cream 231, **232**
Ayurveda 17–18, 182

B

bacteria
    harmful 215
    see also SCOBY
banana and cacao ice cream **232–3**, 234
barley, milled 43–5, **44**
basil pesto 240, **241**
bean(s)
    5-minute minestrone 220, **221**
    activation 45
    black-eyed bean, black turtle bean and soybean pasta 87–8, **89**
    canned/jarred 104–6, **105**
    milled 43–5, **44**
    mung bean & marrowfat pea pasta 87–8, **89**
berry sauce **211**, 212
Bin, The 26, 114–41
biotin 72, 74
Biscoff and coconut ice cream **233**, 235
black-eyed bean, black turtle bean and soybean pasta 87–8, **89**
blanching 54, 130, 215
blood sugar regulation 36, 40, 73–4, 79, 101, 122–3, 151, 219
bouillon (vegetable stock powder) 115, **116**, 118
brain, gut and heart coherence 17
    see also gut-brain connection
breakfasts 19, 45
brine 112, 244, 247
broccoflower 81–2
butter(s)
    activated 72–4, **75**
    vegan 156, **157**

C

cabbage, sauerkraut 110
Cabinets, The 26, 62–113
cacao
    banana and cacao ice cream **232–3**, 234
    super granola 66
cakes, camille **135**, 136–7
calcium 58, 74, 182–3, 190, 208
camille **135**, 136–7
candied ginger, lemon & orange 130, **131**
canned produce 104–6, **105**
capsaicin 248
carob "chocolate" 68, **69**
carrot 86, 128, 220, 245–7
    carrot muffins **135**, 136–7
cashew nut(s) 160, 228–9
    fermented cashew spread 202, **203**
central nervous system 15, 17
    see also brain
chard and fennel kimchi 245–7, **246**
"cheese"
    melty mozzarella 160, **161**, 224–5
    vegan cream cheese 162, **163**
    vegan Parmesan 158, **159**, 240
    vegan ricotta 164, **165**
chia seed 190
    seed crackers 70, **71**
chicken seitan escalopes 174, **175**
chickpea (garbanzo bean) 86
    canned/jarred 104–6, **105**
    flour 32–3, **34**, 36
    red lentil & chickpea pasta 87–8, **89**
chilli
    crispy chilli oil 248, **249**
    garlic chilli-infused oil **249**, 250–1
chive oil 238–9, **238–9**
chocolate

carob 68, **69**
  Italian hot 76, **77**
  The Magnum 228–9, **229**
choices 11, 30
coconut cream, vegan
  whipping cream (coconut) 155, **155**
coconut flour 68, 126, **127**
coconut milk
  avo and matcha ice cream 231
  coconut and Biscoff ice cream **233**, 235
  seamoss panna cotta 212
coconut oil 156, 158, 160
coconut pulp 68
coconut (shredded)
  homemade coconut milk 148
  super granola 66
coconut water, smoothies **188–9**, 190–1
coffee, date seed 124–5, **125**
cognitive decline, age-related 146
coherence, routines for 19–21
companion planting 239, 242
condiments 56–61, **61**
convenience foods 78–88
cookbooks, failure 7, 10
cooking, as sanctuary 12–13, 18, 21–4
courgette (zucchini) 86, 220
crackers, seed 70, **71**
cream
  vegan cooking 152, **153**, 218–19
  vegan whipping (coconut) 155
  vegan whipping (non-coconut) 154, **154**
creativity 24
crostatina 132–4, **133**
cucumber 190
  pickled 112, **112**

D

dashi, instant powder 96, 98, **99**
date seed coffee 124–5, **125**
defrosting food 215
dehydration 47–9, **50–1**, 52–5
  blanching method 54
  raw method 53
  raw sliced method 55
  sugar-enhanced method 52–3
dehydrators 46–9
detoxification 195
dopamine 186
dreams, big 22
dried fruit/vegetables 47–9, **50–1**, 52–5, 64, 66

E

eating, mindful 21
energy efficiency 30
energy levels 40, 53, 59, 74, 123, 124, 126, 134, 160, 190, 195
engagement 24
escalopes, seitan chicken 174, **175**

F

failure, embracing 23
fennel and chard kimchi 245–7, **246**
fermented foods 20, 98, 107–8, **109**, 110–11, 186
  apple cider vinegar 122–3
  cashew spread 202
  chard and fennel kimchi 245–7
  fermented seed loaf 204, **205**
  fermented seed sauce 206
  kombucha 186–7, 192–3, 195
  live vegan yogurt 207
  rejuvelac 186, 197, 200, 202, 204, 206–7
  SCOBY 192–3, **194**, 195
  tempeh 169–70
  water kefir 196, 198
fiber, sources 36–7, 40, 53, 124, 126, 191, 219
flaxseed 191
  seed crackers 70, **71**
flour 31
  almond and seed **35**, 41
  brown rice **34**, 38, 70
  chickpea (garbanzo bean) 32–3, **34**, 36
  coconut 68, 126, **127**
  gluten-free 126, **127**
  home-milled grain 32–49, **34–5**
  legume 32–7, **34–5**, 40
  lentil 32–3, **34**, 37
  pea **35**, 40
  potato **35**, 39, 84, 86
  rice thickener (flour) 42
focus 23, 29, 40, 53, 74, 82, 123, 126, 134, 151, 170, 190
folate 36, 92, 106, 190
food relationship 6
food sovereignty 237, 256
food waste *see* Bin, The Freezer, The 27, 214–39
  best practice 215
fries, minute 226, **227**
fruit
  dried 47–9, **50–1**, 52–3, 55
  see also specific fruit
fruit powder 55

G

garam masala 60, **61**
garlic chilli oil **249**, 250–1
ginger
  candied 130, **131**
  ginger and hibiscus seamoss gummies **211**, 213
glucoamylase 147
glucosamines 195
glucuronic acid 195
gluten-free 33, 36–42, 70, 87, 96, 100, 102, 126, 132, 136
gomasio 58

grains 31, 32–3
   activation 45
   flaked 43–5, **44**, 64
   home-milled flours 32–49, **34–5**
   milled 43–5, **44**
   sprouted 197, 200, **201**
   see also kefir grains
granola, super 66, **67**
gravy powder, DIY 96, **97**
gummies, seamoss **211**, 213
gut 15, 17
   health 19, 186–213
   as second brain 15, 17–18
gut microbiome 20, 38, 170, 186, 195, 197–8, 208–9
gut-brain connection 16, 18–19, 98, 170, 209

H
heart 17, 18–19, 20
hemp seed
   fermented seed loaf 204, 195
   hulled hemp milk 150
   seed crackers 70, **71**
   unhulled hemp milk 149
herbs 116
Holistic Kitchen 27, 252–7
Homegrown Heaven 27, 236–51
hongcha 192
hot chocolate, Italian 76, **77**

i
ice cream
   avo and matcha 231, **232**
   banana and cacao **232–3**, 234
   coconut and Biscoff **233**, 235
   no churn 230–5
   The Magnum 228–9, **229**
immune boosters 17, 53, 55, 59, 74, 110–11, 190, 195, 197–8, 198, 208, 228, 248
inflammation 15, 16, 18
   see also anti-inflammatory foods

intention, living with 255
iodine 98, 208
iron 37, 190, 191
isoflavones 146

J
jam, zero-waste fruit **138–9**, 141
jarred produce 104–6, **105**
jelly, nasturtium 242, **243**
joint health 195, 208

K
kale 81–2, 86, 190, 191
kappa carrageenan 160
kefir 186
   kefir grains 196, 198
   see also water kefir
ketchup, homemade 128–9, **129**
kimchi, chard and fennel 245–7, **246**
Kitchen Zones 26–7
kombu algae 98
kombucha 186–7, 195
   Mensch Cola-flavor 192–3

L
lecithin 156
lectins 147
legumes 31
   activation 45
   canned/jarred 104–6, **105**
   flaked 43–5, **44**
   flours 32–7, **34–5**, 40
   instant veg & legumes soup **85**, 86
   milled 43–5, **44**
   see also specific legumes
lemon 132–4, 140–1, 190
   candied 130, **131**
   lemon-lime water kefir 198, **199**
   preserved lemons 111
lentil(s) 86, 96
   canned/jarred 104–6, **105**
   flours 32–3, **34**, 37
   milled 45, 86

   red lentil & chickpea pasta 87–8, **89**
   red lentil flour **34**, 37
lime-lemon water kefir 198, **199**
loaf, fermented seed 204, **205**

M
magnesium, sources 36–8, 41, 58, 74, 101, 106, 146, 149, 164, 170, 182–3, 190–1, 208, 209
Magnum, The 228–9, **229**
manganese 38
mango 191, 228–9
maple syrup, whole grain mustard with **178**, 180
marmalade, zero-waste crostatina 132–4, **133**
matcha and avo ice cream 231, **232**
meat alternatives, plant-based 172–7
Mensch Chef 13
mental clarity 8–9, 14–19, 23, 28–9, 36, 38, 40, 59, 80, 103, 110, 123, 126, 134, 155, 170, 186–7, 191, 202, 208, 228, 253, 255
milk *see* plant-based milks
mind, morning practices 19
minestrone, 5-minute 220, **221**
miso 98, 158, 160
mozzarella, melty 160, **161**
   tomato sauce 224–5
muesli 64, **65**
muffins, carrot **135**, 136–7
mung bean & marrowfat pea pasta 87–8, **89**
mushroom (dried) 218–19
mushroom (oyster) 81–2, 98
mushroom (shiitake) 98
mustard
   smooth yellow mustard **179**, 181
   whole grain mustard with maple syrup **178**, 180

N

nasturtium
  nasturtium capers 244
  nasturtium jelly 242, **243**
neurodivergence 6–7, 9, 11, 16–18, 30–1, 79–80, 90, 124, 186, 216, 255
  see also Attention Deficit Hyperactivity Disorder
neurons 17
nigari 166
no-fish sauce 102–3, **103**, 245–7
nori 102–3
nutritional yeast 158, 162, 240
nut(s) 31, 64, 66, 68
  activation 64, 72

O

oat(s), rolled 66
  homemade oat milk 147
  milled 43–5, **44**
oils 31
  chive 238–9, **238–9**
  crispy chilli 248, **249**
  garlic chilli **249**, 250–1
okara 132–4, **133**, 168
omega-3 fatty acids 70, 149
omega-6 fatty acids 149
orange, candied 130, **131**
organic produce 73
overwhelm 9, 14, 23, 25, 30–1, 55, 78–80, 82, 172, 253
oxidative stress 38, 74, 124

P

panna cotta, seamoss **211**, 212
pantries 26, 28–61
  clearing out 29, 31
  open 29–30
  organization 30
  Predictability, Simplicity, Empowerment (PSE) 31
  staples 31–61
Parmesan, vegan 158, **159**, 240
passata 93
pasta 90
  high protein 87–8, **89**
  instant tagliatelle **217**, 218–19
pastry dishes, crostatina 132–4, **133**
peanut(s) 72
  activated peanut butter 74, **75**
pea(s) 81–2, 86
  canned/jarred 104–6, **105**
  mung bean & marrowfat pea pasta 87–8, **89**
  pea flour **35**, 40
pectin, homemade apple 141, 242
  recipe **138–9**, 140
pelati 84, 128
  recipe 92
pesto, basil 240, **241**
photography 8
phytic acid 45, 64, 72, 86, 147
pickling 107–8, **109**
  nasturtium capers 244
  pickles 112, **113**
  pickling solution 244
pineapple 191
pizza, anytime **222–3**, 224–5
plant-based meat alternatives 172–7
plant-based milks 143–51, **144–5**
  almond milk 164, 234
  coconut milk 148, 212, 231, 235
  hemp milk 149–50
  Italian hot chocolate 76
  live vegan yogurt 207
  oat milk 147
  rice milk 151
  seamoss panna cotta 212
  vegan butter 156, **157**
  vegan cooking cream 152, **153**
  see also soy milk
potassium 55, 92, 101, 208–9
potato 220
  minute fries 226, **227**
  potato flour 84, 86
  recipe **35**, 39
  potato starch 96, 158, 160
prebiotics 186, 208
probiotics 20, 98, 107, 110–11, 123, 169–70, 186, 192, 195, 197, 202, 207
processed foods 78–9
protein
  high protein pasta 87–8, **89**
  sources 36–7, 40, 134
pumpkin seed
  fermented seed loaf 204
  seed crackers 70, **71**
purée, tomato 94, **95**, 220

R

rajasic foods 17
ready-to-enjoy meals 78–88, 215, 216–26
Refrigerator, The 26, 142–213
rejuvelac 186, 197, 202, 204, 206–7
  recipe 200, **201**
rice
  brown rice flour **34**, 38, 70
  garden risotto 81–2, **83**
  homemade rice milk 151
  rice thickener (flour) 42
ricotta, homemade 164, **165**
risotto, garden 81–2, **83**
rye, milled 43–5

S

salame, vegan 176, **177**
salt alternatives 58
sattvic foods 17
sauces 90–103
  berry **211**, 212
  fermented seed 206
  tomato **222–3**, 224–5
  vegan Worcester 100, **101**
sauerkraut 110
SCOBY (Symbiotic Culture of Bacteria and Yeast) 192–3, **194**, 195

seamoss (Irish moss) 186–7, 208–13
   gel 210, **211**
   gummies **211**, 213
   panna cotta **211**, 212
seed(s) 31, 66
   activation 72
   almond and seed flour **35**, 41
   fermented seed loaf 204, **205**
   fermented seed sauce 206
   seed crackers 70, **71**
   see also specific seeds
seitan chicken escalopes 174, **175**
serotonin 186
sesame seed 58–9, 182–5, 248
   fermented seed loaf 204
   fermented seed sauce 206
   tahini 183–5, **184**
Slow Food movement 107–8
smoothies
   green blend **188–9**, 190
   tropical green **188–9**, 191
soaking 146–7
soups
   5-minute minestrone 220, **221**
   instant tomato 84, **85**
   instant veg & legumes **85**, 86
soy milk
   homemade soy milk 146–7
   homemade tofu 166–8, **167**
   vegan cream cheese 162, **163**
   vegan Parmesan 158, **159**
soybean(s)
   black-eyed bean, black turtle bean and soybean pasta 87–8, **89**
   homemade soy milk 146–7
   tempeh 169–70, **171**
spelt, milled 43–5, **44**
spices 31, 56–61, **61**
spinach 190–1

spread, fermented cashew 202, **203**
sterilization, jars 106
stocks 90–103
   stock cubes 115, **117**, 119
   stock powder 115, **116**, 118
structure 8–9
sugar, refined 15, 18
sun-drying 48
sunflower seed 72
   activated sunflower seed butter 74, **75**
   fermented seed loaf 204
   fermented seed sauce 206
   seed crackers 70, **71**
sweet potato 220
sweeteners 31

T
tagliatelle, instant **217**, 218–19
tahini 183–5, **184**
tamarind paste 100–1
tamasic foods 17
tea 193, 195
tea kvass 192
tempeh, homemade 169–70, **171**
thyroid health 98, 103, 186, 208
tofu, homemade 166–8, **167**
tomato
   instant tomato soup 84, **85**
   passata 93
   pelati 92
   super concentrated tomato purée 94, **95**, 220
   tomato sauce **222–3**, 224–5
   see also pelati
triangular connection 21
turmeric and black pepper seamoss gummies **211**, 213

V
vegetable powder 55
vegetable stock powder 115, **116**, 118
vegetables
   dried 47–9, **50–1**, 54–5

   freezing 215
   see also specific vegetables
vinegars 31
   see also apple cider vinegar
vital wheat gluten 174, 176
vitamin A 53, 190, 208, 228, 248
vitamin B complex 92, 170, 195, 208
vitamin C 53, 55, 59, 110–11, 190, 208, 228, 248
vitamin E 41, 74, 152, 208
vitamin K 190, 208

W
water kefir 196
   lemon-lime 198, **199**
wheatgrass 19
   wheatgrass and spirulina seamoss gummies **211**, 213
wholefoods 16
Worcester sauce, vegan 100, **101**

Y
yeast
   activation 224
   see also SCOBY
yogurt, live vegan 207

Z
za'atar mix 59
zero-waste see Bin, The
zinc 182–3

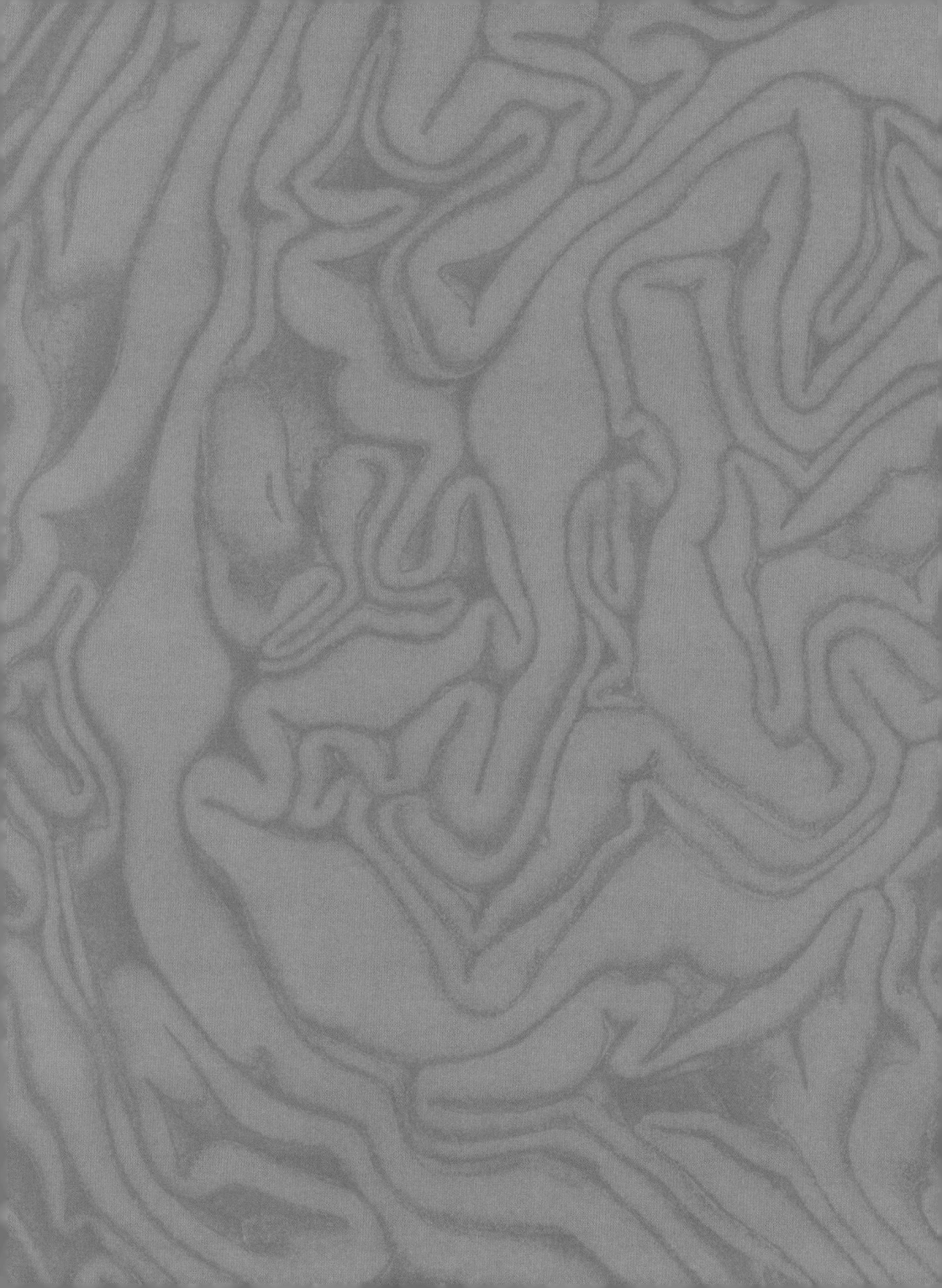

THE MINDFUL KITCHEN MAP
Tomaso Mannu

First published in the UK and USA in 2025 by Nourish, an imprint of Watkins Media Limited
Unit 11, Shepperton House, 83–93 Shepperton Road, London N1 3DF

enquiries@nourishbooks.com

Design and typography copyright
© Watkins Media Limited 2025
Text © Tomaso Mannu 2025
Photography copyright © Myles New

The right of Tomaso Mannu to be identified as the Author of this text has been asserted in accordance with the Copyright, Designs and Patents Act of 1988.

All rights reserved. No part of this book may be reproduced in any form or by any electronic or mechanical means, including information storage and retrieval systems, without permission in writing from the publisher, except by a reviewer who may quote brief passages in a review.

Editorial Director: Ella Chappell
Copyeditor: Emma Hill
Proofreader: Nicola Deschamps
Head of Design & Art Direction: Karen Smith
Typesetting: Eleri Stanton
Production: Uzma Taj
Commissioned photography: Myles New
Food Stylist: Jack Sargenson
Prop Stylist: Julie Patmore

A CIP record for this book is available from the British Library
ISBN: 978-1-84899-433-1 (Hardback)
ISBN: 978-1-84899-434-8 (eBook)

10 9 8 7 6 5 4 3 2 1

Typeset in Natom Pro
Printed in China

FSC MIX Paper | Supporting responsible forestry
FSC® C104723

The manufacturer's authorised representative in the EU for product safety is: eucomply OÜ - Pärnu mnt 139b-14, 11317 Tallinn, Estonia, hello@eucompliancepartner.com, www.eucompliancepartner.com

Publisher's note
While every care has been taken in compiling the recipes for this book, Watkins Media Limited, or any other persons who have been involved in working on this publication, cannot accept responsibility for any errors or omissions, inadvertent or not, that may be found in the recipes or text, nor for any problems that may arise as a result of preparing one of these recipes. If you are pregnant or breastfeeding or have any special dietary requirements or medical conditions, it is advisable to consult a medical professional before following any of the recipes contained in this book.

Notes on the recipes
Unless otherwise stated:
Use medium fruit and vegetables
Use fresh herbs, spices and chillies
Do not mix metric, imperial and US cup measurements:
1 tsp = 5ml 1 tbsp = 15ml 1 cup = 240ml

nourishbooks.com

NOURISH
EAT WELL, LIVE WELL

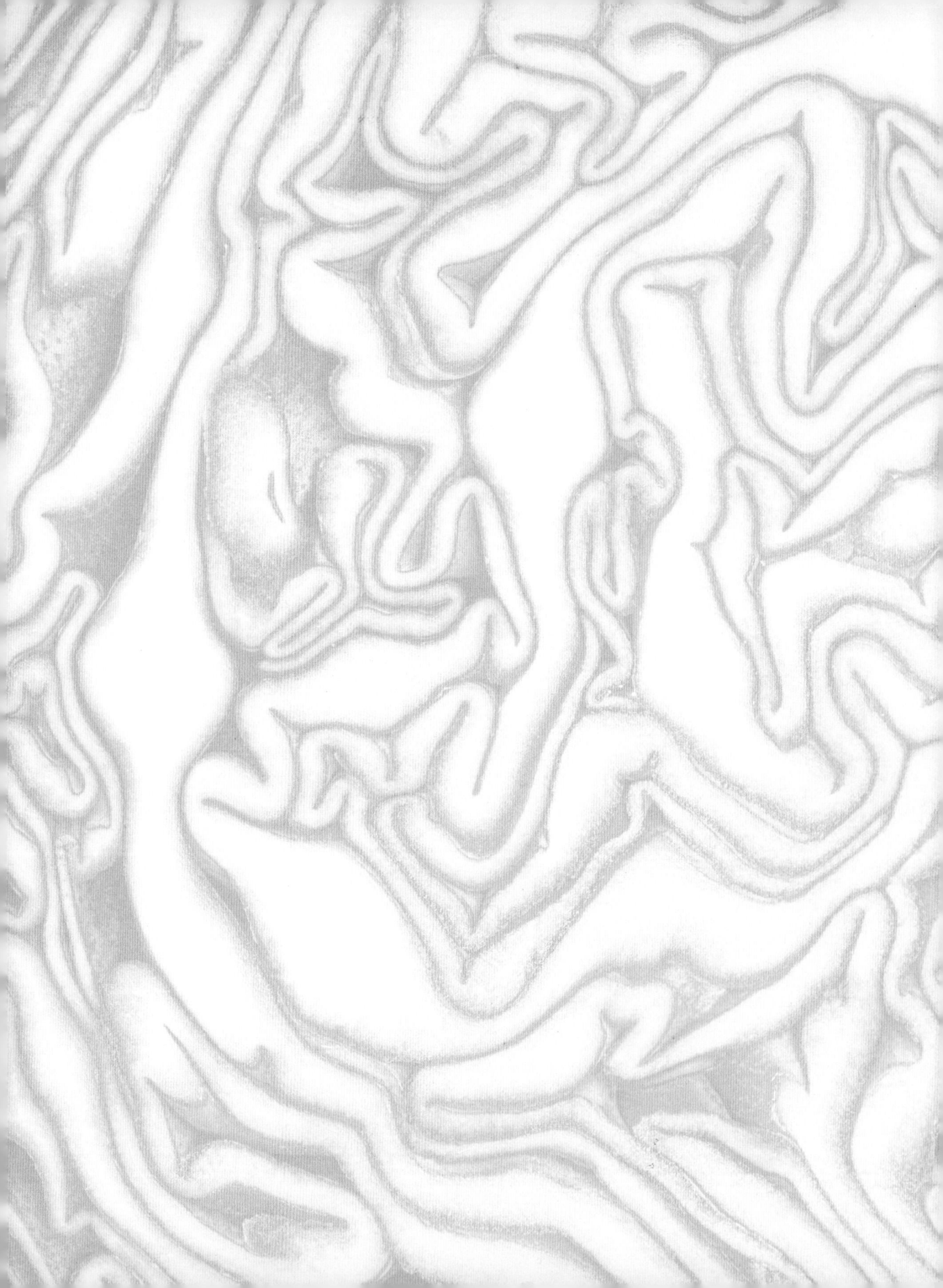